A MILITARY HISTORY OF MODERN CHINA

A MILITARY HISTORY OF MODERN CHINA

From the Manchu Conquest to Tian'anmen Square

Peter Worthing

PRAEGER SECURITY INTERNATIONAL
Westport, Connecticut · London

Library of Congress Cataloging-in-Publication Data

Worthing, Peter, 1964–
   A military history of modern China: from the Manchu conquest to Tian'anmen Square /
   Peter Worthing.
      p. cm.
   Includes bibliographical references.
   ISBN-13: 978–0–275–98780–0 (alk. paper)
1. China—History, Military—1644–1912. 2. China—History, Military—1912–1949.
3. China—History, Military—1949– I. Title.
DS754.15.W65 2007
355.00951—dc22   2007020657

British Library Cataloguing in Publication Data is available.

Library of Congress Catalog Card Number: 2007020657
ISBN-13: 978–0–275–98780–0
ISBN-10: 0–275–98780–9

First published in 2007

Praeger Security International, 88 Post Road West, Westport, CT 06881
An imprint of Greenwood Publishing Group, Inc.
www.praeger.com

Printed in the United States of America

∞™

The paper used in this book complies with the
Permanent Paper Standard issued by the National
Information Standards Organization (Z39.48-1984).

10 9 8 7 6 5 4 3 2 1

Contents

Preface

Even a cursory review of the history of modern China reveals the frequency of warfare over the last four centuries. While military history is just one approach to the study of modern China—along with social, political, economic, cultural, intellectual, and economic approaches—one cannot escape the fact that much of China's modern history has been influenced by war. Warfare and the military have figured decisively in the rise and fall of imperial dynasties, the suppression of internal revolts, the emergence of revolutionary movements, the conduct of China's foreign relations, the development of political parties, the structure of governments, the rise of modern nationalism, and the drive for modernization, all of which have shaped modern China. This work focuses on the causes, conduct, and consequences of war and the role of the military in the historical development of the modern Chinese nation. The military history of China is essential to an understanding of the Chinese state that has now emerged as a twenty-first-century military and economic power.

This book is organized chronologically, covering the period from 1644 to the end of the twentieth century. It can be divided into three sections dealing with Imperial China (1644–1911), Republican China (1912–1949), and People's Republic of China (1949–2000). Part I, Imperial China (Chapters 1–6), begins with a brief review of military developments through to the Ming dynasty. It then describes the Manchu conquest and military rule over China, the devastating defeats at the hands of Western powers in the nineteenth century, the massive revolt of the Taipings, early attempts at military reform and modernization, the wars against France and Japan, and the late Qing reforms that gave rise to China's first modern armed forces. Part II, Republican China (Chapters 7–10), traces the development of military rule after the 1911 Revolution. The military played a dominant role in the search for a viable, modern political state during this period, which experienced intense fighting between independent "warlords," contending political parties that used military force against their rivals, and a Japanese invasion. Part III, People's Republic of China (Chapters 11–14), explores the Chinese Communist role in the Korean War, border clashes with India, the Soviet Union, and Vietnam, changes in military doctrine, organization, and technology, the People's Liberation Army's violent suppression of the 1989 student demonstrations, and the military situation in the Taiwan Straits.

Those who study Chinese history inevitably encounter problems of Romanization of the Chinese language. Professional historians and China specialists tend to use the Pinyin system (Mao Zedong), while general readers are typically more familiar with the Wade-Giles system (Mao Tse-tung). I have chosen to use the Pinyin system with the exception of a few Chinese names that are well known to nonspecialists, such as Chiang Kai-shek (rather than Jiang Jieshi) and Sun Yat-sen (rather than Sun Zhongshan). I have also retained the traditional spellings of commonly used terms such as Manchukuo, Kwantung Army, and Whampoa Military Academy.

This book is based on the work of many historians, but I owe particular debts of gratitude to two colleagues, Jin Qiu of Old Dominion University and David Graff of Kansas State University. Each read the manuscript and provided insightful comments and criticisms. I would also like to acknowledge Larry Bartlett of Texas Christian University, who helped with the early research for this book, and the "Clydesdales" of my spring 2006 class on Chinese Military History. My friends and teammates on the J.D. Highlanders Hockey Club provided both support and much needed distraction during the writing of this book. Finally, I would like to thank my wife Mona and our daughter Tanushri for their love and support.

CHAPTER 1

War and the Military in Traditional China

Warfare has been a part of Chinese history from its earliest days. According to legend, Chinese civilization emerged through the efforts of "culture heroes" and legendary kings, each of whom made technological and cultural contributions. Among these heroes, Huang Di, the "Yellow Emperor," introduced wooden houses, sericulture (silk), boats, carts, writing, military formations and drill, and the bow and arrow. He fought a great battle against alien tribes, securing control of the Yellow River plain for his people. The legends go on to describe three ancient dynasties, the Xia, Shang, and Zhou, each established by force of arms. As historical sources these legends have limited value, but they suggest that the military and warfare played decisive roles in the formation of the earliest political states in Chinese history.

The archaeological record offers more reliable evidence of the military history of ancient China. From approximately 5000 to 1200 BC, various Neolithic cultural groups established settlements across the Yellow River plain. These groups occasionally came into contact with one another, spreading ideas, technologies, and practices into new areas beyond the banks of the Yellow River. These contacts also brought frequent conflict between groups, and warfare became a prominent part of life. In order to protect themselves from attacks, the inhabitants of Neolithic settlements built walls of rammed earth, sometimes up to 20 feet high and equally thick. Weapons from burial sites provide further indication of fighting between different groups, as does evidence of human sacrifice, most likely of war captives.

The Shang Dynasty, c. 1750–1050 BC

Sometime after 2000 BC, these Neolithic people developed into a more complex civilization in the Yellow River basin of north China marked by a formal writing system and advanced technological abilities, primarily the use of bronze and chariots. Primitive written characters from this period etched on cow bones and tortoise shells identify a new civilization known as the Shang dynasty, which lasted from circa 1750 to 1050 BC. The Shang ruled the north China plain from several different capitals, including the modern cities of Anyang and Zhengzhou, and numerous large settlements. The walls surrounding the Shang settlement at Zhengzhou measured

60 feet wide, 30 feet high, and over 2,300 feet long, protecting the capital from attack by non-Shang peoples who lived on the periphery of the state.

The Shang dynasty made important developments in military technology, including bronze technology. Skilled craftsmen manufactured bronze-tipped weapons such as spears, halberds, dagger-axes, and arrow heads, along with military equipment such as helmets, shields, and chariots. Bronze weaponry gave the Shang soldiers an advantage in combat against less sophisticated opponents armed with weapons of wood and stone. Infantry forces typically numbered 3,000–5,000, although some may have reached as many as 10,000. Organized in units of multiples of 100, Shang rulers divided the infantry force into the Left, Right, and Center "armies," along with separate units of archers using composite bows made of wood, horn, and sinew. These foot soldiers supported the chariots, which offered greater mobility and speed on the battlefield. Chariots also served as a mobile platform for the commander, allowing him to observe troops across a larger area than if on foot. In combat, three men typically rode in the chariot: a driver, an archer, and a spear or halberd bearer.[1]

Shang kings engaged in constant warfare, campaigning aggressively against perhaps as many as thirty other groups in north China. In fact, campaigning served as the basic Shang policy for dealing with its less "civilized" neighbors. War booty provided resources such as captives to work as slaves or to be sacrificed, the need for which likely kept the Shang in constant conflict with its neighbors. These campaigns may have been a factor in the fall of the Shang, as chronic warfare strained Shang resources and rendered it vulnerable. Sometime near 1050 BC, a group of people who later called themselves the Zhou succeeded in overthrowing the Shang dynasty.

The Zhou Dynasty, c. 1050–256 BC

Like the people of the Shang dynasty, the Zhou people descended from the various Neolithic groups of north China. The Shang had considered the Zhou "barbarians," a term used to describe all non-Shang people. Living on the western edge of the Shang state, the Zhou developed an alliance with the Shang, helping to protect the frontier and creating a buffer zone between the Shang and the more primitive "barbarians" to the far west. This provides an early example of the Chinese practice of "using the barbarian to control the barbarian." The Shang perhaps also saw the Zhou as growing power and potential enemy and therefore preferred to establish an alliance rather than to fight. The Zhou gradually developed its military strength, including the use of the war chariot which likely played a decisive role in the Zhou conquest of the Shang.[2] As the Zhou grew stronger, the Shang weakened because of strained resources and poor leadership, paving the way for the Zhou to attack and destroy the Shang dynasty near the year 1050 BC. The Zhou took advantage of a weakened Shang force that had been campaigning against another group and could not prepare for the attack. The Zhou conquest culminated in a major battle at Shepherd's Wild, south of the Shang capital at Anyang. The *Shiji*, or Historical Records written in the first century AD, state that the Zhou king led 50,000 troops against 700,000 Shang forces, but popular discontent with Shang rule led most to give up with only token resistance. The best estimates of modern historians put Shang numbers at around 170,000 while the Zhou probably put approximately 45,000 men in the field. Despite its numerical inferiority, the Zhou army scored a decisive victory, putting an end to the Shang dynasty.

The military overthrow of the Shang is better documented than earlier conflicts as the Zhou left far more written records than the Shang. Moreover, the victorious Zhou conquerors felt an obligation to explain why they had attacked and defeated the Shang, attributing their actions to the corruption and cruelty of its last rulers. The Zhou people embraced the concept of "Heaven," an amorphous, cosmic moral force that governed the universe and demanded the overthrow of immoral rulers. Linking Zhou authority to Heaven's will, the new rulers claimed they had acted as a part of Heaven's intention to remove the evil Shang rulers. According to Zhou political thought, a dynasty could rule only so long as the king retained Heaven's favor, later to be described as a "Mandate of Heaven." Thus, the right to rule came from Heaven, the supreme moral force of the universe, which demanded a moral ruler. Conversely, if a king neglected his sacred duties and acted like a tyrant, Heaven would take away its mandate and the ruler could be removed, usually by rebellion, and replaced with a "moral" successor. Zhou records describe the excesses and abuses of the last Shang ruler who tortured for his own amusement and engaged in debauchery and drunkenness. As a result of the Zhou need to justify its military conquest of the Shang, moral virtue became part of the cosmos and history read as a morality play—moral men triumph, immoral men are vanquished. This became the standard justification for political change in traditional China, with a successful conqueror claiming to enjoy the Mandate of Heaven. Military strength and moral virtue would remain the ideal characteristics of rulers and generals in Chinese history.

The Zhou rulers divided the conquered territory into numerous territorial units, each administered by a member of the royal family or a trusted subordinate. These men took titles that became hereditary in return for an oath of allegiance to the Zhou ruler. Each of these regional "lords" had an obligation to render military service when called upon to support the Zhou ruler. They ruled their domains from walled garrisons and maintained their own military forces, creating what amounted to a Zhou military occupation of eastern China. As the head of this hierarchy of lords, the Zhou king reigned from his capital as the "Son of Heaven." Unlike the Shang, the Zhou rulers did not campaign to keep order on the fringes of the state, perhaps understanding that this practice had left the Shang vulnerable.

This system of Zhou rule worked well for a few centuries, but the bonds of loyalty that held the Zhou realm together gradually weakened. Over time, the hereditary lords identified less with the Zhou ruling family and put their own interests before their obligations to the Zhou. As the lords withheld resources from the center and grew stronger, the Zhou ruler grew correspondingly weaker. Eventually, conflict developed between various lords, who began to fight amongst themselves. Moreover, increasingly aggressive "barbarian" pressure on the fringes of the state posed an additional threat to the Zhou. In 771 BC, a group of "barbarians" known as the Rong sacked the Zhou capital, forcing a move to the secondary capital at Luoyang, to the east. This marked the beginning of a prolonged period of military separatism without a strong central authority as the Zhou never regained full control over its lords.

Warfare During the Spring and Autumn and Warring States Periods

Historians of China divide the Zhou dynasty after 771 BC into two distinct periods: the Spring and Autumn period (722–481 BC) and the Warring States period (403–221 BC). During the Spring and Autumn period, the regional lords started transitioning to rulers of independent states and in the fourth century BC began abandoning their traditional titles in favor of calling themselves "king." The Zhou king ruled in name only, clinging to nominal power but unable to control the other "states" that had emerged. The kings of these states often went to war against each other in order to enhance their own prestige or to avenge an insult, rather than for territorial conquest. The king himself or one of his family members usually commanded armies in the field. The chariot took center stage in this aristocratic warfare, with large and powerful states fielding as many as 4,000 chariots while a small state might deploy only a few hundred. It is unclear how many foot soldiers accompanied each chariot, but armies ranged from 10,000 to 30,000 soldiers. Battles rarely lasted more than a day or two, and victors did not pursue the defeated as they left the field. Rules of engagement prohibited fighting during the planting or harvesting seasons, and proscribed an attack on any state in mourning for its king.

The various states entered into alliances for mutual defense against other states or barbarian tribes, which had a distinct influence on the fighting of the period. As a part of such alliances, rulers regularly married their sons and daughters into the ruling families of other states. Whether truly related or not, the heads of the great families of the various states tended to treat each other as family members, often referring to each other as "cousin" or "brother." Such familial considerations influenced the conduct of interstate relations and tended to reduce the brutality of warfare during this period, which featured civility, etiquette, and deference to rank. Elaborate ceremony and ritual preceded battle and a code of chivalrous conduct regulated the fighting. Hsu Cho-yun tells the story of a noble from the state of Jin who doffed his helmet in the midst of battle when he encountered a higher ranking officer from the state of Chu. Another officer of Chu escaped capture because on two occasions the lower ranking Jin nobles gave up the chase out of deference to his rank.[3]

By the sixth century BC, important changes had begun to alter the nature of warfare in China. As competition between the states increased, larger states conquered and annexed smaller states, amassing greater military power. The number of battles and wars actually decreased in the Warring States period, but combat now took place on a much larger scale. Armies of ten times the size of those of the Spring and Autumn period took the field, and military engagements lasted weeks or months instead of days. As the size and scope of warfare changed during the Warring States period, unrestrained and brutal combat replaced the highly ritualistic and regulated fighting of the Spring and Autumn period. Kings and generals increasingly engaged in ruthless campaigns of conquest that resulted in hundreds of thousands of casualties.

The warfare of the Warring States period stimulated changes in military organization, technique, and technology. Rulers began to organize their states for large-scale military campaigns, implementing such institutional practices as population registration, universal military service, and establishing ranks of merit based on military service. Since victory went to those who could outfit the largest armies, rulers began registering land in order to tax the peasants directly through bureaucratic officials, rather than awarding land grants to subordinates from which to take revenue. Others sought to bring new land under cultivation, draining marshes or building new irrigation works. The corresponding rise in agricultural productivity and in tax revenues made it possible for these states to expand their armies, putting men under arms in unprecedented numbers and supplying them with better and stronger weapons.

Another important development involved the rise of large infantry forces, featuring hundreds of thousands of peasant soldiers, supported by cavalry troops. Infantrymen used lances and halberds as thrusting weapons, along with short swords and daggers, all of which required less training and resources than the chariot. Rather than deploy their forces as single units, the larger armies of the Warring States period required commanders to divide their forces into smaller units and employ them individually over great distances. In the fourth century BC, the cavalry techniques of the nomadic people to the north and west of China proper began to find a place in Chinese warfare. An army of 200,000 soldiers might include 5,000–6,000 cavalry troops, employed mostly for scouting and pillaging rather than combat. Chariots proved less useful away from the flat plains of the Yellow River, and the more mountainous or soft, marshy areas of China proved more suited to cavalry. The chariot did not disappear, but its cost and inefficiency reduced it to a minor role in fighting of the Warring States period.

Important technological developments of the period, such as the crossbow and iron weapons, also contributed to the brutality of the Warring States period. In about fifth century BC, Chinese craftsmen began producing iron weapons and tools, which proved superior to their earlier bronze counterparts, more sturdy and capable of holding an edge longer. By the late Warring States period, swords grew longer, more suitable for slashing and cutting, and iron body armor and helmets added protection for the individual soldiers. The crossbow, with its bronze trigger mechanism, also made its debut at this time as a powerful alternative to the compound bow. Its use required great strength, loaded by putting one's feet on the bow while drawing the string back to the trigger mechanism with both hands, but it had much greater range and accuracy than the traditional bow. By mounting several crossbows in a row on a portable base, archers could launch a series of arrows in unison or in sequence.[4]

The military changes of this period also meant an important shift in Chinese society. Warfare had previously been the exclusive domain of the nobility, but the Warring States era gave rise to a new class of military professionals who dominated the conduct of warfare by virtue of expertise rather than birth. This allowed ordinary farmers, if endowed with great ability, to challenge the aristocracy for leadership positions in the military. As rulers eagerly sought out men of proven ability, a certain degree of social mobility allowed men of humble origins to rise to prominent positions.

With the rise of men of talent came one of the most famous pieces of writing of Ancient China, Sun Wu's *The Art of War.* Better known as Sun Zi, or "Master Sun," his treatise on warfare appeared sometime in the fifth century BC. In his book of thirteen chapters, Sun Zi describes the best ways to organize a state for war, how to choose the best terrain, offensive and defensive strategies, the use of spies, and offers practical advice for surviving in the dangerous world of the late Zhou. He placed great emphasis on knowing oneself and one's enemy, preparation, maximizing advantages, minimizing weaknesses, deceit and artifice, while eschewing reliance on simple force. "Know yourself, know your enemy," Sun Zi claimed, "and victory is never in doubt, not in a hundred battles."[5] This work of over 2,000 years ago has been studied by military men all over the globe. Napoleon is said to have read this book, and the twentieth-century Asian revolutionaries Mao Zedong and Vo Nguyen Giap utilized Sun Zi's strategies in order to defeat larger and more powerful enemies.

Qin Unification

During the last 100 years of the Warring States period, the pendulum of power swung back and forth between the three major states of Qin, Qi, and Chu. In 256 BC, the state of Qin conquered the remaining Zhou territory and removed its last king, putting an end to the long, steady decline of the dynasty. Qin gradually emerged as the strongest of the states, conquering and absorbing its neighbors one by one. The conquest of the last rival state in 221 BC marked China's emergence as a unified "empire."

Qin military strength rested in part on its political philosophy known as Legalism, which emphasized building a strong military state. Emerging from the Warring States period alongside other prominent philosophies such as Confucianism and Daoism, Legalism stressed the need to manipulate the population with punishments and rewards in order maximize the state's resources and military strength. An amoral philosophy, Legalism rejected Confucian ideas of righteousness and propriety in favor of raw power. The Qin awarded military titles on the basis of performance in battle or service to the state, and all adult males aged sixteen and above faced compulsory military service.

Following the military unification of China in 221 BC, the Qin ruler assumed the new title Qinshi Huangdi, or "First Emperor of the Qin." Whereas rulers of the various states had referred to themselves as kings, the Qin ruler and all who followed him would use the term "emperor" (*huangdi*), denoting their superior status to "kings" of earlier states. Under his rule, a centralized system of rule divided China into administrative districts called commanderies and prefectures. The emperor appointed officials to supervise each of the commanderies and removed them as he saw fit, marking a departure from the Zhou system of giving elite families virtual independence in controlling areas of the realm. As a result, the Qin state exhibited greater centralized control than ever before and set a pattern for future dynasties. To consolidate his new conquests, the Qin emperor laid out a system of roads and standardized weights and measures, coinage, the lengths of wagon axles, and even the writing system. These changes, all made possible by the military might of the Qin, helped China overcome the regionalism of the Warring States period and established the foundation for 2000 years of imperial government and cultural unity.

Our understanding of the Qin military is enhanced by the army of life-sized Terracotta Warriors unearthed around the first emperor's tomb. Archaeologists have uncovered more than 7,000 figures, each created in great detail and armed with authentic weapons and equipment. Individual soldiers take a variety of poses, standing at attention, kneeling to fire an arrow, or even braced for hand-to-hand combat. The hairstyles, uniforms, and armor are standardized, offering a rare glimpse of the imperial Chinese soldier. The Qin emperor continued to campaign after unification, sending his armies to the north and northwest to drive back the nomadic horsemen who occasionally made trouble along the frontier. To secure China's northern border against the pastoral steppes and its raiders, the first emperor used forced labor to link together a series of walls built by the earlier states into a single defense system stretching perhaps 1,400 miles from southwestern Gansu Province to the southern edge of Manchuria. As Arthur Waldron has pointed out, the modern wall that we now know as the Great Wall dates only from the fifteenth century. Yet the collection of rammed earth defensive works and watchtowers of the Qin dynasty might be considered an early version of this wall, which if properly defended could hold up raiding parties of nomadic horsemen until adequate forces could be concentrated against them.[6] Repair and new construction of the walls continued under later dynasties, replacing the earthen construction of the Qin wall with bricks and stones.

Despite his important contributions, the first Qin emperor worked his people hard on public works projects such as new palaces, defensive walls, a huge tomb, and roads. These demanding and costly projects, combined with strict laws, severe punishments, and compulsory military service, alienated the people and created conditions ripe for revolt. Qinshi Huangdi died in 210 BC, leaving the throne to a weak son who proved incapable of filling his father's shoes. Several revolts broke out in the ensuing years, including some involving the military. In 207–206 BC, Qin rule collapsed amidst these revolts and China lapsed back into chaotic civil war among various rival armies.

The Han Dynasty, 202 BC–AD 220

Out of the rubble of the Qin emerged a successor dynasty known as the Han. Its founder, Liu Bang, also known as Han Gaozu, followed the example set by the first Qin emperor by building on the centralized government system established under the short-lived Qin dynasty. He retained the system of commanderies and prefectures, employed a similar system of ranks, and relied on rewards and punishments. At the same time, he moderated the strict laws and severe punishments that had alienated the people and lowered the taxes that had been imposed with a heavy hand prior to the Qin collapse. The Han dynasty would eventually embrace Confucianism as a state ideology, but in reality it represented a blending of practices of the previous

Zhou and Qin states that scholars have called the "Han synthesis." In essence, the Han attempted to combine Confucian moral rule with Legalist emphasis on military strength.

Like the Qin, the Han military conscripted able-bodied adult males between the ages of 23 and 56, supplementing its ranks with volunteers and convicted criminals. Conscripts typically spent one year of training and one year of active service, protecting the capital, keeping order the countryside, guarding the frontier, or on major campaigns. Once discharged, the soldier returned home to serve as a soldier-farmer in the local militia until age 56. By Han times, the chariot had virtually disappeared from military practice and the vast majority of soldiers served as infantrymen, while a few found assignments in the cavalry or small waterborne units. Considering the state's large population, it is possible that Han armies might have totaled over one million men. The emperor appointed officers to command specific campaigns but retained the power to remove or even execute a general who did not achieve the desired results. The standing army remained in the capital, divided into several units. Individual commanders took responsibility for conscripting and training new recruits, usually organizing them in companies of twenty-five to fifty men. On the frontier, troops manned watchtowers, sent alarm signals to warn against foreign invaders, and repaired defensive fortifications and walls.

The military unification of the Qin had ended fighting between rival kingdoms of the Warring States period, but Han emperors faced a serious threat from the nomadic peoples of the northern and western frontiers. These nomads had excellent military skills, particularly in the art of fighting on horseback. In Han times, the greatest such threat came from a group known as the Xiong Nu, who by the third century BC had formed a tribal confederation stretching from western Manchuria across Mongolia. The Xiong Nu frequently raided settlements in north China, their mounted archers striking with speed and ferocity. The task of dealing with the Xiong Nu threat fell to the emperor Han Wudi, who played a prominent role in the military history of the Han dynasty. Even as a teenager, the "Martial Emperor" showed boldness, vigor, and intelligence. Assuming the throne in 141 BC, he ruled for almost sixty years and aggressively expanded the borders of the empire. From 129 to 119 BC, he dispatched a series of great armies, some numbering as many as 150,000 men, against the Xiong Nu and managed to destroy their power south of the Gobi Desert. These conquests in Central Asia allowed the Han to control trade routes between east and west, the famous Silk Road. Rather than a unified road, the Silk Road consisted of a series of trade centers stretching from China, through Central Asia, to northern India, and to the Roman Empire of the Mediterranean. In order to maintain control over this valuable trade route, the Han relied on its military, which established garrisons along the Silk Road. The Chinese garrisons recruited local farmers to supplement their forces, giving them rudimentary military training. A system of flags, fires, and other signals allowed garrisons to pass on information or call for reinforcements to the string of outposts stretching across the Silk Road.

As Han emperors found that military force alone proved insufficient and expensive, they developed the practice of bestowing gifts upon the rulers of Central Asian states or tribes in order to make them more amenable to Chinese control. This not only provided the nomadic people the goods and products they desired and reduced the need to raid Chinese territories but also prevented them from forming alliances with the Xiong Nu. As a symbol of their acknowledgment of Chinese suzerainty, these rulers sent gifts or "tribute" to the Chinese emperor on a regular basis. In return, the Chinese emperor recognized the ruler as a vassal and promised to protect him and his people. This "Tribute System" emerged gradually as a standard method for managing relations with non-Chinese groups. Its origins lie in the military conquests and territorial expansion of the Han dynasty.

Spanning more than 400 years, the Han Dynasty declined because of a combination of economic problems, natural disasters, peasant discontent, and ineffective government. Following a series of Yellow River floods in the AD 180s , a group of messianic Daoist rebels called the Yellow Turbans attacked and seized major cities around the second Han capital at Luoyang. By this time, the Han government had grown so weak and divided that the job of fighting the Yellow Turbans fell to various generals from powerful families. One such general seized Luoyang and deposed the Han emperor. The Han continued in name until AD 220, yet its authority ended as early as AD 190. When the widespread rebellion began, Han generals emerged as independent warlords and soon completely overshadowed the government. In the several decades following the collapse of the Han, various generals established three separate states: the Wei (north), Shu Han (southwest), and Wu (south). Commonly known as the Three Kingdoms of AD 220–280, this period saw many battles between skilled generals and strategists which inspired the famous literary work *Romance of the Three Kingdoms*. The fall of the Han and the ensuing internal division left China's borders defenseless against nomadic invaders from the Steppe. In AD 317, the resurgent Xiong Nu sacked Luoyang, slaughtering 30,000 inhabitants. From this point, north China saw a succession of states ruled by non-Chinese from roughly 317–581. Large numbers of Chinese fled the "barbarian" north seeking refuge in southern China, significantly increasing the population of southern China.

Sui Dynasty, AD 581–618

For more than three centuries after the fall of the Han numerous states rose and fell in the north and south alike, but China would not see empire again until the late sixth century under the Sui dynasty. Like the Qin, the Sui implemented Legalist policies, which placed a significant burden on the people and engaged in large-scale construction projects and military campaigns. The second Sui emperor, Sui Yangdi, ignored growing domestic unrest in order to concentrate on a series of campaigns against the Korean–Manchurian kingdom of Koguryo, which he feared might form an alliance against the Sui with Turks to the northwest. In a major campaign in 612, a large Sui force crossed the Liao River and attacked the walled cities of Koguryo. The Sui forces had planned for a quick expedition but encountered strong resistance and had to return to China in August. Two more campaigns in 613 and 614 also failed to bring Koguryo under Chinese control. Koguryo's leaders took advantage of the difficult terrain and weather by forcing the Sui armies to engage in lengthy sieges during bitterly cold winters and blistering summers. The Chinese forces required a massive logistical supply chain which proved difficult to maintain. Sui Yangdi began preparations for a fourth campaign, but by this time the empire seethed with domestic revolt.

The Tang Dynasty, 618–907

As Sui power crumbled amid domestic revolt and foreign war, a powerful general named Li Yuan revolted against the Sui emperor. A mix of Chinese and Central Asian blood, Li Yuan had played an important role in putting down early rebellions while Sui rulers concentrated on campaigns against Koguryo. In 617, Li Yuan mounted a successful attack on Chang'an, the western capital, and established the Tang dynasty the next year. The task of consolidating the new dynasty fell largely to his second son, Li Shimin, later known as Tang Taizong. Having experienced war and command at an early age by accompanying his father on numerous military missions, Taizong showed a penchant for military campaign. In 630, he launched a campaign against the Eastern Turks, employing over 100,000 Chinese troops in an attempt to reassert Chinese control over the Silk Road. His troops succeeded, slaughtering thousands in the process, and followed up with campaigns in the Tarim Basin in 639–640 and 647–648. The Tang troops pushed further west into Central Asia securing remote outposts along the Silk Road. The Tang military established "Protectorates" in several areas such as Vietnam (Annan or "Pacified South"), Manchuria (Andong or "Pacified East"), and the Tarim Basin (Anxi or "Pacified West").

Such a massive territorial empire required a considerable military force. The Tang divided the empire into over forty military regions under the control of military governors who had full authority over civilian officials in their regions. In order to meet the military's substantial manpower needs, Tang commanders formed local militia units called Fu Bing. Each local area raised its own force of 800–1,200 men, organized into battalions of 200. The soldiers provided their own weapons, equipment, and rations, but the state supplied armor. These part-time soldiers trained when not planting or harvesting crops and occasionally saw service as guards around the capital. Others served for short periods in remote frontier garrisons, safeguarding the empire against attacks by Turks, Uighurs, and Tibetans and protecting the Silk Road. This system proved an inexpensive and efficient way of meeting the needs of the large Tang army.[7]

The Fu Bing system ultimately proved inadequate in the face of increased pressure from the nomads, which required larger numbers of soldiers than the Fu Bing militias could provide. By the middle of the eighth century, frontier defense required almost 500,000 men and 80,000 cavalry troops, approximately 85 percent of the Tang military, spread across nine frontier command zones. Few Fu Bing soldiers relished the idea of spending long periods of time on the frontier and resisted these assignments. As a result, the Tang government began to replace them with longer-serving conscripts and professional soldiers, many of whom came from non-Chinese groups on the frontier. These professional troops served lengthy terms of service and tended to develop ties of loyalty not to the emperor, but to their commanding generals who saw to their provisions and pay. In order to support these troops, the Tang government gave military governors on the frontier increased authority over the resources of their command zone. As a result, some Tang military commanders developed personal military forces and became virtual independent warlords, quite powerful and occasionally involved in court politics.

An Lushan Rebellion, 755–763

The rise of independent military governors on the frontier in command of the majority of Tang troops meant a corresponding weakening of the domestic forces which rendered the government vulnerable to a coup. In the middle of the eighth century, a general named An Lushan rose in revolt against the Tang, inflicting crippling damage to a once powerful dynasty. A career military officer of Central Asian descent, An Lushan had risen through the ranks of the army to a position as a military governor. In 755, he led 200,000 men from his frontier post against a weakened Tang domestic army, taking control of Luoyang and Chang'an. As An Lushan's troops approached the capital, the elderly Tang emperor fled south to Sichuan with the dynasty seemingly collapsing all around him, inspiring the famous scroll painting *Emperor Ming-huang's Flight to Szechuan*.

In order to suppress the revolt, loyal Tang armies returned from Central Asia abandoning that region to the growing Islamic forces. Although An Lushan had a strong force of troops around him, he failed to take adequate steps to secure his position before his murder in 757. With his death, the revolt broke apart as his subordinate commanders fought among themselves, allowing Tang loyalists supported by Uigher troops an opportunity to restore order. By 763, these forces had revived the Tang dynasty, albeit not to its former strength and authority. Tang frontier defense had weakened to the point that Tibetans and Uighurs frequently raided Chinese cities. After the An Lushan rebellion, regional military commanders held defacto power in China rather than the central government. In 907, amidst a widespread rebellion, one such commander took control of the Tang court and murdered the last emperor, formally ending the Tang dynasty.

The Song Dynasty, 960–1279

After a brief period of division from 907 to 960, a general named Zhao Kuangyin established a new dynasty called the Song which restored unity to China. After seizing power in a coup, he immediately took steps to avoid a similar fate by pensioning off his leading generals with suitable rewards or pushing them into minor posts where they could cause little trouble. As a further safeguard against revolt, he limited regional commanders to a single prefecture and as they died off replaced them with civil bureaucrats. He retained control of all military units but kept the best troops, called the Forbidden Army, in the capital and stationed less effective forces, the

Suburban and Country Armies, in the countryside. This assured that the emperor retained personal control of military power and eliminated the "warlordism" of independent military commanders. With his best troops concentrated in the capital and the lesser troops outside, Zhao Kuangyin launched a campaign against the south to unify China, a task only completed under his successor.

The Song dynasty is remembered as a period of great technological development in China, including the use of gunpowder as a weapon. The Chinese used explosive grenades in battle in the eleventh century, combining coal, saltpeter, and sulfur to produce gunpowder. Ironically, Daoist alchemists searching for the elixir of immortality hit upon this incredibly destructive material. The Chinese had long experience using smoke and fire for military purposes, but the Song marked the beginning of true explosives. The Chinese did not encounter heavily armored knights, and gunpowder had limited impact on nomadic cavalry, so the new weapon remained a supplement to traditional weapons. This information gradually made its way west to the Arabs and then to Europe, where Europeans, inspired by the Renaissance ideals of exploring men's capabilities and in the midst of competing nation–states, would make numerous technological improvements in firearms.[8]

The most critical military problem the Song dynasty faced came from non-Chinese peoples who had taken advantage of the collapse of the Tang to occupy parts of north and northwest China. In the eleventh and twelfth centuries, the Song tried to drive these invaders out of north China, yet these nomadic warriors enjoyed a military advantage over the Song because of the speed and mobility of their cavalry. When military efforts failed, the Song had to sign humiliating treaties which forced the Song to pay "tribute" to these groups in order to prevent further encroachments on Song territory. These treaties provided only temporary respite as in the mid-twelfth century a group of people known as the Jurchens overran all of north China, pushing the Song south of the Huai River and establishing a new state in north China called the Jin dynasty.

The Song experience with nomadic invaders can be seen as part of a "Central Asian invasion" of the eleventh to the fourteenth centuries. Despite their small numbers, the people of the Central Asian Steppe had magnificent military skills and frequently demonstrated their talents along China's northern border. In the grasslands of the Steppe, the nomads relied on raising animals, rather than crops, subsisting on a sheep and horse economy. Using horses to control the herds, to hunt, and to make war, the nomad had no need for agriculture, as long as he could trade occasionally with other areas for goods he could not produce himself, such as metal weapons or luxury goods. The nomads of the Steppe moved on a seasonal basis, moving their herds from summer pasture areas to winter shelter in mountain valleys, and then back again. From boyhood, the men of the Steppe lived in the saddle. They could be quickly mobilized for action, turning from herders into warriors without missing a beat. The active outdoor life they led created rugged, independent, and self-reliant individuals who could survive any manner of hardship. The mounted archers of the Steppe had tremendous striking power. The development of the iron stirrup, sometime after the first century AD but certainly no later than the fourth century AD, gave them a firmer plant from which to use a bow while on horseback. Until the introduction of modern firearms near the year 1800, the mounted archers served as the most effective military force in Asia.

Chinggis Khan and the Yuan Dynasty

In the late twelfth century, the Mongols organized a tribal federation under the leadership of a man named Temujin, better known to history as Chinggis Khan. Born into a noble family around 1167, Temujin grew up in the rough and tumble world of the Mongolian grasslands. At age ten, Temujin saw his father murdered by tribal rivals. He lived for several years on the run, avoiding those who had killed his father and scratching out a living on the Steppe. As he grew to manhood, Temujin assembled a group of warriors around him, all attracted by the strength of his personality. He also made important alliances with other families and Mongol tribes that would come to form the foundation of the tribal federation of Mongols. In 1206, he took the title Chinggis Khan or "universal leader" of the Mongols.[9]

Temujin drew his personal bodyguard, eventually to become an elite unit of troops, from the sons of the various clan leaders within the federation. From this group he chose his top generals and administrators. He organized his army into units of tens, hundreds, and thousands, and by 1227, the year of his death, the entire Mongol military force numbered 129,000 men. The key to Mongol military strength lay in its cavalry, a mounted archer using a powerful bow with a range of up to 200 yards. Typically, the Mongols preferred to fight in open areas, which resembled the grasslands of Mongolia. Choosing open, flat terrain whenever possible, the Mongol force concentrated on a weak point in the enemy position. Line after line of cavalry galloped full speed at the enemy, firing arrows in rapid succession as they approached and firing back over the saddle as the riders returned to Mongol ranks. After subjecting the enemy to a seemingly endless barrage of arrows in this fashion, Mongol horsemen typically broke through the enemy line in order to flank and encircle them. The Mongols often used artifice, concealing substantial forces on the wings of the formation while the center force feigned defeat and retreated in apparent disorder. When the enemy pursued the retreating force, fresh Mongol troops attacked their flanks and destroyed them. To apply psychological pressure to their enemies, they occasionally laid waste to defeated cities, executing nearly every man, woman, and child, leaving only a handful of survivors to share their experience and thereby encourage future cities to see the wisdom of surrender. Never attacking more than one enemy at a time, Temujin always fought for limited objectives and only attacked when his chances for success seemed good. After defeating and annexing his neighbors, Temujin turned his eyes to the wealthy and resource rich area to the south, beginning the Mongol conquest of China. In 1215, he captured Beijing, defeating the Jin dynasty and bringing much of north China under his control. Chinggis Khan died campaigning in northwestern China in 1227, but his descendants, most notably his grandson Kubilai Khan, completed the task by establishing the Yuan dynasty in 1271 and destroying the Song in 1279.

The incredible military power that allowed the Mongols to conquer China began to decline at the end of the thirteenth century. Elite Mongol units remained close to the capital at Beijing while regional military units, composed mostly of Chinese troops with Mongol officers, handled security in the areas outside of the capital. The ability of these regional units to deal with problems such as banditry and revolt declined sharply in the early fourteenth century, as the Mongols found they could not rely on the Chinese conscript soldiers to suppress rebel activity. The decline of Mongol military power and factional struggles at court rendered the Yuan dynasty vulnerable to revolt.

The Ming Dynasty, 1368–1644

As the Yuan dynasty collapsed into chaos, Chinese rule returned under a man named Zhu Yuanzhang, founder of the Ming dynasty. Orphaned at a young age, he spent time in a Buddhist monastery and served for a while in the Mongol army. He eventually joined one of the rebel groups fighting against the Mongols and quickly rose to become a leading general. Zhu's rebel army took the southern city of Nanjing and prepared to attack north China in late 1367. Too divided and weakened to mount a counterattack, the Mongols retreated north back into their homeland. As his armies swept north, Zhu Yuanzhang established the Ming dynasty in 1368.

The Ming dynasty achieved a number of impressive military accomplishments, both on land and on sea. In the early fifteenth century, a eunuch named Zheng He commanded a series of seven maritime expeditions across the South China Sea, the Indian Ocean, and as far as the east coast of Africa. Of magnificent scope and scale, one of these expeditions included sixty-two ships carrying nearly 28,000 men.[10] These expeditions came to a halt in 1433, for various reasons. Confucian scholar-officials opposed the expeditions as ostentatious and unseemly attempts to derive commercial profit. Others criticized the expeditions as an unnecessary expense at a time when China could not afford it. Moreover, a resurgence of Mongol activity alarmed Ming officials who felt they needed every resource to go to this line of defense.

Ming military forces also demonstrated their capabilities in a major war against the Japanese from 1592 to 1598. The Japanese hegemon Hideyoshi sent hundreds of thousands of Japanese troops to the Korean peninsula in an attempt to conquer both Korea and China. Kenneth Swope has argued that despite numerical inferiority in almost every major battle, Ming forces prevailed in the fighting in part because of superior technology, including muskets, mortars, and cannon. The war, which ended with Hideyoshi's death in 1598, indicated that China enjoyed a technological edge against its neighbors.[11]

By 1600, the Chinese had long experience in military affairs. Numerous dynasties had risen and fallen because of revolt and independent-minded generals.

The nomadic peoples to the north and west posed a constant threat to China's security and occasionally ruled over part or all of the empire. Dynasties went to great lengths to fund their militaries, devising new methods to meet their security needs and to prevent internal revolt. Despite China's Confucian heritage which eschews the use of force, warfare and the military played decisive roles in shaping the history of imperial China.

CHAPTER 2

Manchu Conquest and the Qing Dynasty

With the experience of the "Central Asian invasion" and an extended period of Mongol rule in China still fresh in their historical memory, Ming dynasty emperors and officials remained painfully aware of the importance of frontier defense. Accordingly, they repaired large sections of the Great Wall, replacing rammed earth with stones and bricks, and established twenty-five frontier garrisons in order to defend China's northern border against nomadic invaders. By the year 1600, border defense suffered as a result of chronic financial difficulties, bureaucratic corruption, weak rulers, and tax shortfalls. Such problems forced the Ming court to seek ways to defend its borders without great expenditures from the government treasury. These attempts proved unsuccessful, which opened the door to foreign conquest and an extended period of non-Chinese military rule under the Qing dynasty.

Ming Frontier Defense

With an eye toward reducing the need to provision the frontier garrisons, the Ming government drew on the example of the Tang Fu Bing militia system to create regional frontier guard units called Weisuo. Each of these units included a "Wei" of approximately 5,600 soldiers, divided into smaller units called "Suo." Rather than draw resources from the imperial treasury, the government provided the Weisuo units with agricultural lands from which to draw provisions and revenue. The Weisuo system led to the creation of virtual military colonies on China's northern frontier, each with its own independent administration and resource base. Although nominally under the authority of the Board of War and local provincial governors, these units operated under the de facto control of garrison commanders, whose positions became hereditary. The lack of central supervision led to a gradual decline in the military effectiveness of the Weisuo system as some commanders concentrated more on financial gain than frontier defense. Some hired out soldiers as laborers to local elite families for private construction projects or accepted payments from soldiers in order to be excused from military drill. As a result, many Weisuo garrisons operated at far less than full strength. By the year 1600, Ming frontier defenses had grown dangerously weak.

In addition to the Weisuo system, the Ming policy toward Central Asia sought to prevent a major alliance among the tribal peoples of the Steppe, such as had emerged under the Mongols in the thirteenth and fourteenth centuries. The Ming did not have the resources to project its military power north of the Great Wall, so it employed the traditional policy of conferring titles and material rewards on the various tribal leaders of the Steppe. If a tribe acquired too much power, the Ming court would show favor to its rivals and encourage competition and conflict. Employing the time-honored tactic of "using the barbarian to control the barbarian," the Ming sometimes incorporated non-Chinese tribes into the Weisuo system by appointing its leader as a Ming garrison "commander."

As Ming frontier defenses grew increasingly weak, a semi-nomadic tribal people from Manchuria known as the Jurchens, whose ancestors had ruled northern China under the Jin dynasty from 1115 to 1234, began building a powerful state. In the sixteenth century, these people inhabited the area of eastern Liaoning Province in Manchuria. Like the nomadic peoples of Central Asia, the Manchus, as they would later call themselves, possessed the formidable military skills of horsemanship and archery honed by traditions of herding animals and hunting. Yet the Manchus also developed an agricultural tradition, borrowed from the Chinese, which gave them a more stable economic base. They lived in small, scattered villages based on kinship groups of dozens of clans spread out over Manchuria.

The Manchus gradually emerged as a powerful military threat to China, but Ming officials tended to worry more over the potential danger posed by the various Mongol tribes. In fact, the Manchu clans of the region to the east of Mongolia played an important role in the Ming strategy for preventing a Mongol resurgence, providing a "counterweight" to the Mongols. Numerous Manchu tribal leaders had accepted titles from the Ming court, nominally taking a place in the Ming military as Weisuo units, forming an extension of Ming military power far beyond the Great Wall. Like others who entered into these "tribute" relations with China, Manchu tribes enjoyed the prestige of alliance with China and the economic benefits of trade that went along with this relationship.[1]

The Rise of Nurhaci and the Eight Banners

In the late sixteenth century, a Manchu named Nurhaci ascended to the head of the Aisin Gioro clan upon his father's murder at the hands of a rival chieftain. Starting with a small band of warriors, Nurhaci warred against other Manchu clans and took revenge on those who had murdered his father. Using a combination of alliance and military force, by 1589, he united numerous Manchu clans and established a territorial base for his growing state. In 1590, he went on a tribute mission to Beijing where Ming officials received him with honor and granted him an official title. Despite recognition from the Ming, Nurhaci faced opposition from within his family and in 1593, he had to defeat a coalition of rival Manchus and Mongols led by his brother-in-law.

Like Chinggis Khan, Nurhaci relied on strong organization, mobility, and speed rather than large numbers. Early in his career, he organized his soldiers in hunting formations of ten to twelve men, all related by blood or marriage, or used the Mongol system of military organization with units of 10, 100, and 1,000 men. He later organized his people by forming a series of companies called *niru* ("arrows") composed of 150 soldiers and their families. In 1601, he expanded the number of fighting men in each company to 300, which remained standard from that point on. Nurhaci then organized these companies into four Banners, each represented by a different color banner: yellow, white, red, and blue. In 1615, Nurhaci doubled the number of Banners to eight, adding four additional Banners with borders on the original colors.[2]

These eight Banners formed the core of Nurhaci's military power, but they represented much more than simply military organization. Mark Elliott has described the Banners as a "cross between the Marine Corps, Civil Service, and Veterans Administration" which facilitated both military and civilian administration of the population of the growing Manchu state. While each Banner provided troops for military service, they also handled nonmilitary duties such as taxation, production, services, and registration of the population. Membership in the Banner included not only the soldier but his family as well, which meant that the vast majority of members of the eight Banners did not engage in military combat.[3]

Each of the eight Banners fell under the command of one of Nurhaci's sons, known as a Beile, or prince. The commanders of the original four Banners served as senior Beiles while the commanders of the four bordered Banners served as junior Beiles. A handful of Nurhaci's closest supporters and most loyal followers, related by marriage rather than blood, served as advisors. Under Nurhaci, the Banners operated with a certain degree of independence with each Beile treating his Banner as his own personal property. By 1615, each Manchu Banner had reached a strength of 200–300 companies or as many as 90,000 troops. This proved an effective fighting force, each soldier's skills developed by a life of riding and hunting, and honed by constant campaigning against other tribes. Nurhaci maintained strict discipline with severe punishments for those who did not follow orders.

In 1616, Nurhaci's relationship with the Ming court took an interesting turn as he established his own dynasty, the Jin, reconnecting with his ancestors who had conquered northern China in the twelfth century. There could be a number of reasons behind this decision including bolstering his prestige by asserting his relationship to a powerful ancestor, increasing his own power *vis-a-vis* the Banner commanders by developing a stronger central command structure, or signaling his intention to attack and conquer part or all of China. It did not indicate a complete break with traditional Manchu tribal organization and traditions, as he still used the term *Khan* to refer to himself and remained firmly rooted in the tribal world of his homeland. Yet it did mark a turning point in the development of the emerging centralized Manchu state and its growing sense of independence from the Ming court.

In 1618, the new Jin dynasty clearly asserted its independence when it announced a series of "Seven Grievances," including support for rival Manchu tribes who had killed both Nurhaci's father and grandfather, which signaled his intention to attack Chinese settlements north of the Great Wall. As Nurhaci's state grew, it outstripped its resources and this economic pressure forced the Jin state to expand to the south. In May 1618, the Jin state began its assault on Chinese towns in Manchuria with an attack on Fushun, a trading center and garrison city ten miles east of modern day Shenyang. Before attacking with a force of 10,000, Nurhaci first contacted the Chinese commander, Li Yongfang, urging him to surrender and threatening certain death if he did not. After an initial skirmish, Li surrendered along with a thousand other Chinese residents. He became a trusted commander in the Manchu military and even married Nurhaci's granddaughter. The Ming court sent a force of more than 80,000 troops to avenge this attack, but Nurhaci's Banner forces destroyed it. These victories convinced several nearby Chinese settlements to surrender to Manchu authority and by 1621 Nurhaci controlled most of the Liaodong peninsula, driving Ming forces south of the Great Wall. He built a new capital at Shenyang in 1625.

Manchu rule over Liaodong meant changes for Nurhaci's state, which now included significant numbers of Mongols and Chinese. Rather than incorporate the Chinese of Liaodong and their families into the various Banners, Nurhaci allowed Chinese officials to retain their positions and to administer to the population through a traditional Chinese system of government. Each city or village with a Manchu population created a separate "Manchu quarter" where they lived apart from the Chinese inhabitants. This marked the beginning of the Manchu practice of segregation and maintaining distinct Chinese and Manchu administrative systems, which would characterize later Manchu rule over all of China. As his state grew larger and more diverse, Nurhaci sought to impose centralized command in place of the loose, tribal alliances of Manchu tradition. He devised ways to assert greater control over the individual Banner commanders, such as by changing the practice of distributing loot after successful battles. Whereas in earlier times each Banner retained whatever spoils of war it could gather after a victory, Nurhaci began a policy of equal distribution of all spoils among the eight Banners. This prevented any one Banner from acquiring more wealth and power than the others and posing a potential challenge to Nurhaci's rule.[4]

The Ming court responded to the emerging Manchu threat with military force, arming the northeast garrisons with cannon. The best cannon at the time came from Macao, where Portuguese foundries produced artillery pieces larger and more powerful than those cast by the Chinese. Although some conservative officials decried the use of foreign contraptions, perhaps associating them with Christianity which they viewed as a divisive force, four Portuguese cannon arrived in Beijing in 1621. By 1630, the Ming court had hired 200 Chinese mercenaries from Macao who had trained with the Portuguese in the use of the cannon. The Ming emperor Chongzhen turned to the Jesuits for assistance in producing cannon in the 1630s and 1640s. Adam Schall von Bell, one of the best-known Jesuits in residence at the Ming court, cast a total of 500 pieces for his patron and wrote a manual on their use entitled *Essentials of Gunnery.*[5] The additional firepower these cannon provided helped the Ming in its defense of Ningyuan, which came under Manchu attack in February 1626. Deliberately abandoning the outer city walls in order to draw the

Manchu attackers into closer quarters, Ming troops defended the inner walls using cannon and cauldrons of boiling oil to great effect. The fighting continued for several days before Manchu forces withdrew after sustaining significant casualties. In his only defeat at the hands of the Ming, Nurhaci himself suffered a wound and died several months later in September 1626.

Hong Taiji and the Turn to the South

Nurhaci's death came as the developing Manchu state still struggled with organizational and economic issues that came with territorial expansion. With no designated successor, a brief power struggle ensued in which Nurhaci's eighth son Abahai, better known by his imperial title Hong Taiji, emerged as the new Khan of the Jin state. His strong military record and personal command of two Banners provided him with essential leverage against other candidates for succession. Hong Taiji continued his father's policy of expansion and incorporation of new territories and people. As they pushed south, the disciplined Manchu forces treated the Chinese population well, welcoming surrendering Chinese officers and soldiers to join the Manchu military. Hong Taiji also followed in his father's footsteps by moving away from tribal organization toward more centralized, bureaucratic rule. Under his control,

Contemporary China. Cartography by Bookcomp, Inc.

the Manchu state made even greater strides away from a loosely organized state based on tribal and family relationships toward a Chinese style state with an autocratic ruler supported by bureaucratic officials. The greatest obstacle to such change came from Banner commanders, who favored individual autonomy over central control. Hong Taiji gradually undercut the power of the other Banner commanders, using some of the same methods as his father. He further revised the policy for the divisions of war booty, asserting his right to distribute all spoils as he wished, keeping nearly one-third for the imperial treasury.

Hong Taiji further reduced the power of the Banner commanders by incorporating Chinese and Mongol Banners into the Manchu military. As Nurhaci and Hong Taiji warred against neighboring Mongol tribes and Chinese settlements, they absorbed captured or surrendered soldiers into their own forces. They initially created separate ethnic companies of Mongol or Chinese troops attached as supplemental units to one of the eight Manchu Banners. As the number of non-Manchu troops grew with conquest and alliance, Hong Taiji created separate Mongol and Chinese Banners, using the same colored banners of the eight original Manchu Banners. Between 1626 and 1643 he established eight Mongol Banners and eight Chinese Banners. On the eve of the Manchu conquest of China in 1644, the so-called Banner System had reached full maturity with a total of twenty-four Banners: eight Manchu, eight Mongol, and eight Chinese. The Manchu Banners remained the largest forces, but the support of Mongol and Chinese Banners would prove invaluable when Hong Taiji turned his forces against China proper.

Shortages of food and resources drove the Manchus to additional attacks on north China. In 1629, Hong Taiji made his first attacks on China proper, breaching the Great Wall north of Beijing and plundering the countryside. Manchu cavalry forces excelled at raiding operations in the open stretches of north China, but ran into trouble when attacking walled cities, as illustrated by Nurhaci's inability to take Ningyuan in 1626. Hong Taiji remedied this situation by employing captured Chinese soldiers who had experience in casting cannon and using artillery in battle. These men helped the Manchus produce forty artillery pieces in 1631, which shifted the balance of power decisively in favor of the Manchus who now possessed both the power of cannon and the speed of cavalry. In September 1631, the Manchus tested their new artillery capabilities in the siege of Dalinghe, a walled town between Shenyang and Jinzhou. Hong Taiji led 20,000 troops in the assault, first bombarding and capturing the smaller forts on the outskirts before turning their guns on the city itself. In less than two months the Manchus captured Dalinghe and defeated two larger Ming forces sent in relief.

Rather than attempt to breach the Great Wall in the northeast, the strongest point of the Ming frontier defense, Hong Taiji moved west to conduct raids in Shanxi. Along the way, the Manchus secured the allegiance of various Mongol tribes, either through negotiation or through conquest. The incorporation of these Mongol forces increased Hong Taiji's military power, but more importantly provided access to a valuable source of horses which otherwise might have been available to the Ming military. Frederic Wakeman has estimated that in the fifteenth century the Ming court had approximately 1.7 million horses, yet in 1634 it maintained only 100,000 in its stables.[6]

As the Manchu state grew under Hong Taiji, he continued his movement toward a more centralized, bureaucratic government, facilitating rule over his growing Chinese population and curbing the power of the Manchu elites. Numerous Chinese officials now served in the Manchu administration, and Hong Taiji began creating new government structures based on the Chinese imperial model. In 1631, he approved the creation of a Manchu version of the Chinese "six boards," or government bureaus that dealt with civil affairs, finances, rites, war, justice, and public works. He then added an office of the Censorate, a traditional Chinese bureau that supervised the work of the government, identifying and rooting out corruption and abuse of power. The clearest indication of his intention to embrace the Chinese bureaucratic model came in 1636 when he rejected the dynastic title "Jin" in favor of the new dynastic title "Qing" or "pure." This represented yet another step away from the tribal traditions of his Manchu ancestors and a closer association with Chinese tradition of bureaucratic empire. In doing so, Hong Taiji made the transition from "Khan" of the Jin State to "Emperor" of the "Great Qing" or Manchu Empire. It also perhaps represented Hong Taiji's intention to extend his rule to the central China plain, south of the Great Wall. Yet Hong Taiji did not achieve his goal of ruling over all of China, as he died of illness in September 1643, leaving the throne to his six-year-old son with Hong Taiji's younger brother Dorgon serving as regent. This young boy would rule as the Shunzhi emperor, the first Qing emperor to rule over China.

Li Zicheng's Rebellion

As Ming officials concentrated on the growing Manchu threat to the northeast, they neglected affairs in other parts of the empire, especially in the northwestern region around the city of Xi'an. Devastated by government inattention, economic problems, and natural disasters, many in this region faced dire circumstances that compelled them to turn to banditry for survival. Out of these bandit groups emerged rebel armies which rose in revolt against the Ming, which now found itself caught between the Manchus to the northeast and rebel groups to the west. Of these rebels, Li Zicheng, a one-eyed army veteran, proved the most capable and successful. The Ming tended to treat Li more like a bandit than a genuine threat to the throne, periodically sending pacification forces to defeat his rebel armies, but more often simply offering amnesty in return for promises to cease his activities. Even when Ming troops did use force against Li's rebel army, he found that he could easily refill his ranks with a seemingly endless supply of desperate peasants and others who found little reason to support the corrupt and inefficient Ming government. In the early 1630s, Li commanded a force of 40,000 troops, but by 1641 his numbers ballooned to perhaps as many as 400,000.

Taking advantage of the fact that the Ming had transferred its best commanders to the east in order to deal with the Manchu threat, Li Zicheng's forces took control of Luoyang and Kaifeng in 1641 and 1642. In order to facilitate the capture of Kaifeng, he destroyed the dikes that held the Yellow River in its bed, causing a massive flood in which perhaps as many as one million people lost their lives. In February 1644, Li took Taiyuan, in Shanxi Province, where he divided his force into two columns. One moved north to attack a Ming garrison at Datong while the other marched east toward Beijing. In April Li Zicheng's massive force arrived at Beijing and began a siege, but after brief negotiations the demoralized defenders opened the city gates and surrendered. The last Ming emperor, Chongzhen, hanged himself in a garden behind the palace. Meanwhile, Li Zicheng presided over the arrest, torture, and execution of numerous high-ranking Ming officials, except those who agreed to serve Li Zicheng or make a substantial financial "contribution" to Li's treasury.[7]

One of the most capable of the remaining Ming generals, Wu Sangui, commanded the garrison at Ningyuan, just north of the strategic pass at Shanhaiguan where the Great Wall meets the ocean, affording access to the north China plain from Manchuria. As Li Zicheng's force moved toward Beijing, the emperor called Wu Sangui and his 40,000 troops to return to Beijing. Wu had reached only part way when he learned that Li's rebels had taken the city, so he returned with his force to the strategic pass at Shanhaiguan. Li sent Wu Sangui a letter, urging him to forget his loyalty to the Ming and to join Li in return for a lofty title and rewards. Wu considered this offer for a few days, primarily because his father and other family members resided in Beijing under Li's control. Li Zicheng interpreted Wu's delay in responding as a rejection of his offer and in a fit of fury tortured and executed Wu Sangui's father, hanging his head from the city walls.

With both the Ming emperor and his own father dead, Wu Sangui turned to the Manchus for help in exacting revenge. Wu himself had both Chinese and Manchu ancestry and several of his cousins already served the Manchus. He contacted Dorgon, proposing an alliance in order to destroy Li Zicheng's rebel force and to restore the Ming. Wu Sangui saw this as a temporary alliance for which he would offer material rewards to the Manchus and then send them back through the pass at Shanhaiguan to their homelands. Dorgon accepted Wu's offer, but turned the tables, informing Wu that while together they would indeed defeat Li Zicheng, rather than restore the corrupt and decadent Ming they would establish Qing dynasty rule over all of China. Seeing few alternatives and eager to avenge his father's murder, Wu accepted Dorgon's terms. In late May Li Zicheng sent a large force toward Shanhaiguan hoping to crush Wu Sangui's troops, but Manchu Banner units combined with Wu's army to defeat Li's force, sending the survivors reeling back toward the capital. With Manchu, Mongol, and Chinese Banners rapidly heading for Beijing, Li Zicheng fled to the west leaving a looted and smoldering capital to the Manchu forces, which entered the city in early June 1644.

After securing control of the territory around Beijing, Banner units pursued Li Zicheng's retreating forces which turned to the south. Li's forces dissipated as he reached Jiangxi Province, where he died in 1645. Meanwhile, remnants of the Ming court pledged loyalty to a cousin of the last Ming emperor and established a "Southern Ming" dynasty, based at Nanjing. The military forces of this Southern Ming fell under the control of Shi Kefa, formerly minister of war. The Manchus attacked with a force of 100,000 Manchu, Mongol, and Chinese Bannermen supported by nearly 130,000 Chinese troops who had surrendered or defected to the Qing cause. The final destruction of the Southern Ming came with a bloody siege of Yangzhou in May 1645. Southern Ming defenders directed unobstructed artillery fire on Qing soldiers as they made a direct assault on the city walls, killing thousands. Qing artillerymen had ample experience of their own and used cannon to create a breach in the wall, although according to some sources the dead piled up so high that Qing forces needed no ladders to scale the city walls. The gates opened and Qing troops began a ten-day massacre that claimed the lives of perhaps as many as 800,000 people.[8]

Li Zicheng's attack on the Ming court and capture of Beijing had indeed rendered China vulnerable to the Manchus, but the organizational strength and striking power of the Banner forces provided the essential element that made the conquest possible. Mongol and Chinese Banners in particular proved critical to both the defeat of Ming forces and the consolidation of Qing rule over all of China after 1644. Mongol cavalry formed the spearhead of the Manchu attack, and Chinese Bannermen occupied important administrative positions across north China in the wake of the conquest. Having governed Liaodong and its Chinese population for decades, the Manchus had a small but effective Chinese style bureaucracy ready to begin administering to northern China. The Manchu, Mongol, and Chinese Banner troops showed strong discipline in executing their operations, providing stability and order to war-ravaged parts of the capital and north China.

The Military Basis of Qing Rule

Despite the rather quick collapse of the Ming in 1644, it took nearly two decades of fighting to pacify the countryside and consolidate Qing rule over China proper. The Chinese population only grudgingly submitted to foreign rule, ensuring that Manchu rule rested upon a basis of military strength. As a precaution, most of the Banner units remained around the capital to defend against any attack. Members of the Banners, Manchu, Mongol, and Chinese alike, considered themselves a distinct group of elites and prided themselves on their traditional skills of horsemanship and archery. In contrast to Chinese officials who saw their loyalty to the emperor in terms of Confucian-style reciprocal relationship, like that between parent and child, the Bannermen viewed themselves as obedient servants of the ruler, more akin to the relationship between master and slave. In return for this unswerving loyalty and military service, each Bannerman could expect cradle to grave support for himself and his family. The government allotted lands specifically for the support of Banner units and paid active duty Bannermen a monthly stipend in silver, a rice ration, and additional funds to maintain three to six horses.[9]

Cavalry lay at the core of the Banner forces, but they also included foot soldiers divided into archers, lancers, and musketeers. Eventually, each Banner had a company of musketeers with artillery experience, but these units remained of secondary importance, lagging behind the cavalry in terms of prestige. The cavalry soldier typically carried a compound bow and full quiver of arrows, which he could fire accurately while at a full gallop. The infantry soldier carried a short sword and occasionally used additional weapons such as cudgels, flails, or swords of longer length. Each soldier wore a uniform that identified his Banner unit, along with "armor" of padded cloth that facilitated riding and shooting arrows from the saddle. The number of soldiers in any given Banner is difficult to estimate, but Elliott's research in Manchu language documents reveals that in 1644 the total number of Bannermen fell between 300,000 and 500,000, approximately 43 percent Manchu, 22 percent Mongol and 35 percent Chinese. In the eighteenth century, the Qing maintained approximately 681 companies in the eight Manchu Banners, 204 companies in the eight Mongol Banners, and 266 companies in the eight Chinese Banners all under the direct control of the emperor. A commander of an individual Banner might supervise as many as 25,000 troops in one of the larger Manchu Banners or as few as 8,000 in a smaller Mongol Banner. Although the Chinese and Mongol Banners provided important support for the Qing and enjoyed privileges, they remained secondary to the Manchu Banners in terms of rewards and prestige.[10]

The Manchu emperors understood that their position as military rulers over a massive Chinese population and made internal pacification, rather than external defense, the top priority of the Qing military. Elite members of the Banners staffed an imperial guard which protected the emperor and his palace, the Forbidden City in Beijing. A guard unit of 15,000 stood watch over the palace, a vanguard unit of 1,500 traveled with the emperor, leading the way whenever he went outside the gates of the Forbidden City, and an imperial bodyguard of 1,500 men, exclusively Manchu, provided personal protection at all times. Additional Banner units took up garrison duty in a number of major cities and strategic points. These garrison units stood separate from the traditional twenty-four Banners, providing additional security against rebellion and protection for Manchu inhabitants of Chinese cities such as Xi'an, Nanjing, and Hangzhou.

Despite the formidable skills of the Banner forces, they required the support of additional Chinese military forces to maintain order across the width and breadth of China. The Manchus recruited surrendered or captured Chinese soldiers for a separate force called the Army of the Green Standard. These forces took up the task of policing the countryside by maintaining bases in rural towns and prefectures. The Green Standard forces handled day-to-day police matters, pursued local bandit gangs, and assisted local officials with tax collection. In essence, these forces kept the peace in rural areas while the Banners stood in reserve. The Qing court made a conscious decision to rely heavily on the Army of the Green Standard for rural pacification, preferring to preserve the fighting strength of the Banners and feeling that the presence of Chinese soldiers would arouse less resentment than would Manchu or Mongol soldiers. Because the Army of the Green Standard outnumbered the Banner forces, averaging around 600,000 troops during the Qing period, rising and falling because of military need, the court appointed only trusted Manchu and Chinese Bannermen to command them.[11]

Revolt of the Three Feudatories, 1673–1681

The fact that Manchu rule over China depended on the support of Chinese military forces posed a problem for early Qing rulers. In fact, the same forces that facilitated the Qing conquest also posed the greatest challenge to Manchu rule in the early years of the dynasty. Beginning in 1673, Chinese generals who had earlier sided with the Manchus turned against the Qing court in what historians call the Revolt of the Three Feudatories. The term three feudatories refers to three men who defected to the Manchu cause, contributing in no small way to the Qing victory. These three men, Wu Sangui, Geng Jimao, and Shang Kexi, all played critical roles in the conquest by pursuing and destroying remnants of the Ming court in the south and southwest. Wu Sangui himself had seen to the execution of the last claimant to the Ming throne. As a reward for this valuable service, the Shunzhi emperor gave them titles and official appointments in parts of the south. They assumed wide-ranging civil and military authority in their respective territories—Wu Sangui in Yunnan and Guizhou, Geng Jimao in Fujian, and Shang Kexi in Guangdong. Together they controlled the entire south and southwest. Moreover, each took control over tax collection in their domains and enjoyed subsidies from the Qing court to support their military forces. By 1660, Wu Sangui, the most formidable of the three with 65,000 troops under his command, cost the Qing court nine million silver taels in annual subsidies. At times this may have represented as much as 40 percent of the state's cash reserves. Whenever Qing officials suggested reducing the subsidy, Wu began a new campaign on the Burmese border or against one of the ethnic minority groups in the region, thus reminding the government of his value in protecting and pacifying the southwest.[12]

In 1673, almost thirty years after the conquest, Shang Kexi petitioned the Kangxi emperor for permission to step down from his position and to return to his native Liaodong in Manchuria. The Kangxi emperor saw this as an opportunity to begin removing all three feudatories from their bases of power in the south and gave his consent. He also informed Wu Sangui and Geng Jimao that they should do the same. Some Qing officials warned against such a move, fearing that it might provoke a revolt, but the young Kangxi emperor had decided the time had come to deal with the problem of the three feudatories and boldly sought their retirement. Wu, now over sixty years old, had contemplated retirement but expected that his son and family would retain control of his feudatory. When he learned that the Kangxi emperor intended to uproot his entire family and replace them with Chinese and Manchu officials, he instead revolted against the Qing court. He began by executing those officials in Yunnan and Guizhou who refused to join him and in early 1674 declared his intention to establish a new dynasty called the Zhou, invoking the name of the ancient Zhou dynasty which all Confucian scholars regarded as the golden age of Chinese history.

Wu Sangui commanded significant military forces, but not enough to defeat the combined strength of the twenty-four Banners and the Army of the Green Standard. More than his military strength, his ability to arouse anti-Manchu sentiment among the Chinese population of the south gave him an advantage. His call for a restoration of Chinese rule and the expulsion of the Manchus from Chinese soil proved effective as large numbers of Chinese officials in the south abandoned their offices or even killed their Manchu counterparts and joined his forces. One of the other two feudatories, now under the control of Geng Jimao's son Geng Jingzhong, joined the revolt and within a matter of months Wu took control of six provinces in the south and southwest. Hoping to take advantage of his momentum, Wu Sangui offered the Kangxi emperor a deal whereby the Manchus could return to their homeland north of the Great Wall, while Wu would rule over the rest of the Chinese empire through his Zhou dynasty. The young Kangxi emperor showed no desire to compromise. He responded by executing Wu Sangui's son, who had been in Beijing and had allegedly been implicated in a plot to burn down the imperial palace.

Despite Kangxi's determination to crush the revolt, reports from the south that numerous officials and military men had defected to Wu's banner caused great consternation in the capital. Hoping to stem the tide and perhaps win back the support some of these defectors, Kangxi offered amnesty to those who had joined Wu Sangui if they returned to their positions as loyal subjects of the Qing. He also personally directed the military campaign against Wu's forces, first establishing two staging areas from which to distribute troops and supplies. In the east, the city of Yanzhou in Shandong Province served as a base for operations along the coast and into Hunan. In the west, Taiyuan in Shanxi Province served as a staging area for campaigns in the west and protected Beijing from attack. He then reinforced cities across Anhui, Jiangsu, and Jiangxi provinces, forming a perimeter to the north of the territories in revolt and securing the financial resources of the Yangzi River basin.[13]

The Qing military forces showed little of the success in battle that had characterized the conquest of China some thirty years prior. Perhaps hindered by the unfamiliar terrain and climate of the south, the poor performance of Manchu generals and Banner units led the Kangxi emperor to make greater use of Chinese generals and the Army of the Green Standard, another indication of Qing dependence upon Chinese military support. Perhaps emboldened by Wu's early success, in 1676 the third of the three feudatories, Shang Zhixin, son of Shang Kexi, joined the movement bringing Guangdong Province into the conflict on the side of Wu Sangui. As Qing armies bogged down and made little progress in fighting in several provinces, it appeared as though the Qing might not survive and Manchu rule in China would come to an abrupt end.

Despite the lackluster performance of the Banner forces, by 1676 the tide had turned and the movement to unseat the Manchus lost steam. The difference in resources began to influence the fighting, as the larger and better supplied Qing armies began to wear down the individual forces of the three feudatories. Moreover, each of the three feudatories tended to fight on its own with little coordination or cooperation, occasionally even attacking each other. As the tide of battle turned, those who had joined Wu's initial revolt began to drop out of the fighting one at a time. Geng Jingzhong surrendered in November 1676 as did Shang Zhixin shortly thereafter. Kangxi's judicious use of offers of amnesty undoubtedly contributed to the unraveling of the anti-Manchu forces. Wu Sangui's forces continued to fight until his death in October 1678 and then under his grandson, Wu Shifan, until his defeat and suicide in Yunnan Province in December 1681. This marked the end of the Revolt of the Three Feudatories and the complete consolidation of Manchu rule over China.

In the wake of the revolt, the Kangxi emperor executed numerous high-ranking officials and military men who had joined the movement. Two of the three leaders of the feudatories, Geng Jingzhong and Shang Zhixin, among others, suffered "death by slicing" at the hands of Kangxi's executioners. Lists of Manchus and loyal Chinese had already been prepared, allowing the emperor to immediately begin placing new officials in the south and southwest, extending Qing control to those areas that had been virtual Chinese fiefs under the three feudatories.

Pacifying the Borders

The suppression of the three feudatories marked an important step in the consolidation of Manchu rule in China and eliminated the greatest internal threat to the Qing dynasty. Yet there remained serious threats from the periphery of the empire, where Ming loyalists on the island of Taiwan, Russian traders on the northeastern border, and resurgent Mongols on the Steppe each posed problems for the Qing. The Kangxi emperor acted decisively to meet these threats and in doing so carved out the modern borders of the Chinese state.

Since the time of the Manchu conquest, the Zheng family from Fujian Province had been a thorn in the Manchu side as leaders of the most enduring of the Ming loyalist movements. Zheng Chenggong, the most famous member of the family sometimes known in the West as "Koxinga," had established a base on the island of Taiwan from which he continued his anti-Qing resistance. The Qing court initially attempted to deal with this problem by evacuating the coastal region of Fujian, moving the population twenty miles inland in order to deny Zheng Chenggong's forces access to supplies. Zheng died in 1662, but his descendants continued to hold out on Taiwan. Only after the suppression of the three feudatories did the Kangxi emperor turn his full attention to Taiwan, relying on one of the Zheng family's former admirals to lead a large naval force against the island. In 1683, this force of 300 ships and 20,000 men defeated the remnants of the Zheng family force, making Taiwan a formal part of the empire, garrisoned by Qing troops.

The Kangxi emperor next took decisive action against the Russians who had been expanding through Siberia to the northeast border of the Qing empire, building a trading fort at Albazin on the northern bank of the Heilong (Amur) River in 1666. Kangxi had long experience with Westerners, Jesuits having been active in China for roughly a century at that point, but he feared a possible alliance between the Russians and the Zungar Mongols, a group emerging as a powerful force on the Steppe. Kangxi authorized two attacks on Albazin, razing the post and driving the Russian traders out. Peace negotiations, accomplished through Jesuit missionaries translating Russian and Chinese into Latin, resulted in the Treaty of Nerchinsk in 1689. The first treaty in which China addressed a foreign ruler on relatively equal terms, it established regulations for Sino-Russian trade and set the border at the Heilong River, approximately the same as the current border between the PRC (People's Republic of China) and the Russian Far East.

Having crushed the resistance on Taiwan and established a treaty with the Russians, Kangxi moved against the Zungar Mongols who had formed a substantial territorial empire to the northwest of China under the leader Galdan. The rise of a large tribal alliance under the Zungars threatened Qing relations with other non-Chinese groups and destabilized its borders. Galdan had already intervened in Tibet, asserting himself as protector of the Dalai Lama. The Manchu Banner forces proved more effective when fighting on the grasslands of Mongolia than in the mountainous terrain of south China. In 1696, the Kangxi emperor personally led a force of 80,000 troops against Galdan, cornering him at Jao Modo (south of Ulan Battar) and destroying his military force. Continued Mongol intervention in Tibet prompted Kangxi to send a force to Lhasa in 1720, where Chinese forces installed a new "legitimate" Dalai Lama and established a protectorate over Tibet, preventing any Mongol–Tibetan alliance that might prove detrimental to Qing rule.

In 1644, Manchu Bannermen swept through the pass from Manchuria into north China, establishing the Qing dynasty and ushering in a period of over 250 years of foreign rule. The Manchu emperors made efforts to present themselves as Confucian rulers and worthy of the Mandate of Heaven in order to win acceptance from the Chinese population, yet Manchu rule in China rested on the basis of military strength. The Qing dynasty relied heavily on the Banner forces and the Army of the Green Standard to protect the borders of the empire and to put down internal revolt. In the nineteenth century, these military forces would face significant challenges, both internal and external, that would shake the foundation of Manchu rule in China.

The Anglo-Chinese Wars, 1839–1860

The eighteenth century marked the military high point of the Qing dynasty. The Qianlong emperor, who reigned from 1736 to 1796, presided over a large and prosperous empire which had been in firm control of China since the suppression of the Revolt of the Three Feudatories. Like his grandfather Kangxi, the Qianlong emperor worked hard to govern the empire effectively and to secure its borders. He conducted numerous military campaigns against neighboring states, which he referred to collectively as his "Ten Perfections." Repeated campaigns against tribesmen in western Sichuan (1747–1749), the Mongols (1755–1757), Muslim Turks in Xinjiang (1758–1759), the Burmese (1766–1770), the Vietnamese (1788–1789), the Nepalese (1790–1792), and the suppression of a revolt on Taiwan (1787–1788) ensured the pacification of the borders of the Qing Empire. Yet at the same time these campaigns expended valuable resources which exacerbated a growing economic problem and weakened the Qing military on the eve of its greatest challenge.

Deterioration of the Qing Military

Despite the numerous military accomplishments of both Kangxi and Qianlong, the Qing dynasty's military effectiveness gradually eroded over the course of the eighteenth century. Like many Chinese dynasties, corruption posed a serious problem, draining government coffers and placing a greater burden on the taxpaying peasantry. For one egregious example, in the last years of Qianlong's reign he came to rely heavily on a corrupt imperial bodyguard named He Shen, who won the trust of the aged emperor and took advantage of his patronage to amass a personal fortune by plundering the national treasury. On a smaller scale, corruption flourished at all levels of the administration in Qing China, in which underpaid civilian officials and military officers supplemented their incomes through graft, extortion, and drawing payments for "ghost soldiers" who did not exist. When corruption reached excessive levels, it not only caused financial problems for the government but also pushed the largely peasant population, on whom the tax burden fell, into economic desperation.

Such financial problems had a substantial impact on the effectiveness of the Qing military. As a dynasty of conquest, the Qing rulers understood the necessity of maintaining a strong military force and devoted as much as 50–70 percent of the budget to the Banners and the Army of the Green Standard. The Banners in particular required massive funds as each member enjoyed stipends in cash and grain, along with supplements for horses, weapons, weddings, funerals, housing, and old age pensions. Because the Banners included not only soldiers but their families as well, the majority of the funds allocated to the Banners went to the support of those who did not actually serve in the military. The massive financial requirements of the Qing military placed a substantial economic burden on the dynasty, which struggled to meet its needs. Manchu, Chinese, and Mongol Bannermen found it increasingly difficult to maintain their elite lifestyles as stipends remained at levels established during the seventeenth century. While the Banner population increased and prices rose, stipends and living allowances did not. The lack of money with which to maintain their equipment, and the corresponding lack of morale, led to a marked decline in the effectiveness of the Banners. In order to cut expenses, the government eliminated almost all Chinese Banners by 1779. The Manchu and Mongol Banners showed signs of relaxed discipline as many Bannermen became accustomed to soft living. Instead of practicing their military skills, they spent their time gambling, going to the theater, drinking, or running moneylending operations on the side. The Qianlong emperor recognized this trend and attempted to revive them by encouraging a restoration of "Manchuness." He urged Manchu Bannermen to visit the homelands in Manchuria, to return to the practice of traditional military arts of horsemanship and archery, and to use the Manchu language rather than Chinese. For most Bannerman, the quest for pleasure or increased income took precedent over the revival of old traditions.[1]

The decline of the Qing military came amidst the dynasty's general economic distress of the late eighteenth and early nineteenth centuries, which gave rise to a number of revolts. Although most posed little real threat to the dynasty, they revealed weaknesses within the Qing military. The most significant of these revolts, the White Lotus Society Revolt, began in 1796 in response to the declining economic situation in the countryside, lingering anti-Manchu sentiment, and periodic harassment by the Qing government. A quasi-Buddhist secret society, the White Lotus Society began its revolt in Hubei, but quickly spread to other provinces as those who bore a grudge against the Qing joined the movement. In the early years of the revolt, Manchu Bannermen and Army of the Green Standard forces proved unable to defeat the White Lotus fighters. Using primarily guerrilla tactics, the rebels defeated Qing troops and succeeded in capturing several small towns. The tide of the fighting turned around 1800, in part because of the removal of the corrupt He Shen, but also because the court brought in more effective military units from other areas of the empire. Much of the fighting fell to gentry-led militias, organized to defend local areas when regular Qing forces proved incapable of doing so. The fact that the revolt lasted for nearly ten years revealed the degree to which the Qing military had deteriorated over the course of the eighteenth century. The costs of this lengthy suppression campaign served only to exacerbate the already difficult financial situation and fuel discontent.

Western Trade at Guangzhou

In the late eighteenth century, as the Qing government faced profound economic problems and a debilitated military, a new challenge emerged in the form of Western merchants who sailed to China in greater numbers seeking silks, tea, and luxury goods. For the rulers of China, foreign relations had long meant dealing with the nomadic tribes on China's northern border or conducting tributary relations with China's numerous vassal states. The Qing exhibited a certain amount of flexibility in dealing with different foreign groups and recognized that the Europeans required special treatment. Yet Qing rulers worried about the pernicious influence European merchants and missionaries might have on China and so restricted them to remote parts of the southern coast.[2]

Beginning in 1759, the Qing government formalized a system of regulating Western trade called the "Canton System." Named after the port of Guangzhou ("Canton" in the pidgin language of the traders) where trade with Westerners took place, the Canton System reflected the fact that the Qing saw little need for Western imports and reserved the right to control all foreign trade. The Qing court limited Western ships to the single southern port of Guangzhou and designated thirteen or so merchant firms, known as "Hongs," which had the exclusive task of dealing with Western merchants. While at the port of Guangzhou, Qing authorities kept tight control over the movement of the Westerners, restricting them to a walled compound on the banks of the Pearl River which included a long row of warehouses, or "factories," that the foreigners rented from the Hong merchants. Western merchants came ashore to unload their goods, but they could not leave the compound or enter the city. Under such monopolistic conditions, the Hong merchants stood to make substantial profits, charging Western merchants high prices for Chinese goods and imposing arbitrary taxes and fees. Moreover, Western merchants paid for Chinese goods with hard cash, gold or silver, rather than bartering with other goods.

As the leading Western trader with China, the royally chartered British East India Company chafed under the monopolistic restrictions of the Canton System. In an attempt to encourage the Qing government to amend its trade practices, the British government sent veteran diplomat Lord George Macartney to China in the fall of 1792. Arriving the next year in time for the Qianlong emperor's birthday, Macartney intended to present gifts to the emperor and to negotiate a trade agreement between Great Britain and the Qing Empire. In particular, Macartney sought the opening of additional ports for British ships and a commercial treaty regulating the terms of the trade, thereby ending the restrictive and monopolistic Canton System.

Macartney made his way to an audience with the emperor at the summer palace in Inner Mongolia, laden with presents and escorted by Qing troops with flags describing his party as a tributary envoy from England. After an initial dispute over whether or not Macartney would perform the requisite ritual prostration before the emperor, known as the "kowtow," Qianlong granted Macartney an audience and accepted the gifts from the English king, George III. On the issue of trade, however, Qing officials refused to grant his requests. Shortly after Macartney's departure, Qianlong sent his famous letter to George III, explaining his reasons for rejecting the British demands. "We have never set much store on strange or ingenious objects," he informed the king, "nor do we need anymore of your country's manufactures."[3] Further British attempts to negotiate a commercial treaty with the Qing met with similar rebuffs.

Despite the Qing government's unwillingness to alter its trading policies, the nature of the trade with Western merchants changed in the late eighteenth and early nineteenth centuries. Since the Hong merchants had little use for English goods, the British paid primarily in cash for Chinese tea and silks. Throughout the eighteenth century, the balance of trade favored China as British cash flowed into China in substantial quantities. Unable to find a legitimate commodity that the Chinese desired, the British East India Company began smuggling opium into China. Prohibited by Chinese law, opium smuggling took place outside of the confines of the Canton System. Beginning slowly with perhaps 1,000 chests of opium in 1767, the number of chests smuggled into China rose to 40,000 in 1839. In addition to creating a huge number of drug addicts, the illegal trade had a devastating impact on the already beleaguered Chinese economy. As more opium entered China through smuggling routes on a cash and carry basis, more gold and silver flowed out of China, reversing the balance of trade. Lack of an effective navy and rampant corruption hindered Qing government attempts to enforce the prohibition on opium.

Commissioner Lin Zexu at Guangzhou

In 1838, the Daoguang emperor appointed a provincial official named Lin Zexu as Imperial Commissioner in charge of opium suppression. He first cracked down on domestic smugglers and users before addressing the issue with the British. He penned a famous letter to Queen Victoria, asking her why British opium smugglers felt they had the right to "use the poisonous drug to injure the Chinese people?"[4] Unable to convince the British government of the immorality of the opium trade, Lin took the issue directly to the Western merchants at Guangzhou. On March 18, 1839, Commissioner Lin demanded that Western merchants turn over all opium on board their ships within three days. After discussion among themselves and with Hong merchants, the Western traders turned over a token number of chests of opium, believing that such a gesture would allow Lin to save "face" and avoid a further trouble. Lin took possession of 1,036 chests of opium on March 21, but reiterated his demand for all of their stores of opium. British Superintendent of Trade, Charles Elliot, traveled from Macao, a Portuguese trading base since the mid-sixteenth century, to the factories at Guangzhou to mediate the dispute.

Dissatisfied with the response to his demand, on the night of March 24 Lin ordered all Chinese to leave the Western factories, reinforced the armed guard around the compound, and imposed a blockade on the river approach to Guangzhou, effectively shutting down trade. Some 350 foreign merchants remained in the compound, unable to leave or to have contact with their compatriots at harbor downriver from Guangzhou. The military force guarding the compound could not be counted among China's finest warriors, but with a total strength of over 1,000 men they sufficed to keep the Westerners isolated. The force included infantrymen armed with matchlock firearms, supported by servants and peasants armed with pikes and other simple weapons. In order to increase the pressure on the Westerners, at night roving guard units banged gongs and blew horns, preventing those inside from getting a sound sleep and fraying their nerves. Throughout the ordeal, Lin offered incentives for turning over the remaining stores of opium. If the Westerners turned in one-fourth of the opium held on ships outside of Guangzhou, Lin promised to restore cooks and servants to the compound. In return for half of the opium, he would allow small boats to pass through the blockade. With three-fourths of the opium the guards would be removed and once all of the opium had been turned over normal trade would resume.

After less than ten days of confinement, Charles Elliot agreed to produce the remaining opium. He convinced the British merchants to turn all stores of opium over to him so that he could then, as a representative of the British government, turn over the opium to Qing authorities. Commissioner Lin allowed communication between the factories at Guangzhou and ships outside in order to facilitate delivery. A trickle of chests of opium came in slowly, nearing 25 percent of the total, so in a gesture of good faith Lin allowed cooks and servants to return to the compound. On May 4, with the delivery of the promised 21,306 chests of opium and after forty-seven days of blockade, Commissioner Lin removed the guards and set the Westerners free. Lin destroyed the opium by dissolving it with lime and salt in long trenches, draining the residue into a creek, which then washed it out to sea.

Having made his point, Lin Zexu sought to restore normal trade relations, meaning a return to the restrictive Canton System, but insisted that that Western traders first sign a bond promising not to smuggle opium in the future on pain of death. Elliot prohibited British merchants from resuming trade under Chinese terms and demanded compensation for the confiscated opium. He then turned to his government for support in forcing the Chinese government pay compensation and to change the way the British and Chinese conducted trade. The British merchant community joined Elliot in his call for action, as wealthy firms heavily involved in the China trade such as Jardine Matheson lobbied Parliament for action. They sponsored a slew of popular publications describing the injustice of the Chinese incarceration of British subjects and created a substantial fund to finance a military expedition. In October 1839, Foreign Minister Lord Palmerston authorized an expeditionary force to demand reparations from the Chinese government and later issued a declaration of war on February 20, 1840.[5] Palmerston appointed Captain Charles Elliot and his cousin Admiral George Elliot as plenipotentiaries with the mission to obtain reparations for the confiscated opium and the insult to British traders and to obtain greater trading rights in China. The war plan called for a blockade of major coastal ports and the occupation of the island of Zhoushan, in Hangzhou Bay, until the Chinese government paid appropriate compensation and agreed to a commercial treaty.

The "Opium War"

Back in Guangzhou, relations between British traders and the Chinese authorities grew worse. In July 1839, several drunken British sailors got into an argument with Chinese villagers at Jianshacui, a village on the Kowloon side of Hong Kong, and beat a man named Lin Weixi to death. Lin Zexu demanded that the British turn over the sailors involved, but Elliot refused. Instead he paid compensation to the deceased's family and subjected the accused sailors to his own trial aboard a British ship. The court found several guilty and sentenced them to various terms of incarceration and monetary fine. Once back in England, the British government released them, rejecting the authority of Elliot's trial.

When Elliot refused to hand over the accused murderers, Lin Zexu cut off British access to supplies, ordering junks to patrol the river to prevent any Chinese from providing the British with food. He even poisoned sources of fresh water along the river approach to Guangzhou where the British might try to resupply, posting signs in Chinese to warn local residents of the danger. He also pressured the Portuguese officials to expel the British from Macao, forcing them to relocate to the barren island of Hong Kong. On September 4, 1839, Elliot sailed from Hong Kong aboard the *H.M.S. Volage* with a small force of armed merchant ships across the bay to Kowloon to demand provisions. When the Chinese refused to accommodate his demands, Elliot fired a warning shot. Chinese junks returned fire in what historians call the "Kowloon Incident," the first battle of the "Opium War." The fighting resulted in two killed and eight wounded on the Chinese side and two British wounded.

While the British expeditionary force made its way to China, the Qing court did not make immediate preparations for war, in part because of a lack of accurate information. In a memorial to the throne of September 18, two weeks after the Kowloon Incident, Lin Zexu reported a victory in which the British had fired on the Chinese without warning, but Chinese junks returned fire and inflicted dozens of casualties on the British. Inaccurate reporting, a chronic problem in the Qing government and military, often came from local officials who sought to enhance their own role in the hope of obtaining a reward or promotion. Such exaggerations and misreporting would have important repercussions on the Chinese war effort, preventing the Qing court from accurately assessing the realities of the fighting.

Following the Kowloon Incident, Elliot returned to Macao for discussions with Qing officials. The talks proved fruitless, as the Chinese still demanded that the British turn over the sailors involved in the death of Lin Weixi and sign the opium smuggling bond and Elliot still refused to do either. In the meantime, British merchants watched American and other traders sign the bond and take on loads of tea. Some British merchants threatened to sign the bond in order to resume profitable trade. In October, the British merchant vessel *Thomas Coutts* sailed upriver to Guangzhou in defiance of Elliot's prohibition on trade, its captain intending to sign whatever documents the Chinese wanted. Meanwhile, Lin Zexu ordered twenty-nine junks into the Bogue, the point where the Pearl River narrows in its approach to Guangzhou, threatening to seize at random British sailors to stand trial for the murder. Elliot sailed upriver aboard the *Volage* to meet this threat in late October. As he approached the Bogue on November 3, a second British ship, the *Royal Saxon* attempted to sail up to Guangzhou to resume trade. Determined to stop these acts of insubordination, Elliot ordered the *Volage* to fire a shot across her bow. Chinese junks in the vicinity came to the defense of the *Royal Saxon,* precipitating the Battle of Chuanbi. The British destroyed four Chinese junks, damaged several others, and killed fifteen Chinese sailors before forcing the rest to retreat upriver. Nonetheless, Lin Zexu reported to Beijing on November 21, 1839, that the Chinese commander Admiral Guan Tianpei had won a great victory, forcing the British ships to withdraw.[6]

Despite the British victories in these early encounters, Lin Zexu and other Qing officials did not believe that the British posed a formidable military challenge. They tended to view the military problem of the Westerners within the context of piracy along China's southeastern coast. Lin regarded the British as little more than seaborne bandits, who depended on plunder and looting to stay afloat. In order to deal with the problem, Lin Zexu supplemented his forces not by calling for additional Qing regular troops but by recruiting popular militia, mainly bandits and local toughs who often did more damage to Chinese villagers than to the British forces. This reflects not only the difficulty of obtaining reinforcements from other provinces but also the general Chinese view that while the British had naval skills, they could not fight well on land. Lin believed that the local militia could deal with the British should they come ashore and engage in a land battle. He also explored unconventional weapons and tactics such as the use of "water devils"—men who claimed the ability to stay submerged for several hours and might be used to destroy British ships from below the surface. When put to the test, the "water devils" did not live up to their reputation. Yet Lin had some understanding of the power of Western artillery, as he had acquired translations of Western military writings and even purchased foreign-made cannon.

Few Chinese at the time understood the degree of the technological advantage the British would enjoy in the Opium War. The nineteenth century brought a series of advances in military technology, including shallow draft steamships that could operate in five to six feet of water. The greater accuracy of their artillery combined with superior flintlock and percussion cap muskets gave the British a tremendous advantage in firepower. By contrast, the majority of Qing troops relied on traditional weapons such as the bow and arrow, spear, sword, and halberd. Those Qing soldiers who used firearms carried outdated matchlocks, unreliable and sometimes deadly to the user. The Chinese had numerous pieces of artillery, but mostly antiquated pieces from the Ming period, set in fixed positions that prevented adjusting fire. The Army of the Green Standard had given up on rigorous training and by 1840 few units displayed adequate discipline and training. Many operated at far less than full strength because of corrupt officers who padded their rolls with nonexistent soldiers.

In addition to the advantage in firepower, British naval technology helped offset the superior numbers of the Qing forces. Because of the traditional continental focus of the Chinese military, the Qing dynasty had no national naval force. Governors-general of the coastal provinces maintained local fleets of war junks, but these could not match the speed, maneuverability, or firepower of the Western vessels. British steamships in particular moved quickly along the coast in relatively shallow waters, training their guns on Chinese forts and cities. Qing ground forces found it next to impossible to move additional troops to the site of a British attack in time to mount an adequate defense. It took months to move military units on foot from one province to another, only to arrive short on supplies and exhausted.[7]

The British expeditionary fleet assembled off the coast of Macao in June 1840, totaling nearly fifty vessels—warships, steamers, and transports—and 4,000 troops under the command of Admiral George Elliot. Lin Zexu believed they would attack Guangzhou and loot it or perhaps simply try to reopen trade by force of arms. He assembled eighty war junks to protect the river approach to the city, increased the number of guns in the forts along the coast, and in some parts of the channel strung huge iron chains buoyed by rafts across the passage. Unknown to Lin Zexu, Lord Palmerston had insisted from the beginning that the British avoid dealing with local Chinese officials at Guangzhou and conduct negotiations only in Beijing. As a result, the British left several ships to blockade the mouth of the river at Hong Kong to prevent Western ships from going into Guangzhou and Chinese junks from leaving. The rest of the fleet sailed up the coast toward Fuzhou, intending to deliver a letter of demands from Lord Palmerston. Lin Zexu and other Qing officials initially believed that the military preparations in the Pearl River had intimidated the British into retreat and reported this to Beijing. Only later did they realize that they had merely misunderstood British intentions.

In early July the fleet approached the Fujian port city of Xiamen, but Qing officials refused to accept delivery of Palmerston's letter. The fleet sailed north to the mouth of the Yangzi River and the approach to the major cities of Shanghai and Nanjing. Elliot favored an attack on this area because its cities lay close to the water, well within range of the fleet's guns. Perhaps more importantly, the British might cut off the Grand Canal and thus the flow of grain to the capital, giving them a powerful bargaining chip in negotiations. The fleet approached the island of Zhoushan where Commander James Bremer demanded the surrender of the Chinese officials. When the ranking Chinese military officer, Zhang Chafa, refused to surrender, Bremer ordered an artillery barrage of several minutes that destroyed the coastal guns and several war junks. British troops then went ashore and the next day took control of the city of Dinghai with minimal resistance, as most of the area's inhabitants had fled.

As the British fleet moved north on August 1 with six ships and two coal transports, news of the latest engagements trickled into the capital. It normally took a week or more for messages to reach Beijing from the Shanghai area and perhaps two weeks from Guangzhou. The occupation of Zhoushan Island and the movement of the British fleet toward northern China and the river approach to Beijing led the emperor to criticize Lin Zexu for precipitating these events and not dealing with the British effectively. He authorized a Manchu official named Qishan to open talks with the British.

When the British force reached the mouth of the Beihe River, which leads to Tianjin and the quickest land route to Beijing, it encountered a series of defensive emplacements known as the Dagu forts. Here the British delivered the letter from

Lord Palmerston that demanded compensation and changes to the Canton System of Anglo-Chinese trade. The approach of "barbarian" military forces to the celestial capital prompted a flurry of activity in Beijing, where Daoguang and his advisors sought a way to get the British to return to the south. The emperor removed Lin from his position as Imperial Commissioner of Trade, appointing Qishan in his place. Like Lin Zexu, Qishan found himself in a difficult position. He had to get the British to return to the south and obtain peace without making major concessions or changing the Canton System. Following lengthy discussions over the course of August and early September, Elliot accepted Qishan's promise that meaningful negotiations would begin as soon as both parties reconvened in Guangzhou at the end of November. The British fleet left north China in mid-September.

Elliot agreed to return to Guangzhou because he believed that Lin's removal had eliminated a major obstacle to a satisfactory settlement. He hoped that new negotiations would yield a commercial treaty and possession of the island of Hong Kong. Yet the new Imperial Commissioner Qishan showed little intention of making major concessions, offering simply to open the additional port of Xiamen to British merchants. Angered and determined to make a show of force to encourage Qishan to offer more substantial concessions, Elliot ordered an attack on the forts in the Bogue in early January 1841. The artillery pieces in these forts, like all those on the Chinese coast, could not be raised, lowered, or otherwise moved to adjust fire. They lacked adequate range to compete with British naval guns, hampered by poor quality powder, and the forts lay too far apart to support one another. As a result, on January 7, one thousand five hundred British and Indian troops landed at Chuanbi and moved around to the undefended sides of the forts. Meanwhile the newly arrived steamship *Nemesis* prepared to bombard the forts from the channel. The *Nemesis* is an example of the technological imbalance of the Opium War. Built secretly by the British East India Company and constructed almost entirely of iron, this 660-ton paddle ship had two pivot-mounted thirty-two-pound guns, five six-pound guns on swivels, and when fully loaded drew only six feet of water. As the ground troops approached the backside of the fort, the *Nemesis* began its barrage with deadly accuracy. The Qing forces returned fire, but as they could not adjust their fire most rounds flew harmlessly beyond the British ships. British soldiers captured the fort while the *Nemesis* steamed upriver to destroy several junks for good measure. Qishan quickly agreed to negotiations that produced the Treaty of Chuanbi on January 20, 1841. According to this agreement, the Chinese promised to pay the British an indemnity of $6 million, to cede the island of Hong Kong to England, to establish diplomatic equality between China and England, and to resume trade at Guangzhou. Ironically, this agreement led to the dismissal of both Charles Elliot and Qishan.

When the home governments in London and Beijing received the terms of the treaty, neither found them acceptable. The enraged Daoguang emperor ordered reinforcements to Guangzhou as a part of an "army of extermination" to drive the British out of the region. Bureaucratic rivalries made Qishan's position even more difficult as his domestic political opponents spread rumors that he had accepted bribes from the British. Daoguang ordered him brought to Beijing in chains and rejected the Treaty of

Chuanbi. Lord Palmerston proved equally unhappy with the treaty. First, it included an indemnity worth only a fraction of the cost of the opium Lin destroyed. Second, the British did not acquire the island of Zhoushan, which he far preferred to the barren, rocky island of Hong Kong. Interpreting this as tantamount to disobeying direct orders, in April 1841 Palmerston sent Henry Pottinger, an Irishman with substantial experience in India, to replace Elliot as Superintendent of Trade and Plenipotentiary. Pottinger left England with orders to resume the war, to increase the amount of monetary compensation, to abolish the Canton System, to open several new ports, and to obtain the right for consular representation in each port.

As his replacement made his way east, Elliot faced renewed opposition around Guangzhou as Qing troops and militia flooded into the region. He chose to abandon the British garrison at Zhoushan, where contaminated water sickened 1,300 soldiers and killed 150, and concentrated his force for attacks on additional Bogue forts and clearing the obstacles that blocked one of its major passages. In complete control of the river passage to Guangzhou, the British force now threatened the great trade city itself. In May, the Chinese launched an attack using fireboats designed to burn British ships. This involved filling small boats with cotton soaked in oil and chaining them together in pairs. "Water Braves" guided the boats with the tide toward the British ships under cover of darkness, waiting until the last moment to ignite the cotton. War junks would then move in and open fire on the blazing British ships. The attack did not go as planned as British sentries observed the approaching boats and sounded the alarm. The Water Braves ignited the cotton, but the British had time to launch their own small boats to deflect them away from their ships. Changes in the tide prevented a second wave of fireboats and hampered the other ships, but the *Nemesis*, with its coal fires already burning, moved along the channel firing on war junks and shore batteries.

In retaliation for this attack, the British landed several hundred troops under the command of Sir Hugh Gough to capture the forts protecting the northern gate of the city. Gough's force breached the city walls of Guangzhou but did not enter. With British forces occupying the high ground above the city and the guns of the *Nemesis* trained directly upon it, the local Chinese authorities had little option other than to come to terms. Elliot demanded a $6 million payment, which amounted to a "ransom" for Guangzhou, and the withdrawal of all Chinese troops not a part of the normal Guangzhou garrison. In return, the British promised to withdraw and return the captured forts to the Chinese. While by no means a settlement to the war and the issues that began it, this settlement did restore a temporary peace to the environs around Guangzhou.[8]

The Sanyuanli Incident

The fighting around Guangzhou produced xenophobic reaction among the local peasantry and gentry that would have an important impact on the war and Chinese nationalism. Rumors spread that British and Indian soldiers raped Chinese women, looted towns and villages, and desecrated tombs, which gave rise to anger among the peasantry and the formation of local militia. Lin Zexu had earlier encouraged the formation of these irregular troops and relied on them to supplement the Guangzhou garrison. Armed for the most part with clubs, hoes, and spears and led by local elites, these peasant-soldiers began assembling over the winter of 1840–1841 for purposes of local defense. On May 29, 1841, British troops went on patrol to plunder for supplies at the market village of Sanyuanli, several miles north of Guangzhou. The next day, several thousand peasants converged on the area and threatened the British camp. Attempts to disperse the militia failed as they temporarily withdrew only to reform and again threaten to attack. In the meantime, the fierce heat took its toll on British troops who suffered from sunstroke. Sir Hugh Gough finally ordered his men to advance and break through the lines of the village militia. They did so, but a sudden severe thunderstorm limited their vision, obscured the pathways, and rendered flintlock muskets ineffective. In the confusion, one company of sixty Indian sepoys and three British officers separated from the main force and engaged a contingent of militiamen. The rain stopped and the company retreated to a small wooded area where the soldiers formed a defensive square, using bayonets against the spears of the Chinese militia. Before long, two companies of British marines armed with percussion cap muskets, which fired despite the rain, arrived to rescue the lost company, dispersing the villagers and escorting the harried sepoys and their officers back to camp. In all, the British suffered one killed and fifteen wounded at Sanyuanli.[9]

Exaggerated accounts that the militia had scored a great victory and had killed eighty to ninety foreign soldiers began to circulate among the local Chinese villagers. The news spread rapidly, and the ranks of the militia swelled to 12,000. Gough informed Chinese officials that if they did not disband the militia, the British would attack Guangzhou. Qing officials persuaded the members of the gentry who commanded the militia to disband their forces and the 12,000 militiamen simply melted away. As tales of the "great victory" at Sanyuanli spread, many local Chinese concluded that while the Manchu Bannermen and Army of the Green Standard forces seemed incapable of dealing with the Westerners, common villagers organized into local militia could rise up and drive them out of China. They blamed Manchu officials and traitorous Chinese elites for holding back the masses and placating the foreigners. This Sanyuanli incident did much to arouse Han nationalism and anti-Manchu sentiment in the latter half of the nineteenth century.[10]

In August 1841 Henry Pottinger arrived to replace Charles Elliot with 14 ships and 2,500 soldiers to reinvigorate the war effort. In the spring of 1842 he supplemented his force with reinforcements from India, which included thirty-eight vessels and troopships carrying 10,000 infantrymen. His mission resembled Elliot's initial orders, a blockade of Guangzhou and Hong Kong while sending the rest of the fleet up the coast. At Xiamen, Qing officials had amassed fifty war junks and 9,000 soldiers to man the three coastal forts with a combined 200 guns spread out over a mile of coastline. On August 26, 1841, the British began shelling the Xiamen forts. As usual, the Chinese artillery could not adjust its fire to prevent the British from putting a force ashore to take the forts with flanking maneuvers. The British captured Xiamen suffering only two dead and fifteen wounded.

The Yangzi Campaign

From Xiamen the fleet sailed north along the coast to Zhoushan Island, which had long been the object of British planning. Despite heavy Chinese reinforcements, the British captured Zhoushan with minimal casualties, as once again the Chinese left their flanks exposed to ground assault. Afterward, the British captured the fort at Zhenhai, which guarded the mouth of the Yangzi River and the approach to Ningbo. Chinese troops abandoned Ningbo, which served as a British camp for the winter of 1841–1842. Their numbers had dropped dramatically, as they had to leave garrisons at each place they captured—Guangzhou, Xiamen, Zhoushan—and from the illnesses that continued to plague British soldiers and sailors.[11]

While the British forces camped at Ningbo, the Qing court planned a counter-offensive designed to drive the British out of the Yangzi River area. The Daoguang emperor appointed his cousin, a man of limited military experience, to command a force of 12,000 regular troops and 33,000 militiamen. The plan called for a ground attack on Zhenhai, at the mouth of the Yangzi River and a naval assault to retake Zhoushan Island. The attack began on March 9, 1842, in spite of heavy rain. The Qing forces managed to fight their way into Zhenhai and reach the central market before the British drove them back. Using cannon at close range in the narrow streets, British grapeshot inflicted hundreds of casualties on the Chinese attackers. The majority of Qing troops stood in reserve while the attackers fell in alarming numbers before British fire. When the initial assault failed, Qing officers refused to commit their reinforcements, ending the siege. The Qing naval assault on Zhoushan Island likewise failed.

The British Yangzi campaign continued from May to August 1842 and eventually produced a negotiated settlement to the war. Moving on from Ningbo, British forces took Zhapu on May 18, where Manchu Banner forces put up some of the fiercest resistance of the war. On June 16, the British attacked and took control of Wusong and did the same to Shanghai three days later. Approximately forty-five miles downriver from Nanjing an estimated 2,000 Manchu Bannermen again put up strong resistance at Zhenjiang on July 21. The British forces numbered closer to 5,000 and managed to breach the wall and open the city gates. The Manchu Bannermen refused to surrender, inflicting over 1,600 casualties on the British. Fighting to the end, many Bannermen killed their families before committing suicide. The fighting at Zhenjiang indicates that the Chinese belief that the British would be vulnerable in a ground war had some validity. Had the British attempted to take major inland cities, the combination of meeting the Manchu forces where they were strongest and vulnerability to illness would have made a British victory unlikely. Regardless, the capture of Zhenjiang blocked the Grand Canal, bisected the empire, and left Nanjing vulnerable to attack. On August 5, British ships arrived at Nanjing.

Treaty of Nanjing

The failure of the Chinese counteroffensive of May and the British approach to Nanjing led to a change in the Qing court's policy. The Daoguang emperor instructed yet another Manchu official, Qiying, to negotiate a settlement and avoid an assault on the city. Peace came at a heavy price for the Chinese in the form of the Treaty of Nanjing in August 1842, which destroyed the Canton System and restructured the nature of China's relations with the West. First, it stipulated that the Qing court must open a total of five ports to British traders and that each port would have a British diplomatic consul in residence. Second, China ceded the island of Hong Kong to the British. Third, it stipulated that the Qing court pay the British and indemnity totaling $21 million to cover the cost of the opium and expenses incurred during the fighting. A supplemental Treaty of the Bogue, signed in October 1843, added more privileges for the British, including the right of British Consuls to try their own subjects for crimes committed in China, a "Most Favored Nation Clause," which meant that any privileges China extended to other Western countries automatically applied to England as well, and fixed customs duties at five percent of the value of the cargo. Soon thereafter, the Americans and the French demanded similar treaties from the Chinese government. Anxious to avoid new conflicts they could ill afford, China agreed and signed separate treaties with these other powers.

The excitement and satisfaction with which the Westerners in China greeted the Opium War and the new treaty system did not last long. Western traders and officials soon found that the opening of five treaty ports did little to satisfy those who desired greater access to Chinese markets. Local authorities in the newly opened port cities dragged their feet on official matters and remained reluctant to accommodate Western merchants. Qing officials in general showed little interest in adhering to the terms of the treaty or adopting the diplomatic and commercial practices of the Westerners. As leaders of the Far Eastern trade, the British continued to press for free access to other ports along the China coast and the fabulous wealth they imagined existed in the vast interior. Christian missionaries joined in, hoping to visit cities in the interior in order to proselytize and win converts. British, French, and American attempts at treaty revision met with staunch refusal, setting the stage for a second clash between England and the Qing court.

The Arrow War, 1856–1860

The second clash came in October 1856, when Qing authorities at Guangzhou boarded the vessel *Arrow* and arrested a dozen Chinese crew members for acts of piracy. Owned by a Chinese but registered in the British territory of Hong Kong, the seizure of crew members from a "British" vessel provided the pretext for a second Anglo-Chinese War, often called the Arrow War, less than twenty years after the first. The British consul Harry Parkes and Hong Kong governor John Bowring complained that Qing authorities needed a warrant to board a vessel registered under the British flag and argued that the crew enjoyed British legal protection. They demanded the release of the crew members and a formal apology. The Imperial Commissioner of Trade at Guangzhou, Ye Mingchen, released the prisoners a few weeks later but refused to apologize. Without official authorization from London, Parkes ordered a British naval force to sail upriver to bombard the Bogue forts that guarded the entrance to Guangzhou. To make known their annoyance with Ye Mingchen, the British force lobbed shells at his residence and in late October occupied part of Guangzhou. In retaliation, the Qing officials closed off all foreign trade at Guangzhou and in December burned the foreign warehouses.

Back in England, now serving as Prime Minister, Lord Palmerston interpreted the seizure of the Arrow and the alleged hauling down of its British flag as an insult to the nation and authorized a British expeditionary force under Lord Elgin.[12] A French expedition under Baron Gros joined the British in retaliation for the murder of a French missionary in China in early 1856, bringing the total force to 5,700 troops. Elgin sought not only redress for the Arrow Incident but also treaty revision and the right of British diplomats to reside in Beijing. In a word, the British again sought through war what they could not achieve through negotiation. Elgin's expeditionary force arrived at Hong Kong in September 1857 where he issued an ultimatum to Ye Mingchen, demanding compensation and treaty revision. Ye refused, prompting British and French forces to attack Guangzhou on December 28. They arrested the imperial commissioner and sent him to Calcutta, where he died a year later. An allied commission governed Guangzhou through a Chinese puppet regime for the next three years until the completion of a new treaty. In mid-April, a combined British–French force of several thousand troops and over twenty ships sailed north toward Tianjin, feeling that only military pressure on the capital would lead to meaningful discussions. On May 20, 1858, Anglo-French forces opened fire on the Dagu forts that guarded the river approach to Tianjin. Within a few hours, the allied forces took control of the forts and then pushed forward to Tianjin, 100 miles from Beijing.

Shocked and again defeated, the Qing court saw little alternative to negotiations with the Westerners. Senior Manchu officials Guiliang and Qiying operated at a distinct disadvantage in the negotiations as British officials warned that anything less than a satisfactory treaty would mean a march on Beijing. The resulting Treaty of Tianjin, signed on June 26, 1858, gave the British the right to post a minister in Beijing, opened ten new treaty ports to British ships, allowed the British free navigation of the Yangzi River, and gave British subjects and missionaries the right to travel into the interior of China. The treaty also legalized the opium trade and forced the Chinese to pay an indemnity of four million silver taels to cover Britain's war costs. The Qing court accepted these conditions, and then agreed to similar treaties with the French, Americans, and Russians.

In the months after the fighting ended, Qing officials regained some confidence and began to back away from the treaty. In July, local militia attacked British and French forces in Guangzhou but withered in the face of superior artillery fire. In January 1859, Chinese militia attacked a detachment of 700 British marines. The British reinforced the marines with 1,300 troops and six gunboats, dispersing the militia and burning the local village in three days of fighting. In preparation for the return of Western envoys after the formal ratification of the treaty by their home governments, the Qing military rearmed the Dagu forts and blocked the mouth of the river with giant chains, scuttled barges, and reed screens. When the allied representatives returned in June 1859 to complete the treaty ratification, Qing officials demanded that allied representatives disembark on the coast and take a longer land route to the capital. Although the American delegation later did take the land route without incident, the British and French envoys refused. As British engineers and marines began removing the obstacles to clear the river passage, Chinese forts on both sides of the river mouth opened fire on the unprepared British, sinking four ships and inflicting over 400 casualties. Emboldened by this military action, the Qing court abrogated the Treaty of Tianjin in August 1859. Back in Britain and France, outraged politicians called for strong action to avenge the honor of the two countries.

In 1860, a second force of French and British troops sailed to China with a combined force of 41 warships and more than 18,000 troops. In August, they again captured the Dagu forts and pushed upriver to Tianjin, threatening to march on Beijing. After suffering repeated defeats in engagements with Western troops, in mid-September the Qing court signaled its willingness to negotiate, again relenting in the face of superior firepower. However, when a group of British and French representatives approached under a flag of truce, the Qing forces took them prisoner after hearing a rumor that the British had detained a prominent Qing official at Tianjin. A dozen of the prisoners found protection and eventual release thanks to a sympathetic Manchu official, but the Qing forces executed twenty others. Outraged by this act, the allied British and French forces took the offensive and defeated Qing armies on the road to Beijing. The emperor and his advisors fled the capital, leaving others to accept another humiliating treaty. In retaliation for the execution of the British prisoners and abrogation of the Treaty of Tianjin, British troops looted and burned the Summer Palace outside of Beijing. On September 14, 1860, the two sides reached an agreement known as the Beijing Convention. It reaffirmed the conditions of the 1858 Treaty of Tianjin, doubled the original indemnity, added Tianjin to the list of open treaty ports, and ceded the Kowloon Peninsula (opposite Hong Kong) to Britain in perpetuity.

At the end of the eighteenth century, the Qianlong emperor felt confident in dismissing British requests for changes to the Canton System of Sino-Western Trade. He had no idea that continued rebuffs would lead to war with the British and a series of "unequal treaties" that would force China to discard its traditional world view and begin accepting a new international order in East Asia. Moreover, Qing officials did not perceive the British as a serious threat, believing that the empire's military forces could make relatively short work of these Western "pirates." Yet the Qing military, which had propped up Manchu rule over the Chinese majority since 1644, had deteriorated over the centuries. Economic problems led many of the Bannermen and Army of the Green Standard forces to worry more about making a living than maintaining their military effectiveness. Traditional forms of military organization and weapons had not changed in centuries. Meanwhile, Britain experienced an industrial revolution that produced military technology far beyond that of the Qing forces. Defeat in the Anglo-Chinese Wars of the mid-nineteenth century began what many Chinese see as a "century of humiliation" during which foreign powers pressed their military advantage over China to acquire territorial and economic concessions. This sense of victimization at the hands of foreign imperialists had a profound impact on the history of modern China, as future generations struggled with military modernization in order to defend China against further external aggression.

The Taiping Heavenly Kingdom, 1851–1864

The Anglo-Chinese Wars represented only part of the military challenge that the Qing dynasty faced in the mid-nineteenth century. As the government and people tried to understand the consequences of the Opium War, China experienced a massive anti-Qing revolt by a force known as the Taiping Heavenly Kingdom. This destructive civil war threatened to topple the government, devastated large swaths of the countryside, and resulted in the deaths of approximately 20 million people. The revolt consumed valuable resources and distracted the court and its officials from any serious attempt at military modernization between the Opium and Arrow Wars. At the same time, in order to put down the revolt Qing officials experimented with new forms of military organization that helped lay the foundation for China's modern armies.

Hong Xiuquan and the Origins of the Taipings

The Taiping Heavenly Kingdom, commonly known as the Taipings, grew out of the socioeconomic problems plaguing southern China in nineteenth century. Rising population during the Ming and Qing periods had not been matched by an increase in arable land, leaving more people struggling with insufficient land. Tenant farmers in some parts of China found themselves poorer than ever, burdened by heavy taxes and rents, and squeezed by landlords and corrupt officials. Countless displaced or unemployed people turned to banditry and created unrest in the countryside, particularly in south China. The economic consequences of the Anglo-Chinese Wars exacerbated the problem as the indemnity payments forced the Qing court to place even greater financial demands on the peasants. Natural disasters added to the misery, with drought in Henan and severe flooding of the Yangzi River over four different provinces leading to famine. In 1852, the Yellow River changed from its southern route to a northern route inflicting untold suffering on millions. These conditions created a ready pool of economically oppressed people who would fill the ranks of the Taiping followers.

Amidst these volatile conditions lived a man named Hong Xiuquan, one of five children of a peasant family in eastern Guangdong Province. His family scraped together enough money to give him an education, hoping that he would pass the Confucian civil service examinations and become a scholar-official. Hong passed the preliminary county exam but failed to pass the prefectural level exam held at Guangzhou. Many failed multiple times before ultimately passing, so Hong supported himself as a teacher while continuing to prepare for his next attempt. He sat for the prefectural exam twice more, but failed each time. On one of these trips to Guangzhou, a Chinese convert handed him a pamphlet on Christianity. Hong gave it a cursory glance and upon his return to his home village shelved it with the rest of his books.

In 1837, after failing the exam for the third time Hong fell ill, most likely because of the nervous strain and the humiliation of having again fallen short. Delirious for several days, he experienced strange visions in which he ascended to Heaven where a "Heavenly Father" gave him a sword and instructed him to cleanse the earth and "slay the demons." After recuperating, he resumed his work as a teacher and prepared to take the exam yet again. In 1843, he tried and failed for the fourth and final time. Shortly thereafter he discovered the Christian pamphlet given to him in Guangzhou. After reading it, he came to a new interpretation of the visions he had experienced during his earlier illness. He concluded that he had ascended to Heaven and met the Christian God, his father, and Jesus, his older brother, and that they had commanded him to combat the demons on earth.

Convinced of his special mission, Hong began preaching the word of God and the Old Testament, as he interpreted it. Accompanied by two early converts to his cause, his cousin Hong Rengan and his friend Feng Yunshan, in 1844 Hong began traveling across Guangdong and Guangxi Provinces preaching his beliefs. Many of his earliest followers came from the Hakka communities, people whose ancestors had moved to the south from northern China centuries before, yet retained their own dialects and traditions. As a Hakka himself, Hong knew that they often lived outside of mainstream Han Chinese society and clashed with other groups. Picking up followers among the disaffected and poverty-stricken groups of south China, Hong formed a God Worshipers Society with some 2,000 devotees who followed a strict moral code. Mostly peasants, unskilled workers, and a smattering of elites, the God Worshipers followed an ideology which combined Christianity and Chinese tradition. Hong's "Ten Heavenly Commandments" forbade worshiping false gods, wickedness and lewdness, killing or injuring others, and demanded filial conduct toward one's mother and father. Other Taiping regulations prohibited drinking alcohol, smoking tobacco or opium, and gambling. Those who violated the commandments or regulations faced severe punishments.[1]

The Jintian Uprising

The God Worshipers Society had grown to several thousand in 1849, sufficient numbers to attract the attention of local Qing officials. Hong's religious espousals began to take on a political and military nature as he identified the Manchus as the "demons" which God had ordered him to destroy. The God Worshipers assembled in the village of Jintian, Guangxi, where the leaders of the movement began organizing their followers for a defense against an attack by Qing forces, collecting weapons and acquiring as much gunpowder as possible. Rather than bring weapons into their villages, which might arouse suspicion, the Taipings purchased iron and had their own craftsmen fashion it into swords, spears, and knives, hiding weapons in various places, including underwater, until needed. They would later capture artillery and use it effectively, but in the early days of the movement the Taipings made primitive cannon from hollow tree trunks, sometimes making their own poor quality but serviceable gunpowder. A system of communication using various colored flags and a back up system of horns and gongs for occasions when the flags could not be seen, facilitated coordination between various military units. From its earliest days the Taiping Movement subjected its followers to military organization and planned for conflict.

By the summer of 1850, perhaps as many as 30,000 of Hong's followers had arrived at Jintian. In December 1850, local Qing officials ordered an attack on Jintian hoping to disperse what they viewed as a troublesome group. An initial assault by the Army of the Green Standard failed as Taiping fighters killed fifty Qing soldiers. On January 11, 1851, the Taiping military soundly defeated the Army of the Green Standard in a second battle at Jintian. In the weeks following this victory, Hong Xiuquan declared the establishment of the *Taiping Tianguo* or "Heavenly Kingdom of Great Peace," giving the movement its more common name, the Taipings. Hong himself took the title of *Tian Wang* or "Heavenly King."

Following the initial fighting around Jintian, the Taipings engaged Qing forces in several locations around southeastern Guangxi. Their numbers swelled with impoverished peasants and laborers, bandit gangs, and even the occasional disillusioned scholar. As the movement grew in size, it began to take on a more formal organization based on an ancient Chinese written work of the Zhou dynasty called the *Zhouli* or "Rituals of Zhou." This ancient work called for an integrated civil and military system of administration based on the Zhou "farmer-soldier" model. The leaders of the Taipings divided their military into squads, platoons, companies, battalions, and army corps. According to this system, each army corps would include 13,516 officers and enlisted men. Hong and the top leaders maintained complete control over the organization of units and promotion of officers, carefully combining men from different areas in individual squads to prevent any from building a local power base. In their early days, the Taipings showed skillful leadership and organization, removing local or regional cohesion from their followers and replacing it with complete loyalty to the Heavenly King, Hong Xiuquan. This sound organization helps explain their success on the battlefield against Qing forces.[2]

It is doubtful that all members of the God Worshipers Society believed wholeheartedly in Hong's "Taiping Christianity." The majority came from peasant and laboring classes who saw little to lose and potentially much to gain by joining the Taipings, who seemed destined for greatness or at least better mannered and disciplined than the Green Standard forces, which served as the local constabulary. Others gravitated to the Taiping Movement because its religious doctrine and anti-Manchu nationalism tapped into long simmering resentment and hatred of the Manchus and those who served them. This had great appeal among those less inclined to embrace Hong's religious doctrine, and drew many disaffected individuals from different segments of Chinese society. Yet others joined the movement because of Taiping social and economic policies, which featured equality between men and women, support for all through a communal treasury, and equal redistribution of land. Regardless of their reasons for joining, followers had to adhere to strict discipline and submit to Taiping forms of organization.[3]

The Taiping leaders separated their followers into men's and women's camps and strictly forbade sexual contact, even between husband and wife, on penalty of death. This policy of separation proved sporadic as the leaders applied it to early followers and the populations of some cities they later controlled, but never to the entire area that they occupied. Nor did the ban on sex apply to the top leaders, each of whom took multiple wives and exempted themselves from the discipline imposed on the rank and file. Hong Xiuquan used this policy as incentive for his soldiers to fight hard against the Qing forces, promising that the policy of segregation would cease with the end of Manchu rule. The Taipings exhibited egalitarian practices in some areas, such as allowing women to participate in combat. Qing reports detail the presence of female fighters among the Taipings, mostly Miao tribeswomen and Hakka.

In August 1851, the Taipings divided the army into three forces under the command of Hong's highest ranking officers: an advance force under the command of Xiao Chaogui and Shi Dakai, a central force under Yang Xiuqing, and a rear force under Feng Yunshan and Wei Changhui. Together these three forces moved through Guangxi, defeating government forces in several engagements before marching along the Meng River to the walled city of Yong'an. A small vanguard force reached the city on September 24, kicking up great clouds of dust by dragging baskets of rocks behind them in order to give the impression of a much larger force. Rather than wait for the main force to arrive, the vanguard began the assault. At night they positioned their cannon to assail one of the city gates, using firecrackers to give the impression of greater firepower, and sent men to scale the walls. The Taiping force captured Yong'an and 800 government troops defending the city.

The Reorganization of the Taipings at Yong'an

The Taipings spent nearly eight months at Yong'an, resting and reorganizing their force. In preparation for a lengthy stay, they constructed a ring of defensive works outside the city walls to protect them from the Qing forces that would certainly attempt to surround them. As a part of the reorganization, Hong's core supporters—Yang Xiuqing, Feng Yunshan, Shi Dakai, Wei Changhui, and Xiao Chaogui—all took titles of subordinate "kings." Yang Xiuqing proved most important among the subordinate kings, taking control of central administration and serving as commander of the Taiping "Heavenly Army." At lower levels, the Taipings sought to incorporate and indoctrinate the large number of people who had joined them along the way from

Jintian. The Taipings made no effort to force the inhabitants of Yong'an to join the movement or to embrace their religious views, but they did have to adhere to the Taiping moral code or face strict punishment.[4]

Recruits formed new squads for incorporation into the Taiping military under the command of Yang Xiuqing. Soldiers learned a series of regulations for conduct while in camp, on the march, and in battle, which included prohibitions on looting, stealing, and killing civilians. In cases in which soldiers violated these regulations, officers carried out the death penalty on the spot by beheading, burning, or dismemberment, depending on the severity of the transgression. Lesser infractions called for beating, wearing the cangue, or demotion in rank. In addition to insisting on iron discipline, the Taiping leaders promised heavenly rewards for those who performed well. Hong claimed that those who fought and died in battle would ascend to Heaven to receive rewards and titles. If one survived, earthly rewards would follow victory. In the meantime, the soldiers accepted a small stipend distributed on Sundays and drew their daily necessities from the common treasury. The Taiping military benefited greatly from these new recruits, including approximately 1,000 coal miners who had experience in digging tunnels and working with explosives.

By contrast, the Army of the Green Standard and local militia forces that faced the Taipings showed little discipline or military strength. Poorly trained and often unpaid, the Green Standard troops could not match the zeal of the Taiping soldiers who fought for both spiritual and material reward. After the failure to defeat the Taipings at Jintian in January 1851, the Qing court dispatched a force of 40,000 troops to surround Yong'an. Suffering from poor morale and malaria, these troops applied a halfhearted blockade against the city. In December 1851, Qing forces began an assault on Yong'an, slowly moving closer to the city walls over the next three months. This strengthened the blockade and created shortages of food and supplies that eventually forced the Taipings to break out of the city in April 1852. Choosing the east gate where the Qing forces had the fewest troops, more than 40,000 Taiping followers hurried through the lines of the Qing troops under cover of darkness and escaped into a mountain pass to the north. A Taiping rear guard of 2,000 soldiers covered this maneuver, creating smoke and confusion with homemade incendiary devices, wooden tubes filled with gunpowder ignited by a corn silk fuse. The rear guard followed the main Taiping force into the mountains, sending rocks tumbling down on the pursuing Qing troops and engaging in hand-to-hand combat. This ensured the safety of the main force and killed perhaps as many as 5,000 Qing troops, but also cost the lives of virtually all of the Taiping rear guard.

From Yong'an the Taipings moved on to assault Guilin, a large city with imposing walls situated on the bank of the Li River. A detachment of several hundred Taiping soldiers put on uniforms taken from dead Qing troops along with their unit flags and attempted to fool the guards on the outskirts of the city, but the defenders discovered the ruse and prepared for a siege. Approximately 2,000 Qing troops and militiamen initially defended the city, but reinforcements arrived bringing their numbers up to 20,000. Having sent many of their cannon to support the attack on Yong'an, the defenders of Guilin lacked sufficient artillery, a situation they attempted to remedy by digging up several old but serviceable cannon that had been buried near the city during the Ming dynasty. The Taipings set up their artillery in the hills to the southwest, as they did not have sufficient numbers to completely surround such a large city. They began a barrage and attempted to scale the walls with ladders, to no avail. After a month, they broke off the siege, commandeering a number of boats to transport some of their men along the Li River toward the city of Xing'an, which they took easily on May 23.

The Taipings proceeded from Xing'an in two columns, one on the river and the other on land. They avoided the defended city of Quanzhou but suffered a significant loss in doing so. As the Taipings marched past at a distance, a gunner on the city wall took a random shot with a small cannon at a covered sedan chair, believing it belonged to a ranking Taiping leader. The round ripped through the sedan chair and mortally wounded Feng Yunshan, one of the earliest and most effective Taiping leaders. The angry Taipings stopped and assaulted the city, bent on revenge. After a week's siege, the Taipings succeeded in breaching the city wall by placing explosives in a tunnel below. Quanzhou fell on June 3, with Taiping soldiers slaughtering its inhabitants. This was the first time the normally strong discipline of the Taipings broke down and soldiers committed such atrocities, but it would not be the last.

From Quanzhou, the Taipings continued toward Hunan Province, acquiring more boats along the way. They tended to pass through remote, mountainous border areas between Guangxi and Hunan Provinces with Qing forces pursuing them from the rear. Although the Taipings enjoyed success against the Army of the Green Standard and generally proved superior to Qing forces, they did not always triumph in battle. In one notable defeat along the banks of the Xiang River, they encountered a devastating ambush and suffered significant losses. Jiang Zhongyuan, a scholar-official from Hunan, had heeded a call from the Qing court to form a local militia to defend Hunan against the Taipings. In June 1852, with a force of 2,000, he laid a trap at the Suoyi Ford, a point in southern Hunan where the Xiang River makes a sharp bend and narrows considerably. Aware that the Taipings would move north along the river after assaulting Quanzhou, Jiang had his men pile logs on top of each other and spike them into place with iron rods, creating a formidable barrier just after the bend in the river. With Jiang's troops waiting in ambush on the west bank of the river, Taiping boats made the turn at Suoyi Ford where they rammed into the log barrier. Boats at the rear collided with those at the front halting all movement, spilling the Taipings into the river, and rendering them vulnerable to the fire of Jiang's troops secluded in the dense woods of the river bank. The Taiping column moving on foot managed to avoid the ambush, but an estimated 10,000 Taiping followers traveling by river died by gunfire or drowning. Many of those killed had been among the most dedicated and experienced followers and soldiers. The Taipings would replenish their losses with new recruits while on the march, but these did not possess the same level of indoctrination and discipline of the original Guangxi followers.[5]

The surviving Taipings left the river and spent six weeks recuperating before continuing their slow advance into Hunan. After training 20,000 new recruits and casting hundreds of new cannon, the Taipings prepared to attack Changsha, the capital of Hunan Province. Yet this delay also gave the government time to strengthen the force defending Changsha, eventually massing 50,000 troops inside the city walls. In September, the Taipings began the assault against Changsha, pounding the walls with cannon fire and attempting to ignite city dwellings with flaming arrows. Another prominent Taiping leader, Xiao Chaogui, fell in the fighting, again shot by a marksman from the city wall. Engineers built floating bridges which allowed attacking troops to cross the Xiang River to open a second front at the western wall. Tunnel diggers worked diligently to get under the city walls where Taiping miners placed explosives. Qing defenders relied on the acute hearing of blind men to identify the location of Taiping tunnel digging and then attempted to collapse the tunnels by pounding on the earth with heavy iron balls or by diverting water into the tunnels. The Taipings succeeded in bringing down sections of the city walls but could not get past the defenders. After two months, the Taipings moved on without taking the city. Capturing a fleet of boats at Lake Dongting on which to transport a portion of the force down the Yangzi River, they withdrew from Changsha in late November.

Moving down the Yangzi, the Taiping army captured the river bank cities Hanyang and Hankou, in preparation for an attack on Wuchang. After the initial frontal assaults brought too many casualties, the Taipings once again showed their engineering skills by building floating bridges that allowed their troops to attack Wuchang from both banks of the river. Unlike Changsha, Wuchang had less than 5,000 soldiers with which to mount a defense. Anticipating the attack, the governor of Hubei had ordered his soldiers to burn all homes and buildings between the city walls and the river, intending to deny the Taipings any shred of cover from the city's guns. To prevent tunneling under the city walls the defenders dug deep pits into which they sunk listening posts which would alert them to the digging. These measures proved inadequate as in January 1853 a tunnel explosion brought down a large section of city wall and Taiping soldiers poured into the gap. As usual, the soldiers had orders to kill all government officials and troops, but to spare the common people. They already enjoyed the support of local residents who resented the governor's destruction of their homes and businesses and offered the Taipings information on the city's defenses. Yet at Wuchang the Taipings departed from their usual practice of relying on volunteers and began conscripting men into the army in order to bolster their force.[6]

The Taipings briefly considered halting their march and making Wuchang their capital. Word of large numbers of government troops massing for an attack led the leaders to drop this plan and push on. Rather than head north toward Beijing, where they expected to encounter the strongest resistance, the Taipings turned east toward Nanjing, a major city in the populous and resource-rich Jiangnan region. Following the Yangzi River, they captured Jiujiang in February 1853, after the garrison of 800 Qing soldiers fled, followed by Anqing in March, which cleared the way to Nanjing. These victories helped revive Taiping fortunes and replenish their resources as they captured vast amounts of silver from city treasuries, significant pieces of military equipment, and thousands of boats. Along with these materials good came hundreds of thousands of new followers who swelled the ranks of the Taiping force to nearly one million soldiers and followers. Not all new members joined willingly, as the Taipings now tended to incorporate entire towns and cities into their ranks. With each conquest the Taipings went through substantial reorganization and indoctrination of local inhabitants who found themselves separated into men's and women's camps and drafted into Taiping military units. Yet the indoctrination, training, and dedication of the new followers never reached the level of the original Guangxi Taipings, detracting from the overall effectiveness of their military.[7]

Representing the most formidable city the Taipings had yet faced, Nanjing's city walls measured 40 feet high and stretched for 25 miles around the city. Approximately 14,000 Chinese soldiers, Manchu Bannermen, militia, and mercenaries guarded the ten gates and thousands of battlements. As usual, the Taipings placed their cannon on the hills outside the city and then set to work digging tunnels under the city walls. Upon completion of a suitable tunnel under the northern section of the wall, the Taipings prepared a diversion. During the night, Qing troops guarding the western wall saw riders with torches massing for an attack. They sounded the alarm, drawing the defenders to the western wall, yet when they fired on the horsemen they knocked not men but straw dummies off their mounts. Meanwhile, a series of explosions rocked the northern wall, opening a small breach. The Qing forces managed to stop the Taipings from passing through the opening, but panic spread through the city. Troops defending other gates fled, allowing Taiping forces to scale undefended portions of the city wall at the southern gate. Other Taiping soldiers had earlier infiltrated Nanjing, disguised as Buddhist monks. At a prearranged signal, they set fires across the city, spreading confusion and fear. The Manchu garrison held the city's inner citadel, where a large force of Bannermen made their stand. Facing certain defeat and death, many opted to kill their families and then commit suicide. The siege of the citadel resulted in the slaughter of tens of thousands of Manchu men, women, and children. Hong's Taiping force controlled the city on March 29, 1853.

The Heavenly Capital

The capture of Nanjing, which Hong Xiuquan renamed *Tianjing* or "Heavenly Capital," meant a strategic change for the Taipings. Early success came in part from speed, mobility, and avoiding battle when they chose. They now remained static in a defended position which the Qing forces could assault. They built defensive works around Nanjing, digging ditches and planting bamboo stakes in the ground outside the city walls. Each of the city's ten gates had two cannon, and soldiers manned the city walls, keeping piles of rocks ready to hurl down on attackers. Horns and drums sounded the alarm in case of attack, and a series of signal flags directed defenders to various points of the city as needed. They maintained a string of postal stations around the city in order to keep the leaders informed during the inevitable Qing counterassault. These preparations did not mean that the Taipings gave up all offensive action, as they periodically sent forces to campaign far beyond Nanjing's city walls. Yet when Taiping armies did venture outside of Nanjing, they did so independently rather than as a unified force. For example, in the spring of 1853, a mere two months after capturing Nanjing, the Taipings sent out two expeditions, one to the north and the other to the west, designed bring the entire northwest under Taiping control. Although both campaigns saw some successes, by 1855 Qing forces managed to defeat the divided Taiping units.

The Taipings did derive certain benefits from the occupation of Nanjing, a wealthy and resource-rich area. The city's treasury held millions of taels and food stores sufficient for several years. This allowed the Taipings to continue to reorganize and even begin implementing some of the socioeconomic changes outlined in the most famous of Taiping writings, the "Land System of the Heavenly Dynasty." Among other things, this 1854 document called for equal distribution of land among all followers of the Taipings and organized the entire population of Nanjing into units of twenty-five families, mirroring the military system. Each twenty-five family unit fell under the command of a sergeant who served as a civil administrator, monitoring behavior, distributing rewards, meting out punishments, judging disputes, presiding over education and religious services, and supervising the communal treasury. The sergeants reported all decisions upward through the ranks to the Taiping leadership, which still held complete control. This represents a further militarization of Taiping society, subjecting individual families to the rigid discipline and control of the military. It also set the people of Nanjing apart from the surviving original members of the movement, who remained separated into men's and women's camps.

Zeng Guofan and the Hunan Army

While the Taipings launched their northern and western campaigns, the Qing court began putting together a more effective force to defend the dynasty. Already reeling from defeat in the Opium War, the Army of the Green Standard and Banner forces had proved of limited ability in dealing with the Taipings. In desperation, the court called upon regional gentry to organize provincial military forces to defeat the Taipings. Zeng Guofan, a prominent Confucian scholar from Hunan Province, took the lead in organizing a new force that would eventually defeat the Taipings. A holder of the *Jinshi* degree which came from passing the highest level of the Confucian civil service examination, Zeng had returned from his official post to his native province at the death of his mother in 1852. As he prepared to observe the traditional Confucian period of mourning, the emperor ordered him to organize a military force to attack the Taipings. The Qing court issued such orders to scholar-officials in numerous provinces, inspired by the success of Jiang Zhongyuan's attack on the Taipings at Suoyi Ford. Confucian to the core, Zeng hesitated to accept the order until he had fulfilled his filial obligations to his departed mother, but he cut short his mourning ritual because of the severity of the situation.

Zeng understood that the traditional local militia, usually assembled to deal with bandits, could not stand up to the disciplined and experienced Taiping troops. He therefore began building a new force, larger than traditional local militia, centrally directed with a clear chain of command, disciplined, and well funded. This force took the name *Xiangjun,* or Hunan Army. Zeng Guofan began with 1,000 men drawn from preexisting local militia. He recruited new soldiers and officers, drilled and equipped them, and even assembled a small naval force. He drew his soldiers from local villages, accepting only hardy peasants from good families and rejecting drifters and transients whose character might be suspect. Similar to the Taiping army, Zeng imposed strict discipline on his troops with prohibitions against opium, gambling, and abuse of civilians. Many of Zeng's troops used the traditional sword and spear, but others carried muskets and employed artillery. Officers came from the gentry, mostly men who had personal ties to Zeng Guofan. Such personal relations made this a cohesive force that proved far more effective than the forces of the Army of the Green Standard. The first officers, all carefully scrutinized to ensure that they possessed character and courage, came exclusively from Hunan, but Zeng eventually turned to men of talent from other areas, including Li Hongzhang from Anhui, who would go on to build a similar force of his own. In fact, Zeng produced a number of protégés who would play important roles in the military development of China after 1864.[8]

In order to finance this new force, Zeng relied on contributions from the gentry and a local tax on goods transported through the province called the likin (*lijin*). The Qing court allowed Zeng and other regional officials to collect this customs duty in order to fund their military efforts. As a result, stipends for Zeng's soldiers averaged as much as twice the normal salary for Chinese soldiers in the Army of the Green Standard. Beyond forming a well-paid and disciplined military force, Zeng Guofan utilized his own form of propaganda to rally people to his cause. While the Taipings won support from the disaffected elements of Chinese society with promises of equal land distribution and "heavenly rewards," Zeng attempted to rally others in defense of Chinese tradition. He saw the Taipings as a threat to the Confucian core of Chinese civilization. Their espousal of foreign religion, their destruction of Confucian ancestral tablets, their attitudes toward women, and their policies of separating the sexes ran contrary to the deeply entrenched Confucian world view of all Chinese, but especially the Confucian-educated scholar-gentry. This helped ensure a steady stream of recruits and financial contributions. As commander of this provincial force, Zeng enjoyed considerable power which led the Manchu rulers to view his activities with a healthy degree of suspicion. The kinds of personal loyalties cultivated in the Hunan Army had always been discouraged in the Qing military as potentially dangerous. Zeng understood that a powerful provincial army under the independent command of a Chinese official would alarm the ruling Manchus and therefore made every effort to include a Manchu on his staff, hoping to allay their fears and suspicions.

Initially intending to simply defend Changsha and Hunan against the Taipings, Zeng's Hunan Army became the striking arm of the Qing dynasty against the Taiping capital. Yet rather than rush headlong into a clash with the Taipings as the Qing court might have preferred, Zeng first tested his forces in a battle against local bandit gangs in December 1853, giving his men experience before attacking Taiping units. Even with this experience, the Hunan Army lost its first few engagements with the Taipings. Only in May 1854 did Zeng see success in a battle at Xiangtan, followed by another victory at Yuezhou. Although the Hunan Army eventually grew to more than 100,000 troops, it typically operated in small units of 10,000 or less, stressing quality over quantity. Often outnumbered by the Taiping forces, Zeng's units made up for this disadvantage with good training, proper equipment, careful planning, and use of local strongholds and defensive fortifications. This initial success proved a turning point in the lengthy struggle, clearly demonstrating the effectiveness of Zeng's provincial force. Further victories in late 1854 at Wuchang and Hanyang on the upper Yangzi blunted the Taiping western expedition and began the process of chipping away at the perimeter of the zone of occupation surrounding Nanjing. The Taipings would take back Wuchang in April 1855 but could not hold on to it against Zeng's troops who recaptured it for good in December 1856.

The rise of the Hunan Army meant a revival of fortunes for the Qing court, which faced a number of difficulties in suppressing the Taipings. Financial shortages forced the court to exact "contributions" from prominent officials, causing resentment within the ranks of the bureaucracy. Other rebellions forced the Qing to spread its already thin military resources rather than concentrate them all on the Taipings. Conflict between Muslims and Han Chinese in Yunnan Province led to a revolt and the establishment of a "Panthay Kingdom" from 1856 to 1873. Under the influence of Sufi leaders, Muslims in Gansu and Shaanxi rebelled against Qing authority in the 1860s and 1870s. A third major revolt, known as the Nian, rose in poverty-stricken areas of central China and continued until 1869.[9] Moreover, between 1856 and 1860, the court found itself once again at war with Western powers, this time Britain and France in the Arrow War. Not until the conclusion of the Beijing Convention of 1860 could the Qing court give its full attention to the Taipings. Beyond material shortages, the Qing attitude toward the Taipings perhaps prolonged the war. Jonathan Spence has suggested that had the Manchu government not insisted on the complete destruction of all Taipings, there might have been greater incentive for defectors to leave the Taiping ranks. Manchu intransigence gave those who might consider defection little choice but to fight with the Taipings to the death.[10]

The formation of Zeng's Hunan Army posed a significant challenge to the Taiping Movement, which had already begun to suffer from serious internal problems. After years of fighting, the situation in Nanjing grew desperate as food and supplies became scarce. In September 1854, the Taipings allowed a large contingent of noncombatants leave Nanjing to alleviate the food problem. In early 1855, Taiping leaders reversed their policy of segregation of the sexes in the face of growing discontent among their followers. Moreover, Nanjing itself fell under constant threat from two large Qing military camps, one to the north and the other to the south, which blockaded the city. The Taipings broke the blockade and overran the Qing southern camp in June 1856, which lifted the pressure for time, but internal factors crippled the movement. Hong Xiuquan, perhaps mentally unstable from the start, withdrew into his palace and provided little leadership. Meanwhile, his subordinate kings began to turn on each other. In September 1856, conflict among the Taiping leaders boiled over into violence as Wei Changhui killed Yang Xiuqing and 20,000 of his followers. Yang had been the Taiping's best military strategist and his death left them without sound leadership and central control. Following this bloodletting, Shi Dakai, another capable general, fled Nanjing in the summer of 1857 leading hundreds of thousands of his troops through Jiangxi, Zhejiang, and Fujian. He then turned west and fled to Hunan and Sichuan where Qing troops would hunt him down six years later. Zeng Guofan's Hunan Army allowed Shi's force to escape, keeping the pressure on Nanjing and the Taiping zone of occupation. At this time of great peril, the remaining Taiping leaders had no overall plan for dealing with this threat.

Zeng Guofan's strategy revolved around gaining control of the upper Yangzi region, that is the territory west of Nanjing, which he considered the key to the defeat of the Taipings. His forces did not always triumph in battle—in a major battle in Anhui in 1858 the Taipings destroyed a unit of the Hunan Army and killed one of Zeng's brothers—but they did maintain a consistent strategy of controlling the upper Yangzi River in order to trap the Taipings at Nanjing. In Zeng's words, it would be like "turning a jar of water over on a high roof," as his forces pushed steadily down-river against the Taiping stronghold at Nanjing.[11] Slowly but surely Zeng's forces took control of the river, even while the Taipings still controlled some isolated cities and towns along its banks.

In 1859, Hong Xiuquan's cousin Hong Rengan, who took the title "Shield King," arrived at Nanjing to attempt a revival of Taiping fortunes. In addition to clarifying religious doctrine and administrative policy, Hong Rengan drew up a new military strategy. Like Zeng Guofan, Hong Rengan hoped to take control of the upper Yangzi to secure the flow of supplies into Nanjing. He first planned an attack on Shanghai, where he would seize government coffers to purchase twenty steamships from foreigners which the Taipings would then use to secure control of the upper Yangzi. In 1860, a Taiping force began with a diversionary attack on Hangzhou, designed to draw the attention of Qing troops. Instead of following through with the attack on Hangzhou, the Taipings attacked at Suzhou and gathered troops for the march on Shanghai.

In August 1860, a 3,000 man vanguard reached Shanghai, warning the Western community that the Taipings would not harm them if they displayed yellow banners outside their homes. While some Western gunrunners had long been supplying the Taipings with weapons and ammunition, by this time the Western governments had ruled out support for the Taipings, preferring to deal with the Qing court which promised to honor the terms of the latest treaties. From the beginning, the Western nations had maintained a pro-Taiping neutrality, avoiding direct involvement but hoping that the Christian views and noticeable discipline of the Taiping might lead to better trade relations between China and the West. Westerners who came into con-tact with the Taipings soon realized that Taiping Christianity smacked of blasphemy and their attitudes toward trade did not differ substantially from those of the Manchu dynasty. After 1860 and the Beijing Convention, the Westerners tended to shift to a position of pro-Qing neutrality. As a result, some Westerners supported the Qing troops with artillery fire and the Taiping attack on Shanghai yielded nothing.

By this time a second powerful provincial army had assembled under Li Hongzhang. Li's Anhui Army operated in the lower Yangzi area to the east of Nanjing. A third force under Zuo Zongtang approached from Zhejiang to the south.

Li Hongzhang's force found support from an experimental military unit called the Ever Victorious Army. Funded by wealthy Shanghai merchants, the Ever Victorious Army combined Chinese soldiers with Western officers, weapons, and training. Its role in the defeat of the Taipings is sometimes exaggerated, but it did contribute to the defense of Shanghai.[12]

By 1861, the Heavenly Capital came under intense pressure from the combined forces of the provincial armies. The Hunan Army recaptured Anqing in September 1861, assuring control of the upper Yangzi River. In the east, Suzhou fell in December 1863, setting the stage for the siege of Nanjing, which began in March 1864. Using the same tunneling techniques as the Taipings, Zeng's forces sought to bring down the city walls with explosives. Taiping gunners aimed their cannon at the ground at the base of the walls, attempting to collapse the tunnels and bury the diggers. Some Taiping forces remained outside of Nanjing, but Qing troops barred their return. Surrounding the city with towers and parapets, each with a healthy garrison of troops, Zeng's forces completely sealed off the roads in and out of the Heavenly Capital. Hunger and shortage of supplies crippled the defenders. In July 1864, tunnelers blew up a section of the eastern wall, allowing Qing troops to pour into the breach. Hong Xiuquan died on June 1 after a lingering illness or possibly took his own life. The conquering forces slaughtered the inhabitants of the city, taking no time to discern loyal Taiping followers from unfortunate residents of Nanjing. The remaining Taiping forces still in the field fled, only to be hunted down and destroyed one by one, bringing the movement to an end.

The Taiping Heavenly Kingdom rose out of the southwest with a powerful army and nearly succeeded in toppling the Qing government. Many of its soldiers fought with religious zeal, and its military commanders provided intelligent leadership. Yet the movement failed for several reasons. First, the decision to halt at Nanjing rather than immediately march north to attack Beijing took away momentum from the Taipings. Had Taiping armies continued northward without pause, before the creation of the provincial armies, they might have been able to defeat Qing forces and control the empire. Second, the Taiping Movement suffered the loss of some of its most effective leaders which it could not replace. The death of Feng Yunshan in 1852, the murder of Yang Xiuqing in 1856, and the departure of Shi Dakai in 1857 deprived the Taipings of their best organizers and military commanders. Hong Xiuquan withdrew deeper into his own world as the leadership collapsed, and attempts by younger leaders to revive the fortunes of the movement after 1856 fell short.

Finally, the contradictions in the Taiping Movement provided its enemies with ammunition with which to attack it and jeopardized the support of its own followers. The anti-Manchu nature of the Taiping Movement won adherents among the Han Chinese and disaffected groups such as the Hakka community. Yet at the same time, Hong's espousal of a foreign religion ran counter to the deep Confucian heritage of the Chinese elites. Zeng Guofan mobilized support among the gentry by presenting his Hunan Army as a defender of China's ancient traditions. Moreover, within the movement the contradiction between Taiping leaders who lived in luxury, such as

Hong Xiuquan who had dozens of wives, and the common followers, who lived in male and female camps, led to dissatisfaction within the ranks and threatened the unity of the movement. These factors, in conjunction with the superior provincial military forces based on Zeng's Hunan Army, spelled the destruction of the Taiping Heavenly Kingdom. Regardless, the Taiping Movement shook the Qing dynasty to its foundation and precipitated attempts at military modernization in the ensuing decades.

CHAPTER 5

At War with France and Japan, 1864–1895

With the conclusion of the Arrow War in 1860 and the suppression of the Taiping Heavenly Kingdom in 1864, the Qing court and its regional officials had time to take stock of the situation and consider the full consequences of China's military weakness. Beginning his reign in 1862, the Tongzhi emperor presided over a period of "restoration" designed to revive the dynasty's fortunes after more than two decades of turmoil. This marked the beginning of a larger program of reform and modernization in China known as the Self-Strengthening Movement or Westernization Drive, which spanned the last four decades of the nineteenth century. The majority of the modernization projects undertaken during the Self-Strengthening Movement involved improving China's military through a combination of new technology and Western style training. Although some Manchu officials appreciated the need to strengthen the empire's defenses, many leaders of this reform movement came not from capital but from the provinces, where forward-thinking Chinese officials who had been on the front lines of the military struggles against the British and the Taipings sought ways to improve China's military capabilities.

The Self-Strengthening Movement

Among these provincial reformers, several stand out. Lin Zexu, one of the earliest leaders of this reform movement, developed a rudimentary knowledge of the West through his own efforts, seeking out translations of Western writings and studiously learning about the great power of the British navy. Lin had been one of the first to advocate the adoption of modern weaponry and had ordered translations of Western manuals for gun making. Zeng Guofan, defender of the Qing dynasty against the Taipings, also advocated upgrading China's weaponry and helped found the first modern arsenal in China, which began producing rifles, cannon, and even iron ships using machinery purchased from abroad. One of Zeng's protégés, Zuo Zongtang, is also known as one of the great forerunners of military modernization in China. Zuo's participation in the fighting against the Taipings and his analysis of the Opium Wars led him to see that China needed to revamp its military in order to protect its coasts. Perhaps more than any other figure in this movement, Li Hongzhang, another of

Zeng's protégés, helped build China's modern military force. Like the others, Li had come to appreciate the power of Western guns and ships and believed that if China did not make great advances in these areas, she would be at the mercy of the Western powers. He emerged as the driving force behind many of the Western style military reforms of the late nineteenth century.

The Self-Strengthening Movement saw many changes designed to improve China's relations with the Western powers, including the establishment of a government office to conduct diplomatic affairs with Westerners (*Zongli yamen*), an interpreter's college to train Chinese students in Western languages (*Tongwen guan*), and the dispatch of Chinese teenagers to study in the United States. Yet the overriding concern among the leaders of the Self-Strengthening Movement remained the need to learn the superior technologies and military techniques of the West. As the movement progressed, some argued that the basis of the West's military power lay in its wealth. Modern weaponry cost much more than traditional weapons, and an effective military required the support of up-to-date communications systems and industry. As part of an attempt to develop profit-oriented enterprises, which would support the development of modern weaponry, numerous projects such as mines, mills, and factories, appeared, funded and operated with private capital but subject to government supervision.

Of the numerous military and industrial projects begun during this period, perhaps the two best examples are the Jiangnan Arsenal and the Fuzhou Shipyard. Established in 1865 under the direction of Li Hongzhang, the Jiangnan Arsenal developed into the largest East Asian arms manufacturer of its time. Its location in Shanghai allowed it to make use of customs duties drawn from the busy port and likin taxes on goods transported across the province. The Jiangnan Arsenal specialized in small arms, beginning with muskets and advancing to breech-loading rifles in the 1870s, but produced artillery and ships as well, launching eleven ships in its first decade. Many of these vessels still had wooden hulls, but the arsenal also produced a number of iron clads. The largest of the ships built at the Jiangnan Arsenal had 1,800 horsepower and 26 guns, still slightly behind European technology but ahead of the best ships produced at Japanese shipyards. In addition to warships, the Jiangnan Arsenal built troop transports and torpedo boats. The Fuzhou Shipyard stood out as the second great military industrial enterprise of the period. Zuo Zongtang established the yard in 1866, which would be the home port of one of China's four naval fleets. Like the Jiangnan Arsenal, the Fuzhou Shipyard produced a number of serviceable vessels in its first decades and established a school of naval administration to train naval officers. In both locations, Westerns experts initially directed production, instruction, and helped with purchases of Western arms and ships to supplement growing domestic production.[1]

Army Reform and the Creation of a Navy

In addition to establishing industrial sites for the production of arms, ammunition, and ships, the Qing court also began attempts to strengthen its existing military forces. Recognizing the contribution of temporary provincial military forces in defending against the Taipings, especially Zeng Guofan's success with the Hunan Army, in the 1860s the court authorized the creation of new permanent regional armies called *Yongying*. These regional armies began with the remnants of the provincial forces that defeated the Taipings as the core, recruiting new soldiers to fill out the ranks. These units differed from the traditional Army of the Green Standard in that they featured the higher wages and personal ties that had helped make Zeng Guofan's Hunan Army such an effective fighting force. Equipped with modern Western weapons, over 300,000 soldiers served in these regional armies. They did not replace existing military forces but rather formed yet another layer of military organization of the Qing dynasty, alongside the Banners, the Army of the Green Standard, and local militia. Each commander chose his own officers who commanded battalions of 550 men. Zeng Guofan advocated bringing this system of organization to the massive Army of the Green Standard, allowing commanders to choose their own officers and providing better pay for the enlisted men. The cost and magnitude of such a reform prevented its full implementation, but the Qing court did attempt to upgrade the equipment of the Bannermen and Green Standard troops, and incorporated Western military tactics and strategy into their training.[2]

While the Army of the Green Standard continued to serve as an internal pacification force, the new regional armies provided China's best hope against outside invasion by a hostile foreign power. Li Hongzhang, governor-general of Zhili Province, commanded the strongest of these new armies, the Anhui Army, also known as the Huai Army. Li built his Anhui Army based on the model of Zeng's Hunan Army, but after the defeat of the Taipings he incorporated a number of Green Standard units into his force. Armed with weapons purchased from the West and drilled in Western military fashion, the Anhui Army emerged as a model for the development of other Chinese regional armies. Yet the very source of the regional army's strength proved its weakness as well. Because these units featured a personal relationship between the commanders, officers, and sometimes even the enlisted men, nepotism and corruption remained a problem. With no objective standard for appointing and promoting officers, commanders sometimes simply chose their relatives or friends, without regard for professional competence.

Since the experience of the Anglo-Chinese Wars, Manchu and Chinese reformers recognized the importance of coastal defense and began assembling a modern naval force in the 1860s. By first purchasing ships from the West and then producing their own at the Shanghai and Fuzhou shipyards, the Qing court created a navy of four distinct fleets: the Beiyang (northern) Fleet, the Nanyang (southern) Fleet, the Guangdong Fleet, and the Fuzhou Fleet. By 1882, China had fifty steamships, approximately half made in China, manned by officers who had studied at naval academies at Fuzhou, Tianjin, or abroad. The size of this naval force may indicate significant advances in coastal defense capabilities, but the naval officers had limited training and the fleets operated independently, with no central command structure or coordination.

The Sino-French War, 1884–1885

While the Qing court and provincial reformers struggled to reorganize the empire's ground and naval forces, the French had been taking steps toward the complete colonization of Vietnam. French merchants drawn by the raw materials and markets of Asia, missionaries eager for converts, and the military which sought bases and coaling stations in Asia collectively pressured the French government to take control of Vietnam. Through a series of military clashes followed by unequal treaties, based on the model of the Treaty of Nanjing, the French gradually accomplished this goal. In 1862, following a three-year military struggle, the Vietnamese court agreed to the Treaty of Saigon which ceded three provinces in southern Vietnam to France. In 1874, the Vietnamese emperor signed a second treaty, once again the result of military force, which gave France free navigation of the Red River and control over Vietnam's foreign relations.

Qing officials took note of French military actions on the southern frontier and prepared to defend against encroachments on China's territory. In 1881, the governor of Guangxi sent a small Chinese military force to northern Vietnam. In 1882, as French ships sailed into the Red River preparing to take the river passage to Yunnan Province, the Qing court sent a fleet of twenty ships to sail toward Vietnamese waters. Chinese troops from Yunnan crossed the border in June 1882, bringing artillery pieces and preparing to defend the border from the Vietnamese side. As both sides tensed for possible military conflict, the court ordered Li Hongzhang to open negotiations with the French minister to China, Frederic Albert Bourée. Meeting in Tianjin, in late November 1882 Li and Bourée reached a tentative agreement that called for a withdrawal of Chinese troops from Vietnam, an end to French attempts to conquer Tonkin (the French term for the northern part of Vietnam), regulated trade between China and France via the Red River, and a buffer zone along the Sino-Vietnamese border under Chinese control. This tentative agreement collapsed when the new French Prime Minister, Jules Ferry, rejected it and resolved to complete the French conquest of northern Vietnam.

Fighting in Vietnam began not with official Qing troops but between the French and a group known as the Black Flags, a Chinese quasi-secret society and pirate organization that operated along the Red River in northern Vietnam. Led by former Taiping rebel Liu Yongfu, the Black Flags harassed and raided French traders and explorers who ventured up the Red River toward China, provoking a clash that initiated the Sino-French War. In May 1883, the Black Flags fought with French troops outside of Hanoi, leading French politicians and the jingoistic public to cry out for revenge. In August, a French force seized control of the capital city of Hue in central Vietnam and forced the Vietnamese emperor to sign a third and final treaty making Vietnam a French protectorate, completing the process of French colonization.[3]

As French troops seized the capital at Hue, a separate force prepared to attack Liu Yongfu's Black Flags in the north. Three columns totaling 1,500 soldiers marched west to drive the Black Flags out of Son Tay, a critical town on the Red River, which guarded the approach downriver to the major city of the north, Hanoi. Liu Yongfu's troops employed guerrilla tactics against the French, preparing ambushes and fighting from behind prearranged defensive barriers. The Black Flags attacked the French columns halfway along the route and over the course of a three-day battle killed forty-two Frenchmen, forcing the rest to return to Hanoi. The rugged terrain and primitive communications systems made it difficult for the French to call for reinforcements or to withdraw, and Black Flags harassed them at every opportunity.

Following the capture of Hue and the final Treaty of the Protectorate, officials in Beijing debated whether or not to initiate military action against French forces in Vietnam. Manchu and Chinese officials, including Li Hongzhang, who feared that China's military reforms had not yet prepared it for another war, argued against inviting trouble with France until China could adequately defend itself with modern weaponry. They believed that China should fight only if directly attacked and favored negotiations to settle the problem in Vietnam. Other officials criticized this position and advocated military support for Vietnam. They described France as one of the weaker Western countries, though they had little knowledge of the outside world, and pointed to the emperor's Confucian obligation to support the legitimate ruler of Vietnam. The Qing court, at the time dominated by the emperor's aunt, the Empress Dowager Cixi, waffled between military action and a negotiated settlement, but ultimately decided in favor of military action to support the Black Flags and protect Vietnam. Cixi therefore ordered Li Hongzhang to go to the south to direct military preparations. Chinese land forces and ships already on the scene in Vietnam had orders to advance, but not to begin hostilities. The court recognized Liu Yongfu's Black Flags as an official part of the Qing military, allocating supplies to them and promising great rewards for the capture of Hanoi.[4]

In December 1883, the French again attempted to drive the Black Flags out of the Son Tay region, this time sending 5,000 troops by land and water along the Red River. A combined force of Black Flags and Chinese provincial troops had prepared defensive works including a substantial earthen wall and water-filled moat surrounding the town. The French attacked Son Tay using artillery to bombard Chinese positions, forcing them to slip away under the cover of darkness, leaving behind 1,000 dead. French losses included 42 dead and 320 wounded. This rout stunned the Qing court, which now feared another defeat at the hands of a Western army but did not want to go back on its obligation to support Vietnam. Still, a number of officials in the capital pressed for an aggressive assault on Hanoi, arguing that the French lacked supplies and suffered from low morale.

Military officials from the border provinces of Yunnan and Guangxi favored more cautious action, delaying further attacks until the end of the monsoon rains. In the meantime, they advocated reinforcing the Black Flags with Qing forces in preparation for future operations. In January 1884, Chen Yuying, Governor-General of Yunnan and Guangxi, led 12,000 Chinese troops over the border to meet with Liu Yongfu, bringing the total number of Chinese troops in Vietnam to 47,000. Chen's force combined with Liu's Black Flags to form a defensive arc across northern Vietnam, blocking the major routes to the Chinese border. In March, 5,500 French troops pushed north from Hanoi to attack Chinese forces at Lang Son, a town on one of these main routes leading to China. Along the way, French troops clashed with a Chinese force at Bac Ninh, where Guangxi troops had some newly purchased artillery. They had, however, little experience in using the artillery and allowed the French to occupy the high ground around the city and employ their own artillery to great effect. The Guangxi troops withdrew in the face of the French barrage, heading toward Lang Son and leaving their new artillery pieces to the French. Liu Yongfu's men stayed to repulse an initial French assault, but when the Guangxi troops left he angrily led his troops in a different direction.

The defeats at Son Tay and Bac Ninh concerned the Qing court but did not lead to significant changes, beyond executing two military commanders. The Empress Dowager Cixi and some of her officials wavered indecisively between the desire to continue the war and the fear of additional defeats. As a result, the court took no steps to change its strategy or tactics, and the military situation continued to deteriorate. When the French proposed negotiations in May 1884, the court accepted and sent Li Hongzhang to Tianjin to begin talks with the French representative Francois Ernest Fournier. The two men had met before and quickly hammered out a tentative settlement. According to the terms of the Li–Fournier Agreement, the Qing court agreed to withdraw all its forces back across the Chinese border and to respect the Franco–Vietnamese treaties of 1874 and 1883. In return, the French promised to give up any demand for an indemnity. As the Chinese and French governments considered this settlement, in June a French force of 900 moved northeast to occupy Lang Son, believing that Chinese troops had already moved back to the border as stipulated in the Li–Fournier Agreement. On the way, they encountered a Chinese force at the village of Bac Le. Although the Chinese commander knew of the Li–Fournier Agreement, he asked the French to delay their march to Lang Son, because he had not yet received formal orders to withdraw back to China. The French commander gave the Chinese an ultimatum for evacuation, which precipitated a battle that lasted for two days and forced the French to retreat. The French interpreted this "Bac Le Incident" as a deliberate ambush and a betrayal of the goodwill France had shown in not demanding an indemnity, which it then insisted upon to the tune of 250 million Francs. As a result, both sides rejected the Li–Fournier Agreement and the fighting continued.[5]

The Destruction of the Fuzhou Shipyard

The French took an unexpected approach to the new round of fighting by attacking the port of Jilong on the island of Taiwan. Using its superior ships and cannon, the French fleet under Admiral Lespes pounded the gun emplacements that guarded Jilong and occupied the city until a Chinese land force of 15,000 forced it to withdraw. Meanwhile, Admiral Courbet led another fleet of French ships up the Chinese coast toward the shipyard and naval base at Fuzhou. He assembled several iron warships and two torpedo boats at the mouth of the Min River, about a dozen miles downriver from the Fuzhou Shipyard where the Fuzhou Fleet had eleven wooden warships, twelve junks, and a number of smaller vessels. The Chinese did not restrict the movements of the French fleet near the coast as there had been no formal declaration of war, and the Qing court did not want to expand the fighting to China. Still, officials at the Fuzhou Shipyard asked Li Hongzhang to send ships from the Beiyang Fleet at Lushun (Port Arthur) to support the Fuzhou Fleet. Li refused, fearing an attack by the Japanese with whom he believed the French had been in contact to arrange a coordinated attack. Zeng Guoquan, brother of Zeng Guofan and commander of the Nanyang Fleet based at Shanghai, also refused to send ships to Fuzhou. This serves as a classic example of the lack of coordination among Chinese naval forces in the nineteenth century that contributed China's continuing military weakness. On August 23, 1884, the French ships opened fire on the Fuzhou Shipyard and within one hour sunk all but two of the fleet, destroyed the dock facilities, and killed more than 2,000 Chinese. The next day the French fleet sailed back downriver to the ocean, destroying the Chinese coastal forts along the way. As usual, Chinese forts had guns in fixed positions guarding the approach upriver, rendering them useless against French ships coming downriver.

To this point, neither side had declared formal war, but the Qing court did so a few days after the attack on the Fuzhou Shipyard. The French did not reciprocate, fearing that in a state of war foreign powers might refuse French ships access to neutral ports in Asia. Moreover, although some favored an expedition against China's ports to the north such as Nanjing, Shanghai, or Tianjin, the French government worried that such a move would trigger a larger war that might require a land campaign in China. Instead, Admiral Lespes led a second French attack on Jilong in October 1884. Once again, after a brief occupation during which 600 soldiers died from diseases such as cholera, the French had to retreat in the face of a substantial Chinese land force. French ships remained off the coast of Taiwan imposing a blockade. The Qing court ordered Li Hongzhang and Zeng Guoquan to send ships from the Beiyang and Nanyang Fleets to break the blockade, but both dragged their feet for fear of losing their own ships. Li again argued that the threat of a Japanese attack made it unwise to send his ships to the south. The court agreed and ordered Zeng alone to send ships to Taiwan. After a nearly three-month delay, Zeng complied only under the threat of punishment and dispatched five ships to break the blockade. As the ships approached the French fleet near Taiwan, they immediately turned back. The French pursued, catching and sinking the two slowest while the other three returned to their home base. The French followed and blockaded the Chinese port of Zhenjiang at the mouth of the Yangzi River.[6]

Meanwhile, back in Vietnam the Qing court attempted to revitalize the land war by commissioning Liu Yongfu as general-in-chief and ordering him to attack French positions. In February and March 1885, Chinese forces went on the attack, reoccupying Lang Son in one of the notable Chinese victories of the war and inflicting significant casualties on the French. Intermittent fighting continued until negotiations produced a peace settlement in June 1885, known as the Treaty of Tianjin. The peace settlement differed little from the earlier Li–Fournier Agreement, in that the Qing court recognized all French treaties with Vietnam and the French demanded no indemnity. Regardless, China suffered substantial economic loss as a result of the war.

As a test of China's Self-Strengthening Movement, the Sino-French War showed that China's military modernization efforts had not made significant progress. The French victory had been far from decisive and the Chinese won a few battles on land, but China still lagged behind in terms of military capability. Chinese victories at Bac Le and Lang Son came as much as a result of French logistical difficulties and inferior numbers as Chinese strategy and tactics. More than a technology gap, the war revealed the degree to which Chinese armies and navies suffered from poor organization, inadequately trained officers, and the absence of a unified command structure. Chinese arsenals and shipyards had produced modern weapons and ships so that at the outbreak of the war the French had only a slight advantage in firepower. Yet the Chinese still did not know how to use these modern weapons effectively. Moreover, each fleet had its own commander and areas of responsibility, and proved reluctant to come to the aid of each other or to coordinate their actions. For its part, the Qing court showed indecision and ineffectiveness in conducting the war, vacillating between waging war and seeking peace. Had it made a clear decision for war and stood firm from the beginning, it might have put forth a stronger war effort. Conversely, had it pursued sincere negotiations from the start, the Fuzhou dockyard might still be intact. In essence, the Sino-French War amounted to a military and economic disaster for China.

Military Reform and Reorganization

In the years after 1885 the Qing court attempted to make changes to the Chinese military in order to rectify some of the obvious shortcomings revealed by the Sino-French War. Since Chinese forces had achieved some success in the land fighting, most believed that China's greatest weakness lay in its naval forces. Li Hongzhang in particular stressed the urgent need for naval development as he believed Japan's growing interest in Korea would eventually mean war between China and Japan. The Qing court had traditionally preferred divided and overlapping commands in order to prevent a unified revolt from within the military, but after the Sino-French War it recognized that China needed a unified naval command to coordinate the four fleets. In 1885, the court created a Navy Board under the direction of the Manchu Prince Chun and Li Hongzhang. In theory, the Navy Board stood at the top of a centralized command, coordinating naval development and operations of all Chinese fleets. Yet in practice, the Navy Board suffered from a chronic shortage of funds, forcing Li Hongzhang to spend most of his time attempting to acquire additional money to support naval development and coastal defense. Beyond modest amounts from the Qing court, Li relied on contributions from the provinces, the sale of offices and titles, and foreign loans to buy additional ships from Germany and Great Britain. Li also had to compete for funds with the Empress Dowager Cixi, who needed money for her gardens and for a new summer palace. A marble boat in the new summer palace, built for her enjoyment with funds earmarked for purchasing foreign ships, is sometimes cynically described as "Cixi's navy."

Despite the creation of the Navy Board, the four fleets still operated independently, as each commander retained autonomy and concentrated on improving his own fleet. The Beiyang Fleet remained the largest of the four because it took the lion's share of the funding, because of Li's position as associate director of the Naval Board. Its home base at Lushun on the Liaodong Peninsula had multiple guns of six to eight inches surrounding it and its secondary naval base at Weihaiwei, on the Shandong Peninsula, had fifty-five guns of four to ten inches. Mines and steel cables protected the ocean approach to major naval bases along the coast, both northern and southern, so as to prevent a repeat of the French destruction of the Fuzhou Fleet in the Sino-French War.

Another important postwar reform involved improving the quality of Chinese army and navy officers. Naval academies at Tianjin and Fuzhou raised the requirements on the entrance exams and expanded their courses of study. Li established China's first formal academy for army officers at Tianjin in 1885, designed to produce professionally trained officers for his Anhui Army. He hired German instructors and included astronomy, geography, and mathematics in the curriculum. He envisioned that these graduates would experience one year of intensive study and then spread out through the army to train others. The course of study later increased to five years, and in its first 15 years the Tianjin academy produced 1,500 officers. This academy also served as a model for others, such as new army and navy academies at Guangzhou, established in 1887 under the direction of Zuo Zongtang. These changes helped China prepare for its next military clash, a war against Japan for control of Korea.[7]

The Sino-Japanese Rivalry over Korea

China valued Korea as a leading tributary state in the Ming and Qing dynasties. Under the Yi dynasty (1392–1910), Korea had closed itself off to most foreign contact since the seventeenth century but sent tribute missions to Beijing and modeled its cultural and political institutions after those of China. In the latter half of the nineteenth century, after the Opium War and Treaty of Nanjing forced China to open its doors to increased trade, Korea also faced great pressure to open up to the West. Having learned some difficult lessons about Western firepower, the Qing court urged the Koreans to seek peaceful relations with the West.

As the Koreans began adjusting to the realities of the new international order in East Asia, Japanese leaders had already developed an intense interest in Korea in the wake of the 1868 Meiji Restoration. The new Meiji government embarked on a massive program of change and modernization, and its leaders understood Korea's economic and strategic value. The Japanese had long viewed the Korean peninsula as a "dagger" pointed at Japan, a potential base for an attack on the Japanese islands. As Meiji Japan embraced Western standards of international commerce and diplomatic practice, its diplomats and merchants demanded a new relationship with Korea. In 1873, the Korean government "snubbed" the new Meiji government by refusing to open Korea up to Japanese diplomats and merchants. Some Japanese officials construed this rebuff as an insult and advocated a military expedition against Korea to "teach it a lesson." Despite significant support for a "Conquer Korea Campaign," cooler heads prevailed, and the Meiji government turned to internal consolidation and development rather than foreign adventure.

Within a few years, Japan once again pressured Korea to accept a new relationship between the two states. In 1875, the Japanese government sent gunboats to Korea to demand trade, where they exchanged fire with Korean coastal forts. The Qing court advised the Korean government to negotiate before the Japanese forced Korea to open up, much as the British had forced China's hand. In February 1876, the Koreans and Japanese signed the Treaty of Kanghwa that recognized Korea as an equal state (rejecting Korea's traditional position as a Chinese tribute state), called for the exchange of envoys, opened three Korean ports to Japanese merchants, and gave the Japanese consular jurisdiction in these ports. In order to counter the rising Japanese influence in Korea, the Qing court urged Korea to open up to the Western powers as well. In 1882, with the help of Qing officials, the United States and Korea signed a treaty by which the two states exchanged diplomats, established consuls at trading ports, and agreed to treat each other on the basis of equality. As usual, the other European powers soon followed, signing similar treaties with the Korean government.

Within Korea, different factions around the Yi court contended for influence, one favoring the traditional alliance with China while the other preferred closer ties to newly modernizing Meiji Japan. The Chinese and Japanese governments occasionally dispatched troops to Korea to quell disturbances and support the Yi court, which led to a developing Sino-Japanese rivalry over Korea that threatened to lead to war. In order to prevent a Sino-Japanese clash over Korea, the two governments agreed in 1885 that each would withdraw its troops from Korea and that if in the future either found it necessary to send troops to Korea, each should notify the other in advance and remove the troops as soon as possible. With this agreement, China and Japan temporarily resolved their competition by serving as "co-protectors" of Korea. This agreement by no means ended the Sino-Japanese rivalry over Korea, as both sides remained intent on controlling the Korean peninsula. For China, preserving its relations with Korea meant retaining its traditional dominant position in East Asia. For Japan, control over Korea meant additional raw materials and markets for its growing industry and preserving Japan's national security by preventing a hostile power from attacking Japan from Korea.

A Korean revolt known as the Tonghak Movement provided the spark that ignited the Sino-Japanese War. Led by a frustrated Korean scholar who billed himself as a messianic leader against Western influence and religion, the Tonghak Movement began as a new religion in the 1860s. Although Korean authorities captured and executed its leader, his followers continued to call for the expulsion of Westerners and government reform. In 1894, the Tonghaks rose again and marched on Seoul, which prompted the Korean government to request help from the Chinese resident general, Yuan Shikai. The Qing court agreed to send 2,000 troops over the border to help crush the Tonghak rebels, and a few days later informed the Japanese government of its decision. This prompted Meiji leaders to send Japanese troops to Korea, but in much larger numbers than the Chinese, though the Korean king had specifically requested that Japan not send troops. In July, following the defeat of the Tonghaks, Japanese troops seized control of the Korean palace, disarmed the palace guard, and detained the King. They appointed the king's son, known to be friendly to the Japanese, regent for his father and announced a plan of sweeping reform that would bring Korea under Japanese influence.

The Sino-Japanese War, 1894–1895

As had been the case prior to the war with France, Li Hongzhang, the commander of China's strongest land and naval forces, preferred to avoid war. Li hoped for Western mediation of the dispute over Korea and therefore did not rush into preparations for war with Japan, which he felt might jeopardize a peaceful settlement. As a result, when no Western power agreed to mediate and war began, Japanese forces heavily outnumbered Chinese forces in Korea. To prevent the Beiyang Fleet from transporting additional Chinese soldiers to Korea, Japanese warships patrolled the northwestern coast of Korea. In late July 1894, several days prior to a formal declaration of war, Japanese cruisers attacked Chinese transport ships returning to China from Korea after dropping off troops. In the process of pursuing a damaged Chinese vessel fleeing the scene, the Japanese ships encountered two other Chinese vessels heading toward Korea with reinforcements. Without warning, the Japanese fired on these vessels, damaging the *Zao Qiang* and sinking the *Gao Sheng* on July 25, 1894. Over 1,000 Chinese soldiers drowned, many unable to swim. On August 1, the two sides declared war on each other.

By the early 1890s, China had rebuilt much its military strength, led by the Anhui Army and the Beiyang Fleet, both under the command of Li Hongzhang. The four fleets had a total of sixty-five large ships and forty-three torpedo boats. Japan, by contrast, had thirty-two warships and forty-three torpedo boats, giving China the advantage in terms of naval tonnage and leading some observers to predict that China would triumph over its smaller neighbor. In formulating a naval strategy, Chinese naval commanders had been deeply influenced by the destruction of the Fuzhou Fleet in the Sino-French War. As a result, the Chinese adopted a defensive strategy designed to protect the naval bases along China's coast from Liaodong to the Yangzi River. Rather than contest the waters along the Korean coast, Li Hongzhang chose to concentrate his strength closer to Chinese waters, holding a line from the Yalu River to the port at Weihaiwei. In order to protect the new ships and ports, Li hid his fleet behind a string of floating mines in Weihaiwei and Lushun harbors. This had the advantage of shortening the Chinese logistical chain and protecting the ocean approach to Tianjin and Beijing, but it also allowed Japan to transport its troops to Korea uncontested. Taking advantage of control of the waters around Korea, the Japanese took the offensive both on land and on sea, planning naval attacks on Chinese bases on the Liaodong and Shandong peninsulas while ground forces moved overland through Korea to attack Manchuria.

The Japanese landed troops on both coasts of Korea, at Wonson in the east and later at Inchon in the west, sending both groups overland toward Chinese positions. These troops first attacked Chinese forces around Seoul, executing a flanking maneuver and routing the Chinese. The Qing court, as had been the case in the Opium War, received inaccurate reports of a great victory over the enemy "dwarfs." The Japanese moved north intending to lay siege to Pyongyang, which if captured would clear the way to the Chinese border. More than 20,000 Chinese troops defended the walled city against 23,000 Japanese attackers. Over the course of two days in September 1894, the Japanese attacked in multiple columns, using diversions to distract Chinese attention from the main thrusts. The Chinese had adequate weapons and time to prepare for the attack, but chose to entrench themselves behind the city walls rather than attack Japanese forces as they crossed the Taedong River which runs through Pyongyang. The outnumbered Chinese forces withdrew under the cover of darkness, leaving substantial amounts of weapons and supplies, pulling back to the Yalu River and abandoning Korea to the Japanese.[8]

Meanwhile, Li Hongzhang had dispatched five steamships to escort troop transports carrying reinforcements to Korea. On the return voyage to Lushun, Li's fleet fought the battle of the Yalu River on September 17. The Chinese and Japanese had twelve ships each, China with the advantage in tonnage and firepower, but the Japanese enjoyed greater ship speed and proved faster and more accurate in firing their guns. Japan also had superior naval officers and had broken the Beiyang Fleet's communications code. Moreover, the Chinese southern fleets refused to send ships to support the Beiyang Fleet, taking revenge for Li Hongzhang's refusal to send his ships to help protect the Fuzhou Shipyard against the French in 1885. Taking advantage of the fact that the Chinese ships lined up abreast with the weakest ships to the outside, the Japanese divided into two squadrons and positioned their ships on the wings of the Chinese formation where they launched devastating broadsides against the outer ships. In the face of this withering fire, Chinese ships broke formation and fought individually. The Chinese lost four ships while the Japanese lost none. Several damaged Chinese ships made their way back to Lushun.

With the Japanese navy in complete control of the Yellow Sea, its ground forces pushed toward the Chinese–Korean border for an attack on Manchuria. As they had at Pyongyang, rather than challenge the Japanese as they attempted to cross the Yalu River, Chinese forces remained behind fortified positions on the northern bank of the river, allowing the 25,000 Japanese troops to cross unmolested on pontoon bridges. In October the Chinese abandoned their positions at the Yalu, falling back on Shenyang in the heart of Manchuria and hoping that the bitterly cold weather would halt the Japanese advance. While Japanese ground forces crossed the border into Manchuria, crushing Chinese troops at Haicheng in December 1894 and moving rapidly southward, naval forces planned attacks on the Chinese naval bases at Dalian, Lushun, and Weihaiwei that would allow the Japanese access to the Bohai Sea and the river route to Beijing. This meant a two-pronged attack on the capital, one moving southwest from Manchuria and the other moving northwest from Tianjin.[9]

The Fall of Lushun and Weihaiwei

In November 1894, Japanese forces landed on the east coast of the Liaodong Peninsula, quickly knocking Chinese artillery emplacements out of commission and capturing the city of Jinzhou, which guarded the land approach to the naval bases at both Dalian and Lushun. Moving down the peninsula, the Japanese took Dalian several days later with minimal resistance, setting the stage for the battle of Lushun. Although they enjoyed a significant numerical superiority, the Japanese did not have appropriate artillery for a massive bombardment, which forced them to attack Chinese gun emplacements surrounding the base one at a time. Although updated with improved artillery, Chinese officials did not coordinate their fire to put up an ineffective defense. Lushun fell after a single day's bloody fighting in which Japanese soldiers massacred thousands of Chinese soldiers and civilians. The fall of Lushun left the critical naval base at Weihaiwei as the last obstacle to complete Japanese control of the Yellow and Bohai seas.

In preparation for an attack in Weihaiwei, the Chinese had laid mines and reed screens to block access to the harbor. A series of impressive forts with heavy guns surrounded the base, and smaller forts at the mouth of the harbor provided extra protection against any attempt by the Japanese navy to enter the harbor. Japanese forces began the attack on Weihaiwei in January 1895 by landing troops to the west of the base as a diversion. A separate force landed to the east of Weihaiwei and approached the base, which housed fifteen ships of China's prized Beiyang Fleet. Capturing the outer forts one at a time, the Japanese turned these guns on the remaining forts and used them against the Chinese. After several days of bombardment both from their own guns on land and from Japanese ships outside the harbor, the Chinese commander Ding Richang surrendered on February 12, committing suicide later that same day. This defeat left the road to Beijing wide open.[10]

Under the circumstances, the Qing court saw little alternative to surrender and quickly sued for peace. Japanese negotiators intended to press for substantial concessions and a heavy indemnity, but limited their demands when a Japanese fanatic shot Li Hongzhang, the Chinese chief negotiator, wounding him in the face. The embarrassed Japanese government quickly ended the war and agreed to a peace settlement. The Treaty of Shimonoseki, signed on April 17, 1895, provided for the recognition of Korean independence and the end of its tributary relationship with China; an indemnity of 200 million taels to Japan; cession of Taiwan, the Pescadores, and the Liaodong Peninsula to Japan; the opening of four internal river ports to Japan; and the right of Japanese nationals to open factories and industries in China. Weeks after the conclusion of the treaty, in what is known as the Triple Intervention, Russia, France, and Germany demanded that Japan return the Liaodong Peninsula to China in return for a larger indemnity. In no position to challenge three Western powers, the Japanese had no choice but to agree. The war not only marked the rise of Japan as a modern, imperialist nation but also set the stage for Japan's later war with Russia and expansion into Manchuria.

As had been the case in the war against France, Qing army and navy forces showed that they had improved on a technological level but still suffered from divided regional commands. The four Chinese fleets continued to operate independently and offered little support to each other. The Japanese, on the other hand, had created well-funded national land and naval forces, a unified command system, and a system of universal male conscription to provide large numbers of well-trained recruits. China had more ships than Japan but lost this advantage because it did not commit all of its ships to battle. Fighting against only part of the Chinese fleet, the Japanese used smaller, faster ships to destroy the Chinese ships in the Yellow Sea and to capture naval bases at Dalian, Lushun, and Weihaiwei. In Manchuria, the Anhui Army did most of the fighting, and troops sent from the southern provinces arrived only after the war had ended. This humiliating defeat, not at the hands of a Western power but a much smaller Asian state, revealed the limits of the Self-Strengthening Movement even more clearly than had the Sino-French War of ten years earlier.

The Sino-French and Sino-Japanese wars starkly revealed the limits of China's attempts to build its military into a modern force. The defeats increased criticism of the Qing court for its inept handling of the wars and demonstrated the need for even greater efforts at military reform. With its weaknesses completely exposed, the Western powers descended on China to exact territorial and economic concessions from the Qing government. In 1897 under the pretext of compensating for the murder of two German missionaries in Shandong, Germany seized the area around Jiaozhou harbor, including the city of Qingdao. The Germans then compelled the Chinese government to lease the area to Germany for ninety-nine years. Encouraged by the German success, the Russians took two ports on the Liaodong Peninsula, Lushun and Dalian, the very ports Russia had forced Japan to relinquish after the Sino-Japanese War, compelling the Chinese government to lease the area for twenty-five years and grant Russia rights to construct a South Manchurian Railway from these two ports to the Chinese Eastern Railway, which connected to the Trans Siberian Railway. The British leased the naval base at Weihaiwei for twenty-five years, and the French leased Guangzhou Bay in the south for ninety-nine years. The Chinese refer to this renewed bout of imperialism in China as the "carving up of the melon," which further discredited the Qing court and accelerated the pace of a growing revolutionary movement within China that would eventually put an end to Manchu rule.

CHAPTER **6**

The New Armies and the 1911 Revolution, 1895–1916

The Self-Strengthening Movement of the late nineteenth century had involved mostly Chinese provincial reformers who focused on technology such as artillery and steamships with an eye toward naval development and coastal defense. The wars with France and Japan revealed that technological development alone had not been sufficient and that China's military remained incapable of defending its borders. Moreover, China's two greatest military forces, the Anhui Army and the Beiyang Fleet, had been largely destroyed in the fighting. This prompted the Qing court to finally offer genuine support for military development, joining provincial officials by authorizing significant military reforms that went beyond the scope of the Self-Strengthening Movement. Recognizing that adopting modern weapons and technology did not solve China's military problems, the court began a larger program of Western style military training and organization. This new round of military reform resulted in the creation of new military forces that would help overthrow the Qing dynasty and precipitate an extended period of military rule in China.

The Self-Strengthening and Newly Created Armies

These organizational changes began in late 1895 with the creation of two experimental military units, the Self-Strengthening Army under the command of Zhang Zhidong and the Newly Created Army under the command of Yuan Shikai. If successful, these two units would serve as models for the development of additional forces. Both these armies drew on the model of the Hunan and Anhui Armies and the policies set by Zeng Guofan and Li Hongzhang, such as recruiting carefully and accepting only sturdy peasant recruits in good health, who could verify their good conduct. While Zeng's Hunan Army had been largely recruited locally, the Self-Strengthening and Newly Created Armies took in recruits from several provinces as long as they met the standard for induction. Soldiers enjoyed good pay, adequate rations, and decent treatment from their officers. Yet they differed from the earlier regional armies in that they relied completely on Western methods of training and organization. Specifically, they followed the German model of combining infantry units with cavalry, artillery, and engineers. Drilling and training took place under the watchful eye of German advisors. In order to train officers for the Self-Strengthening Army, Zhang Zhidong established a military academy at Nanjing, offering a three-year curriculum focusing on strategy, tactics, artillery, and cartography. Based in Zhili Province, Yuan Shikai's Newly Created Army employed the same training and organizational model and quickly grew to a force of 7,000 men. Like Western armies, these forces had staff officers who specialized in transportation, communications, supplies, and weapons and ammunition.[1]

These changes can be seen as a part of a larger call for reform of the government and the military that followed the Sino-Japanese War and the "scramble for concessions" in which foreign imperialists established concessions or "spheres of influence" in China. The changes also reflected the views of prominent reformers, such as Kang Youwei and Liang Qichao who caught the attention of the young Guangxu emperor. Together these three presided over the "Hundred Days Reform" in the summer of 1898, which initiated a series of reforms designed to modernize China and its military. Among other things, this Hundred Days Reform included replacing the old military examinations, which emphasized physical strength and archery skills, with a modern examination that stressed knowledge of weapons, strategy, and tactics. They hoped this change would produce a new generation of military officers more capable of commanding a modern army. The reformers also called for a centralized system of universal military training and the creation of a reserve force. Kang and Liang also called for sweeping changes to the government, including the creation of a national assembly and adoption of a political constitution. The Empress Dowager feared that these reforms would pose a threat to Manchu rule and plotted with conservative officials, including Yuan Shikai, to kidnap the emperor. Claiming that an illness had incapacitated the Guangxu emperor, she reasserted her authority as regent and put an end to the Hundred Days Reform in September 1898. She reversed almost all of the reform edicts issued the previous summer, held the young emperor under house arrest for the rest of his life, and issued arrest warrants for Kang, Liang, and other prominent reformers. As a result, for the time being the Chinese military remained divided into regional forces with a divided command structure and nonstandard weapons.

The Boxers, 1899–1901

The next great impetus for military reform came as a result of an event known in the West as the Boxer Uprising. Westerners used the term Boxers to describe the members of a quasi-religious secret society who launched attacks on foreigners and Chinese converts at the turn of the twentieth century. The Chinese refer to them as *Yihequan* (Fists United in Righteousness) or *Yihetuan* (Militia United in Righteous). The Boxers rose in Shandong Province in a border area rife with poverty and banditry. Far from the protection of government authority, local people organized for self-defense and protection against predatory bandits. Influenced by superstition, popular culture, and folk theater, the Boxers believed in spirit possession and claimed that they could render themselves invulnerable to weapons, including Western firearms, through the practice of Boxer rituals. They had no coherent organization or command structure but rather emerged as jumbled body of diverse "Boxing" groups united by the practice of spirit possession and antiforeignism. Claims of such extraordinary powers proved critical to the rise of the Boxers, as it attracted those who had suffered and sought empowerment. The fact that anyone could learn spirit possession, as opposed to the years of study necessary to learn a traditional martial art, rendered the movement accessible to the masses and facilitated its spread across Shandong and north China. Flooding and drought brought dissatisfaction and hunger, which made people more likely to join such a movement and to seek someone or something to blame for their troubles.[2]

In addition to the socioeconomic factors that contributed to the rise of the Boxers, the presence of Western missionaries in Shandong added cultural conflict to the movement. German missionaries had been particularly active in the region as their presence grew significantly in the years after the "scramble for concessions" following China's defeat in the Sino-Japanese War. They occasionally intervened in Chinese legal cases, offering protection to those accused of crimes if they agreed to convert, which angered the local Chinese community and made them suspicious of the missionaries. Tensions flared in late 1897 when a group of unknown assailants murdered two German missionaries in what is known as the "Juye Incident." The German government pressed the Qing court to take action against those responsible and demanded funds for the construction of new churches in Shandong as compensation. Taking advantage of the incident to increase its territorial concessions in Shandong, the German government also forced the Qing court to grant it a lease on the port at Jiaozhou. Tensions between the missionary community in Shandong and local Chinese continued, contributing to the rise of antiforeignism in the area. In early 1898, the Boxers began a campaign of hostility and violence against local Christians.

In late 1898, the ranks of the Boxers swelled with refugees from severe flooding of the Yellow River, which brought increased anger and resentment to the Boxer movement. Many Chinese blamed the Western missionaries and their churches for angering Heaven and bringing natural disasters down on the people of Shandong. Foreign governments began to pressure the Qing court to suppress the Boxers and prevent acts of violence against missionaries and Christian converts. Chinese local authorities originally viewed the Boxers as bandits and tried to suppress them, fearing that violence against missionaries would lead to conflict with the foreign powers. Yet as the number of Boxer groups increased and local authorities found it difficult to suppress the movement, they took a different approach by recognizing the Boxers as a local militia.

Boxer groups expanded over the course of the winter of 1898–1899, numbering in the hundreds as "teachers" who instructed people in martial arts and spirit possession moved across Shandong. Wearing red turbans or sashes to identify themselves, the Boxer groups had no overall commander or unified leadership, spreading from village to village under different leaders. Female Boxers formed a separate group called Red Lanterns, mostly young, unmarried women who wore red handkerchiefs and like their male counterparts practiced martial arts. The Red Lanterns supposedly possessed special magic powers, which they employed in support of the male

Boxers. Most Boxer bands carried out their antiforeign activities in their home areas, attacking local churches and the homes of Chinese converts or foreign missionaries. They gradually began to move from the countryside closer to larger towns and cities and broadened their attacks to anything foreign, such as telegraph wires or railway stations. By early 1900, accounts of the actions of the Boxers had begun to appear in foreign newspapers, and missionaries reported increased hostility in Shandong. This expansion of the movement had a chilling effect on the foreign community in north China, which made repeated calls for the Qing court to take action against the Boxers.

The Qing court showed little interest in punishing the Boxers and issued an official decree in January 1900 approving of villages which assembled militia for self-defense or for protection against bandits. Local authorities had orders not to suppress any particular Boxer group but rather to concentrate on preventing disorder in general. Great Britain, the United States, France, Germany, and Italy sent protests to the Qing court, arguing that this only encouraged acts of violence against foreigners and converts, and demanded that the court take steps to disband the Boxers in Shandong. While the Qing court chose not to move aggressively to meet these demands, government forces did occasionally clash with the Boxers, which made it increasingly difficult to describe them as official militia forces. As the Boxers moved beyond Shandong into the areas around Tianjin and Beijing in late May and early June 1900, they killed French and Belgian railway engineers and British missionaries. The foreign diplomatic community responded by calling for a relief force of international troops to march on Tianjin and Beijing to provide protection. A relief force landed at the Dagu forts in mid-June and succeeded in reaching Tianjin, but made slow progress from there and eventually had to turn back as Qing troops blocked their way and destroyed the railroad tracks leading to the capital.[3]

In early June, some provincial governors advised the Qing court to take decisive action against the Boxers in order to avoid provoking another foreign military expedition against China. In contrast to these calls for suppression of the Boxers, a number of conservative officials argued that the Boxers could provide the solution to the problem of foreign imperialism in China. As the court debated its position in mid-June, the Boxers attacked the foreign community in Beijing, setting fire to foreign churches and homes and killing a member of the Japanese legation. Emboldened by this action, the Empress Dowager and the Qing court declared war on all the Western powers and Japan on June 19, 1900, and told the foreign diplomats to leave Beijing within twenty-four hours. This amounted to an impossible demand since to step foot outside the diplomatic compound would have meant certain death for any foreigner. With the support of some elements of the Qing military, the Boxers laid siege to the foreign legation for approximately two months, using traditional weapons and attempting to set the legation on fire. Inside the barricades, over 900 foreigners and 2,000–3,000 Chinese Christians desperately organized a defense. Qing troops offered artillery support to the Boxers in the capital but did not press the attack wholeheartedly as many commanders doubted the wisdom of this military action.

In fact, a truce in mid-July brought a halt to the fighting during which the attackers sent in supplies of food and fresh water.[4]

As the Boxers besieged the diplomatic legation compound in Beijing, attacks on foreigners and converts took place in scattered communities across north China. In one of the most notorious cases, a Qing provincial official in Shanxi Province named Yu Xian offered protection to foreigners in the area. When more than forty men, women, and children accepted his offer of sanctuary, he promptly executed them. Yet in many other regions of China, provincial officials ignored the declaration of war and came to agreements with Western consuls in the treaty ports to protect each other. The elite forces of the Self-Strengthening Army and the Newly Created Army did not participate in the attacks on foreigners.

On August 14 a second international relief force composed of more than 18,000 troops from several nations (8,000 Japanese, 4,800 Russians, 3,000 British, 2,100 Americans, 800 French, 58 Austrians, and 53 Italians) arrived in Beijing to relieve the beleaguered defenders. Marching from Tianjin and fighting their way toward the capital, the relief force scattered the poorly organized Boxers. Although relatively brief, the fighting featured great brutality on both sides. The Boxers raped and tortured while Western troops engaged in widespread looting and plundering. Hundreds of Chinese women committed suicide fearing rape by Western soldiers. As the international force approached Beijing, the Empress Dowager fled to the west, leaving her officials to make a peace settlement, known as the 1901 Boxer Protocol. This agreement stipulated that the Qing court must pay an indemnity of 450 million taels over 39 years, destroy the Dagu forts and other military installations along the Beijing–Tianjin corridor, and allow foreign troops to remain at a number of strategic points and at the legation headquarters. Finally, the Boxer Protocol called for the execution of several officials deemed guilty of encouraging the attacks. The financial burden of this agreement, perhaps the most damaging consequence of the Boxer movement, drained funds away from the military reforms of the next decade.

Late Qing Military Reform

The Boxer Uprising cannot compare to earlier wars against foreign powers, but it served to once again reveal the continuing problems of the Qing military forces and provided renewed incentive to reform the military. In its wake, the Empress Dowager and the Qing court showed genuine interest in a program of institutional reform for China, including plans to create a truly national army and to establish military educational facilities based on the Japanese model. As a first step, in August 1901 the court abolished the traditional military exam, ending the antiquated system for procuring officers. Of all of the post-Boxer military reforms, the establishment of a national system of military education had the most dramatic impact by creating a new generation of professional officers. In addition to attending new military schools in China, significant numbers of Chinese students began going abroad to study at foreign military academies. The majority chose Japan because of its location, its lower cost, and lesser language barrier. In 1900, forty Chinese students enrolled in

Japanese military academies, but by 1904 this number had grown to more than 200. The Japanese government opened a special school for Chinese students called the Shimbu Gakko, which prepared them for entry into a formal Japanese military academy. Many returned to serve as instructors in new Chinese military academies, such as the Baoding Military Academy, which Yuan Shikai established in Zhili Province.

Historically, the best and brightest of China typically chose to sit for the prestigious Confucian civil service examination, but when the Qing court abolished the entire examination system in 1905, study in military academies took on a new appeal. Students from educated families flocked to the military schools, drawing more elites of Chinese society into military service. This created a new generation of professional military officers who replaced the Confucian-educated, scholar-official military leaders of Zeng Guofan's generation. These new professionals not only strengthened the Chinese military but also contributed to the revolutionary movement that had gained momentum in the early years of the century. The late Qing military reforms helped sow the seeds of the destruction of the dynasty by separating China's traditional elites from support of the ruling dynasty. No longer drawn into government service, graduates of military academies might just as likely consider how to overthrow the Qing court as how to protect it.

Under the guidance of these new officers and Japanese and German advisors, Chinese soldiers improved greatly in terms of discipline and drill. The court identified weak elements of the Army of the Green Standard for elimination and subjected the remaining units to retraining and reorganization into battalions of approximately 500 men, which served as provincial standing armies or constabulary and border patrol forces. Banner forces also underwent retraining and reorganization into brigades of 3,000 men. Although the Empress Dowager agreed to reforms designed to produce a national army, she rejected the idea of a general staff, clinging to the tradition of decentralized commands that the Manchus had preferred throughout the Qing dynasty. Too much power in the hands of a single official or small group, she feared, would make the standing army a potential tool for revolt against Manchu rule.

The Beiyang Army

In 1901, Yuan Shikai assumed the posts of Governor of Zhili Province and Superintendent of Northern Administration, making him the most important figure in this era of military reform. From these offices, Yuan utilized central government funds and customs revenues to transform the Newly Created Army and elements of the Self-Strengthening Army into a single force known as the Beiyang Army, which emerged as China's premier military force in the early twentieth century. He created his own staff sections and appointed officers to oversee planning, military preparation, and training and instruction. Like many others, Yuan saw the creation of a single, national standing army as the most important goal of the postwar period.

In 1902, the Beiyang Army provided the first two divisions of what would become a national standing army, known as the New Army, and served as a model for other forces to emulate. In order to begin planning for this national force, in December 1903 the Qing court created a CAR (Commission for Army Reorganization), under the direction of the Manchu Prince Qing and Yuan Shikai, designed to centralize policy and standards for the New Army. The commission made preparations for a total force of thirty-six divisions, each of approximately 12,500 men, by standardizing plans for pay, training, weapons and ammunition, medical services, and by creating a uniform system of ranks and terminology. A large reserve force, with ten years of service, would support the thirty-six divisions. The soldiers would be volunteers between the ages of 20 and 25, in good physical condition, and from respectable peasant families. The CAR also called for a new system of elementary-level military schools in each province, four middle military schools, and a number of full-fledged military academies in other parts of the country. These elementary and middle schools would prepare students to attend the military academies or to serve as noncommissioned officers in the new force. Seeking a better-educated military force, the CAR even stipulated that 20 percent of the enlisted men in any given unit must be literate.

By the autumn of 1905, the New Army had six divisions of the planned thirty-six in place, all of which belonged to the Beiyang Army, based in north China. Partly as a result of the 1904–1905 Russo-Japanese War, which threatened Qing control of its Manchurian homelands, the court moved up the deadline for the completion of the thirty-six divisions from 1916 to 1912. The CAR planned to accomplish this accelerated development by ordering each province to reorganize its forces—Banner, Green Standard, and regional armies—combining the best of all of these units into new divisions and demobilizing the rest or organizing them into a reserve force or police units. The plan called for each province to create at least one division to contribute to the total of thirty-six in the planned New Army. Although the quality of Chinese military forces improved as a result of these late Qing reforms, it remained a diverse and decentralized force commanded largely by provincial officials. In fact, the "national army" the Qing court envisioned would actually be a combination of regional forces, collectively called the New Army. This also put the financial burden on the provinces rather than on the Qing court.[5]

These provincial New Armies typically combined infantry and cavalry but remained short on artillery, and their quality varied widely, as did their loyalty to the government. In 1907, the Qing court took the dramatic step of disbanding the Manchu Banner garrisons and ending the policy of segregation between Manchus and Chinese, which led many Bannermen who had manned the garrisons to join the New Army. The traditional Manchu and Mongol Banners remained intact.[6]

The Qing court moved ahead with these military reforms, yet Manchu officials still feared that the Chinese officials who commanded these New Army divisions might turn against the dynasty. To forestall such an event, in 1907 the court removed both Yuan Shikai and Zhang Zhidong from direct command over their military forces by "promoting" them to the Grand Council in Beijing. The Empress

Dowager, who had dominated the court since the 1860s, died in 1908, but her successors continued to guard against giving regional Chinese military officials too much power. The new regent Prince Chun dismissed Yuan Shikai from service, pressing him into an early retirement. Zhang Zhidong died in 1909, the same year that the CAR and the Board of War merged to become the Ministry of War, putting all armed forces, military academies, and arsenals under direct Manchu control. Although the Manchus clung to military authority, within the Beiyang Army Yuan's subordinate officers remained loyal to their former commander. Their loyalty grew out of professional relations rather the locally based personal loyalties of the earlier regional armies of Zeng Guofan and Li Hongzhang. Regardless, the New Army divisions represented a break from the tradition of the regional armies that had supported the dynasty since the days of the Taipings. Their training and organization closely resembled those of modern armies in Japan and Europe.[7]

By 1911, the combined forces of the Beiyang Army and the New Army divisions from provinces such as Hubei, Jiangsu, Shanxi, Shaanxi, Jiangxi, Guangxi, Guizhou, and Yunnan numbered only at most twenty divisions of the planned thirty-six, perhaps totaling 190,000 troops. Beiyang Army troops made up as much as one-third of this total. Many smaller provinces found it difficult to fund their New Army divisions and operated at less than full strength. Others proved hesitant to build a military force that they feared would strengthen central authority. While most enlisted men joined because of economic hardship and remained apolitical, many of the officers had become involved in anti-Manchu organizations. They helped spread revolutionary ideas throughout the ranks of the provincial New Army divisions.

Sun Yat-sen and the Tongmenghui

The organization of the New Army took place in the context of the growing revolutionary movement in China. As the Qing court sought to revive its fortunes and preserve Manchu rule through military and political reform, many Chinese intellectuals outside of the government had been thinking seriously about China's future since the Sino-Japanese War. Some argued in favor of a constitutional monarchy while others advocated the violent overthrow of the Qing dynasty. Of the leaders of the revolutionary movement Sun Yat-sen emerged as the most visible and widely recognized. Born to a peasant family outside of Guangzhou, Sun grew up listening to stories of the anti-Manchu movement of the Taiping Heavenly Kingdom, which had ended only two years before his birth. In 1879, Sun and his mother went to Honolulu, Hawaii to join Sun's older brother who had emigrated and started a successful business. Sun attended in the Iolani School and later graduated from Oahu College in 1883. He enrolled in medical school in Guangzhou where he became involved in revolutionary societies and study groups. He moved to a medical college in British Hong Kong where he enjoyed greater freedom of movement and discussion. He graduated first in his class in 1892 and set up a medical practice in Macao.

Prior to 1894, Sun saw reform, rather than revolution, as the best treatment for China's weakness. During a trip to Beijing in 1894, he witnessed firsthand the degradation and corruption of the ruling Manchus and heard the stories of China's poor military performance in battle against the Japanese, on both land and sea. Now convinced of the need to overthrow Manchu rule, Sun began raising money to finance his plans for revolution. He turned to overseas Chinese, the secret societies of southern China, Christian converts, and foreign missionaries for contributions. He traveled to the United States, Europe, and Japan to raise funds and support. In London, he achieved worldwide notoriety when Qing diplomats stationed there recognized him as a known revolutionary and kidnapped him for return to China. Sun managed to get a message to some English friends who got the British Foreign Office to protest the illegal kidnapping on British soil. The Chinese legation reluctantly released him, and the episode made him an instant celebrity and the most visible leader of the anti-Qing movement.

Sun gradually developed and articulated the basic principles of the social and democratic revolution he intended to launch. These principles became known as the Three People's Principles—nationalism, democracy, and people's livelihood—which served as the foundation of the revolutionary philosophy of Sun and his followers. The first principle, nationalism, called for not only the overthrow of the Manchus but also the elimination of foreign imperialism in China. The second principle, democracy, called for the establishment of a democratic republic, which ensured the people's right to vote and participate in government. Finally, people's livelihood stressed the need for regulating capital and land reform in order to alleviate the poverty of China's masses. His following grew slowly but picked up steam in the early years of the new century.

In August 1905, Sun brought unity to the diverse anti-Qing movement by creating an alliance of revolutionary organizations called the Tongmenghui, usually translated as the Revolutionary Alliance. As leader of this new organization, Sun worked out a plan for revolution in three stages. First, Sun envisioned a military power seizure and a brief period of military rule to preserve order. Second, a period of political tutelage, lasting not more than six years, during which the Chinese people would learn about democratic practice in preparation for elections at the local and national levels and the creation of a political constitution. The third and final stage involved dissolution of military government in favor of a constitutional republic governed by popularly elected officials. The Tongmenghui grew rapidly, uniting people of different backgrounds and serving as a rallying point for revolutionary and progressive forces in China. It had particular success recruiting among Chinese students studying in Japanese military academies. These young men joined the Tongmenghui in large numbers and then returned to China to assume instruction duties at Chinese military academies and to serve in New Army divisions in various provinces, quietly spreading their revolutionary ideas to their own cadets and colleagues. Ironically, the New Army that the Qing court envisioned as a force to protect the dynasty actually included many officers who dedicated themselves to its overthrow.

The Wuchang Revolt, 1911

Sun Yat-sen and the Tongmenghui occupied center stage of the anti-Qing movement, but the military action that gave rise to the 1911 Revolution that ended Manchu rule originated with the New Army. The revolutionary pulse in China quickened in the years between 1906 and 1911 as various revolutionaries, often members of secret societies with only limited contacts with the Tongmenghui, attempted revolts in southern China. Each failed but contributed to the unmistakable surge of revolution building in China. These early attempts at revolution had taken place in southern China, most aimed at capturing Guangzhou. In 1911, a group of soldiers from the Hubei New Army planned their own revolt in the tri-city area of Wuhan (Hankou, Hanyang, and Wuchang). Located on the Yangzi River, control of the Wuhan area would put the revolutionaries, if successful, in a position to move either south to Guangzhou or north to Beijing as the situation dictated.

The Hubei New Army began under the direction of Zhang Zhidong when he assumed the office of Governor-General of Hunan and Hubei. Taking one battalion of the Self-Strengthening Army, Zhang began building a new force based at Wuchang. Incorporating reorganized and retrained Green Standard and Banner forces, the Hubei New Army developed into a force of 16,000 in 1911, one of the best of the provincial New Armies in southern and central China. Like other New Army divisions, the ranks of the Hubei New Army included soldiers who advocated revolution. While many Japanese-trained officers joined Sun Yat-sen's Tongmenghui, other soldiers gravitated toward revolution for more practical reasons. Edmund Fung has shown that many noncommissioned officers and enlisted men in the provincial New Armies participated in revolutionary activities because of dissatisfaction with the conditions of service. Corruption, minimal prospects for promotion, and the government's problems in meeting its payrolls drove many soldiers into revolutionary circles.[8]

The soldiers of the Hubei New Army who planned the revolt against the Qing dynasty intended to strike in late October, but a mistake led them to swing into action earlier. On October 9, as several soldiers prepared bombs in an apartment in the Russian concession of Hankou, one made the mistake of smoking a cigarette that detonated one of the bombs and destroyed the apartment. Police who responded to the explosion discovered lists of the names of men involved in the planned uprising, many of whom served in the Hubei New Army. As police began rounding up suspected revolutionaries and summarily executing some of them, other revolutionary elements of the Hubei New Army decided to swing into action on the evening of October 10, 1911, seizing control of government offices and armories in Wuchang. After defeating local Qing government forces, approximately 3,500 New Army troops joined the revolutionaries and helped control the city, putting the Manchu governor and commander of the New Army to flight. Most of the soldiers involved in the revolt came from the ranks of the enlisted men or noncommissioned officers, but they managed to coerce a brigade commander named Li Yuanhong, who had not been involved in the planning of the uprising, to take command of the revolutionary force at Wuchang.[9]

Some progressive officials and members of the gentry joined the revolutionaries and sent telegrams to military and political officials in other provinces, explaining what was happening and urging them to declare independence from the Qing court. On October 12, the two other cities of the Wuhan region, Hankou and Hanyang, fell to the revolutionaries. In rapid succession numerous provinces and cities in China declared independence between October and November. Within 90 days, two-thirds of China had seceded from the Qing dynasty. Sun Yat-sen, traveling through the United States when he learned of the events at Wuchang, decided that he must secure foreign acceptance for the revolution. Moving quickly to London and France, he won the support of those governments and then returned to China, where his colleagues established a provisional government of the Republic of China. They elected Sun president of the provisional government and designated January 1, 1912, as the first day of the Republic of China.

The Qing court sent officials to order the revolutionaries to stand down but also understood that the situation required significant military force. On October 12, the court sent two divisions of the Beiyang Army to the south by rail in order to suppress the revolt. Gunboats from Shanghai sailed up the Yangzi River toward Wuchang, but ended up defecting to the revolutionaries. The court quickly realized that it needed a capable military leader who commanded the loyalty of the Beiyang Army to suppress the revolt. This meant recalling Yuan Shikai from the "retirement" the court had forced on him several years earlier. Even after he left command of the Beiyang Army, his loyal protégés remained in its officer corps, making him the ideal commander to defend the dynasty. Yuan at first refused the Qing invitation, citing the "poor health" that had allegedly caused his retirement. He agreed to take command and negotiate with the revolutionaries on behalf of the Qing court only when the court agreed to create a national assembly and cabinet system and to give him full authority over all Qing military forces. He also demanded amnesty for the revolutionaries. These demands gave the appearance of some common ground with the revolutionaries while simultaneously making himself the most powerful man in China. Desperate to retain control, the Qing court agreed to Yuan's demands and gave him full command over all Qing army and naval forces. The court also agreed to establish a constitutional monarchy, with Yuan Shikai as premier.

Having acquired tremendous authority from the Qing court, Yuan Shikai then attempted to impress the revolutionaries with his military strength by sending his Beiyang troops to retake the city of Hanyang as a show of force. Hanyang fell to Yuan's troops on November 27, and serious fighting took place around Nanjing. Many enlisted men and officers of the New Army divisions in the provinces had joined the revolutionaries, but Yuan's Beiyang Army remained the best fighting force in the country. As a result, both the Qing court and the revolutionaries came to see Yuan as the only man who could help them achieve their goals. Unable to defeat Yuan's force, Sun and the revolutionaries began to fear that continued fighting might lead the foreign powers to intervene, perhaps on the side of the Qing court.

The revolutionaries concluded that they must secure Yuan Shikai's support for the new government, as Yuan seemed to be the only man capable of preventing civil war and forcing the abdication of the Manchu emperor. Ernest Young has pointed out that from the revolutionaries' perspective, Yuan seemed to be the ideal man for the job: he had a reputation as a capable military man, a reformer who had built the Beiyang Army, and had earlier clashed with the Qing court which led to his forced retirement. More than any other, Yuan Shikai could deliver national unity. Lacking the military strength to crush the revolutionaries, Yuan agreed to negotiations and offered to join them in exchange for the presidency of the new republic. Sun saw little choice but to agree.[10]

Sun declared his intention to surrender his position as president of the Republic to Yuan Shikai, who assured Sun that he would induce the voluntary abdication of the Qing emperor and abide by the principles of constitutional government. During a series of imperial conferences in mid-January 1912, Yuan Shikai pressured Qing officials to give up the throne. Since Yuan and his generals had announced their support for the revolutionaries, Manchu authorities reluctantly agreed. The last Qing emperor, the child ruler Puyi, renounced all political power but retained the palace and all its treasures, along with an annual pension of four million Chinese dollars. On February 12, Yuan Shikai announced the formal abdication, ending 268 years of Manchu rule in China. The next day Sun Yat-sen resigned as the provisional president of the Republic, naming Yuan Shikai his successor. On the following day, the provisional parliament formally elected Yuan Shikai provisional president and Li Yuanhong, leader of the revolutionary forces at Wuchang, provisional vice president.

Although Yuan Shikai had agreed to move to Nanjing to assume the office of president of the Republic, he showed no intention of leaving his power base in the north. His men instigated riots to justify the need for his continued presence in Beijing, where he assumed the presidency on March 10. He appointed his own subordinates to important cabinet ministries such as foreign affairs, internal affairs, war, and navy, leaving the ministries of education, justice, agriculture, and forestry to members of the Tongmenghui. Yuan Shikai displayed a great outward deference toward Sun Yat-sen, meeting with him often to discuss affairs of state and listening carefully to Sun's views on land reform and taxation. Yuan appointed Sun director of railways and charged him with drawing up a plan for a national railway system. Yet Yuan proved uninterested in democratic government and almost immediately clashed with other revolutionaries.

The provisional constitution called for parliamentary elections within six months of the formation of the government. By the time of the elections in December 1912, the Tongmenghui had absorbed other parties to form the GMD (Guomindang) or Chinese Nationalist Party under the leadership of Song Jiaoren. Song had studied parliamentary theory in Japan and strongly advocated party government to check the potential abuse of power by the president. In the December elections the Guomindang won a landslide victory. On March 20, 1913, assassins shot Song Jiaoren as he left the Shanghai railway station to take up his new assignment as the

Guomindang representative in Beijing. He died two days later, and subsequent investigations implicated Yuan Shikai's subordinates. In April 1913, Yuan Shikai negotiated a loan of 25 million British pounds from a five power banking consortium, run by Britain, France, Germany, Russia, and Japan. Sun and others opposed such a large foreign debt and urged the parliament to reject this loan. Yuan Shikai had his supporters surround the parliament building with troops, threatening the safety of its members and rejecting a parliamentary voice on the issue.[11]

The "Second Revolution"

Guomindang members in the parliament rejected Yuan's government leading to a "Second Revolution" of the summer of 1913, which began when the governor of Jiangxi Province, Li Liejun, declared independence from the Republic. Several other provinces followed suit in the next month, but others who saw a strong central authority as necessary did not participate. Yuan Shikai and the Beiyang Army had little trouble crushing the divided and poorly equipped southern provincial armies and the fighting ended quickly. In the wake of the fighting, Yuan Shikai dissolved the parliament, purging Guomindang members on the basis of their participation in the Second Revolution. He assembled a new parliament and rammed through a measure that extended the presidential term to ten years, renewable by reelection without limit. In his quest to strengthen central authority, Yuan went so far as to attempt to restore the monarchy and rule as emperor. His American advisor on constitutional matters, Dr. Frank Goodnow, expressed doubts about the appropriateness of republican government in China and argued in favor of constitutional monarchy as a more suitable institution. Japanese advisors likewise stressed constitutional monarchy as the source of national strength, citing the cases of Japan and Great Britain. In December 1915, Yuan announced his intention to restore the monarchy and assume the throne.

In Yunnan Province, a group of revolutionaries formed a National Protection Army in defense of the Republic, demanding that Yuan Shikai drop his plans to restore the monarchy. Together with several southern provinces such as Guizhou and Guangxi, Yunnan declared independence and engaged Yuan's forces in combat. Yuan Shikai wanted to meet this challenge with force, but lack of support among his own generals forced him to abandon his plans in March 1916. He died suddenly in June 6, 1916. The disappearance of a strong central power plunged the country into a period of chaos and disorder.

The military reforms of the late Qing period contributed greatly to the modernization of China's military forces and paved the way for the overthrow of Manchu rule. At the same time, they also helped create a situation in which the military encroached on civil affairs. In the wake of Yuan Shikai's death in 1916, central authority broke down into smaller regional units, each under the control of a military commander or prominent civilian supported by a personal military force. A national government continued to exist in Beijing, dominated by generals of the Beiyang Army, but this national government's authority extended only as far as the army of the general who controlled Beijing. These generals fought each other in numerous battles, most of short duration but on a large scale and widely destructive. In the provinces, military or civilian officials assumed authority with the support of provincial New Armies and acted in accordance with local interests. These regional armies likewise engaged in fighting, contributing to the conflict and disorder of the period from 1916 to 1928.

7

Warlords and the Northern Expedition, 1916–1928

The men who assumed local or regional authority after Yuan Shikai's death are often called "warlords" or "militarists." In simple terms, a warlord or militarist in this era commanded a personal armed force, governed or sought to control a specific territory, and acted more or less independently of any central or national authority. Many of the warlords took the title of military governor, but their size and power varied widely. While smaller warlords might control a district or two, others perhaps an entire province, the most powerful ruled two or three provinces and entire regions of China. Some scholars have avoided the term warlord, viewing it as derogatory and inappropriate as some of these men displayed progressive tendencies and provided sound government, yet the term remains in common use. Regional warlords dominated Chinese political and military history from 1916 to 1928 and many remained important figures until 1949.

The Beiyang Warlords

The immediate years after 1916 saw the rapid rise and fall of different national governments in Beijing as Yuan Shikai's subordinate generals competed for authority in the capital and control of the nominal national government. Between 1916 and 1928, the Beijing government had seven different heads of state and twenty-four cabinets. Feng Guozhang and Duan Qirui, two leading commanders of the Beiyang Army, emerged as two of the most important figures in the capital and became known as the "Beiyang Warlords." Li Yuanhong, Yuan's vice president, assumed the post of president of the Republic of China, but since he had no military power of his own, true authority rested with Duan and Feng, each of whom tried to fill government posts with his own loyal supporters, strengthening his position against potential rivals. In August 1916, Duan Qirui took the office of prime minister and assembled a new cabinet. A dispute between Duan and Feng over whether to declare war on

Germany and join World War I led to a larger conflict among the contenders for power in Beijing and the secession of several provinces from the national government in 1917. Zhang Xun, an ultraconservative general who retained his traditional Manchu-style queue well after the fall of the Qing dynasty, briefly attempted to restore the monarchy until Duan's forces drove him out of Beijing.[1]

Following this brief attempt at imperial restoration, a tenuous balance emerged with Feng Guozhang assuming the presidency of the republic and Duan Qirui resuming his post of prime minister. Feng controlled elements of the Beiyang Army in the area around Shanghai and Nanjing, but since he came from Zhili Province his forces collectively took the title of the Zhili Clique. They opposed Prime Minister Duan Qirui's followers, based in the area around Beijing, collectively known as the Anhui Clique, after Duan's home province. A third major warlord, Zhang Zuolin, led the Fengtian Clique which controlled Manchuria. The maneuvers, intrigues, and battles between these three warlord cliques make this one of the most complicated and chaotic periods of modern Chinese history.

Duan Qirui aroused the opposition of several southern provinces when he attempted to assert control over Hunan Province, which led to two years of fighting between northern and southern China. His plan to unify China by military force led Duan to turn to Japan for financial support, signing secret agreements giving Japan economic concessions in return for substantial loans. These agreements helped pave the way for Japan's later claims to German concessions in Shandong Province at the Versailles Conference in 1919. Duan's pro-Japan policies aroused the opposition of the Zhili Clique, which precipitated the first of three major conflicts among the warlord cliques of north China.

The Anhui–Zhili War of 1920 pitted Duan Qirui, who controlled Beijing and much of north China, against Cao Kun, who had replaced Feng Guozhang as leader of the Zhili Clique upon the latter's death in 1919. Cao Kun controlled the Yangzi region of Hubei, Jiangxi, Jiangsu, and Henan. Zhang Zuolin and the Fengtian Clique supported Cao Kun and the Zhili Clique in defeating Duan's Anhui Clique. Zhang's forces attacked from the north while Cao's forces attacked from the south, destroying the Anhui Clique and forcing Duan to resign as prime minister and flee to Japan in July 1920. Cao Kun and Zhang Zuolin had united out of their common dislike of Duan Qirui, but his removal also eliminated their common ground. The Zhili Clique now controlled the Beijing area, but the Fengtian Clique remained dominant north of the Great Wall. The two cliques temporarily shared power, finding mutually acceptable individuals to take leading positions in the Beijing government. Yet, Cao and Zhang each attempted to place their own supporters in important positions, which eventually led to war between the Zhili and Fengtian cliques.

The first Zhili–Fengtian War erupted in April 1922, resulting in the defeat of Zhang's Fengtian forces which retreated back into Manchuria. This left the Zhili Clique in the dominant position in north China, until Wu Peifu, a Confucian scholar turned soldier and protégé of Cao Kun, led another attack on Zhang Zuolin in the fall of 1924. The resulting second Zhili–Fengtian War lasted less than two months, but featured fighting on a grand scale. According to Arthur Waldron, over

420,000 troops fought in this war with weaponry equivalent to that used in World War I. This large-scale combat, which included prominent betrayals and changing loyalties, concluded in November 1924 only after producing tens of thousands of casualties. A relative peace settled over a devastated north China, with Zhang Zuolin's Fengtian forces in control of the capital.[2]

Regional Warlords

As the conflict among the Beiyang warlords raged in north central China, a second group of regional warlords emerged on the periphery of these conflicts and in the south. These regional warlords came from various backgrounds and had diverse approaches to governing their territories. For example, Feng Yuxiang began life as an illiterate peasant but rose to prominence as the "Christian General" who allegedly baptized his troops with a fire hose. Zhang Zongchang, the "Dogmeat General," controlled Shandong Province. He reportedly traveled with a harem of Russian concubines and his troops excelled in "opening melons" or splitting open the skulls of their enemies. Yan Xishan, the "Model Governor" and former Qing battalion commander who controlled Shanxi Province for decades, promoted reforms in the fields of women's rights and education. Chen Jiongming, a Western educated degree holder from southern China, believed in a federal system of government to unite China and sought to make Guangdong a model province. In all, scores of warlords, great and small, controlled various parts of China between 1916 and 1928.

Many of these warlord regimes operated on a family basis, with close relatives of the warlord serving in important subordinate positions. Because these regimes depended upon military might to maintain their control over a given territory, loyalty between the warlord and his top officers provided the glue that held these cliques together. Beyond blood relationships, ties of marriage, school, and locality also determined appointments to important positions in the regime. The soldiers who filled the ranks of the warlord armies typically came from the peasantry. Poor and landless, they joined these armies primarily for economic reasons even though the material rewards of military service often proved meager. In the worst armies, looting took the place of regular pay, making the appearance of warlord armies tantamount to a disaster for villages and towns.[3]

Since the warlords depended on their military forces to maintain their positions, they required significant resources to support their armed forces. Most warlords raised funds through taxation in their territories, sometimes collecting taxes several years in advance. Others established monopolies over certain commodities such as salt or opium. These revenues went to supply the troops with western weapons such as rifles, machine guns, and artillery. Some of these weapons came from Chinese arsenals, but many warlords relied on imported weapons to arm their troops, despite a ban on weapons exports by the Western powers after World War I.

In the end, no single warlord emerged with enough military strength to defeat all the others and unify China. Warlord armies fought in hundreds of battles in the

1920s, making and breaking alliances as they saw fit, devastating the country and exhausting the people.

The Rise of Nationalism: The May Fourth Movement

While regional warlords contended for power, many Chinese experienced profound changes as a result of what some have called an intellectual revolution. The failure to build a functional republican government after 1911, the chaotic and destructive battles of the warlords, and continuing foreign imperialism combined to produce a rise in nationalist sentiment and a renewed search for a solution to China's problem of national weakness. This new nationalism found expression in a political demonstration known as the May Fourth Movement of 1919.

In many respects, the history of China after 1842 is dominated by ever-increasing efforts to strengthen China's military capabilities in order to defend against foreign imperialism. This common goal motivated reformers from Lin Zexu and Zeng Guofan to the young men who joined the New Armies and participated in the overthrow of the Qing dynasty. Despite high hopes for a new government and military after 1911, China remained vulnerable to foreign military pressure, particularly from Japan. While the Western powers concentrated on the bloody European battlefields of World War I, Japan saw an opportunity to extend its interests in China. In 1915, the Japanese government presented Yuan Shikai with a series of demands for political and economic rights, collectively known as the 21 Demands. Eager for foreign support for his bid to restore the monarchy, Yuan agreed to most of these demands which included joint Sino-Japanese management of important iron-producing ventures, Japanese rights to build railroads and factories in parts of China, and a promise not to offer any other state access to Chinese ports or harbors. Duan Qirui's later secret agreements with the Japanese government gave Japan a claim to German concessions in Shandong Province, acquired in the scramble for concessions after 1895, which set the stage for an explosion of Chinese anger and nationalism.

When the victorious powers presiding over the Versailles Conference which followed the conclusion of World War I turned to the question of what to do with defeated Germany's territorial concessions in China, most Chinese believed they would revert to Chinese control. When they learned of the decision to award these concessions to Japan, young Chinese rose up in outrage on May 4, 1919, to demonstrate in Tian'anmen Square, in what historians have called the May Fourth Movement. This movement not only featured a protest against Japanese imperialism and what the Chinese perceived as unfair treatment at the hands of the Western powers but also gave new impetus to a New Culture Movement that began around 1915 in which young Chinese had been exploring different solutions to the problem of China's continuing weakness. Many intellectuals of this period criticized China's traditional Confucian culture which they believed rendered China weak in the face of foreign imperialism. They advocated discussion of new ideas to modernize China such as literary reform, adding the study of the sciences to school curricula, and political democracy. Some saw Western democratic states as appropriate models for China. Others took note of developments in Russia, where two revolutions in 1917 toppled the imperial government and brought V.I. Lenin and the Bolsheviks to power. The early successes of the Bolsheviks led to increased study of Marxism in major cities such as Beijing and Shanghai. Prominent intellectuals and educators Li Dazhao and Chen Duxiu created independent Marxist study groups which formed the basis for a formal CCP (Chinese Communist Party), established in Shanghai in July 1921.[4]

The Bolshevik Revolution in Russia not only inspired the establishment of the CCP but also prompted a reorganization of the revolutionary party of Dr. Sun Yat-sen. Observing events in Russia, Sun attributed the success of the revolution to the superior organization and strict discipline of the Bolsheviks and attempted to transform his organization into a disciplined revolutionary party. He noted Lenin's stress on organization and leadership, with the party providing a core of dedicated and disciplined leaders to act as a vanguard of the movement. He returned to China from Japan in 1917 and established a revolutionary base in Guangzhou, but had no armed force to support his fledgling government. He remained dependent on the cooperation of various southern warlords, who occasionally turned on him, to protect his base.

The First United Front

As Sun reorganized his party, the new Soviet Russian state sought to establish friendly relations with other countries. Soviet representatives, working for the Communist International or Comintern, made contact with various groups in China, including communist study circles in Beijing and Shanghai, individual warlords, and Sun Yat-sen's Guomindang. In the spring of 1921, a Comintern agent using the pseudonym Maring (Henk Sneevliet) traveled to Guangzhou to meet personally with Sun Yat-sen. While Sun did not embrace Soviet views on radical social revolution, he nonetheless appreciated the organizational skills of the Communists. He also interpreted Lenin's New Economic Policy, which preserved rural markets and private property in Soviet Russia, as evidence that Lenin and the Bolsheviks could show moderation. Sun proved willing to open discussions on cooperation, with an eye toward securing Soviet assistance in organizing and disciplining his own party.

As a condition for its support, the Soviet government insisted on a policy of united front that would bring together different revolutionary groups in China to work toward the common goal of national unification and ending foreign imperialism. The Soviets specifically had the Chinese Communists in mind and suggested that Sun allow members of the CCP to join the Guomindang as full members. Sun knew the Communists' skill at working with the laboring classes, which they had already illustrated by organizing labor strikes in mines and establishing peasant associations in the countryside. Moreover, Soviet material support and advisors, which Sun desperately needed to build his own party and army, depended upon cooperation with the Communists. He might also find it easier to keep watch over the Communists from inside his own organization, rather than let them work against him from outside. Over time, Sun believed that the Communists could be absorbed and won over to the Guomindang position.

In early 1923, Soviet representative Adolph Joffe and Sun Yat-sen worked out the formal agreement for cooperation between the Guomindang and the Chinese Communists, in what is known as the Sun–Joffe Pact. The Soviets agreed to help Sun recast the Guomindang as an effective revolutionary organization and to help build an armed force with which to unify China and carry out the revolution. In return, Sun Yat-sen promised the Soviets rights to the Chinese Eastern Railroad in Manchuria and accepted a Soviet presence in Outer Mongolia. Many on both sides accepted the merger reluctantly. The Communists viewed the Guomindang as a bourgeois party dominated by industrialists and middle-class elements, many of whom worked with foreign imperialists and oppressed the working people of China. The Guomindang tended to view the Communists as wild-eyed radicals who sought to eliminate private property and conduct aggressive land reform. Yet they agreed to this marriage of convenience because each side needed the other and they shared the immediate goal of national unification. Communist Party members joined the Guomindang as individuals, retaining their CCP membership and forming a "party within a party" or a "bloc within." Communists intended to expand their influence within the Guomindang, win over its members, and take control from within. To ease Guomindang concerns, the Soviet representatives declared that China would not be ready for Communism in the near future.

Whampoa Military Academy

With the conclusion of the agreement to form a united front, the Soviet government sent a group of Russian advisors to China under the direction of political advisor Mikhail Borodin (Mikhail Grusenberg) and military advisor General Galen (Vasili Blucher). These advisors went to work reorganizing Sun's Guomindang to create a revolutionary party and army. Borodin focused on building a disciplined political force and mobilizing the local populace to support the Guomindang through a land reform campaign. Galen concentrated on establishing a military force that could defeat the various warlord armies and unite China under a single government. With this latter goal in mind, Sun Yat-sen and his Soviet advisors established the Whampoa Military Academy in February 1924, located on an island ten kilometers downriver from Guangzhou.

Sun chose a young military officer named Chiang Kai-shek, just returned from leading a military mission to the Soviet Union, to serve as commandant of the Academy. Born in 1887 to a salt merchant family in Zhejiang Province, Chiang showed an interest in military affairs from a young age. Like many young Chinese of his generation, he saw military development and modernization as the keys to building a strong Chinese nation. Chiang attended military school first in China and then in Japan, but returned to China to participate in the 1911 Revolution. While in Japan he became involved in the anti-Qing movement and joined Sun Yat-sen's Tongmenghui. After 1911, he rose as a military supporter of Sun Yat-sen in the struggle against Yuan Shikai. Following the Sun–Joffe Pact in 1923, Sun sent Chiang to the Soviet Union as head of a military mission to obtain arms and study military organization. On his return he took a position on the Guomindang military council. As commandant, he handpicked the officers and faculty for the Academy, guided by the example of nineteenth-century scholar official Zeng Guofan whose moral character, integrity, and military leadership skills served as a model for Chiang.[5]

The Whampoa Academy got off to a rocky start as Chiang Kai-shek left only weeks after its establishment, because of disagreements with Soviet advisors over curriculum and management style. After an absence of only a month Chiang Kai-shek worked out his differences with the Soviets and returned to assume the post of commandant. The Academy featured a rigorous training regimen as the faculty expected the cadets to complete a course of instruction in six months that cadets at other Chinese military academies completed in two years. Whampoa also differed in that the instructors sought to prepare cadets for immediate combat service and therefore devoted significant time to field exercises and physical fitness. The instructors and cadets operated under great pressure, as the success of the revolutionary movement depended upon the Academy's ability to produce a group of young officers superior to those of the "warlord" armies and to prepare them for immediate combat. Seeking to produce as many junior officers as possible in a short period of time, instruction at the Academy emphasized basic military drill and practical skills such as weapons and tactics. The Soviet Union provided financial assistance through a monthly stipend and an initial shipment of arms, though Sun's government would have to pay for additional weapons and ammunition.

Cadets followed the training model of the Soviet Red Army, with classroom and field activities from Monday through Saturday and political lectures on Sunday. Since the new force would be a truly revolutionary army, ideological instruction took a prominent place alongside practical military training. Political officers, called commissars, oversaw the political education of the troops, lecturing them on the history of foreign imperialism in China and Sun's Three People's Principles. Political commissars had considerable authority and had to countersign all orders to military officers prior to execution. The majority of political commissars came from the ranks of the Communists and left-leaning members of the Guomindang. Zhou Enlai, future Premier of the People's Republic of China, served as deputy director of the Political Department.[6]

The curriculum at Whampoa resembled that of other Chinese military academies, heavily influenced by Japanese concepts of spirit and aggressive action. Many of the instructors had been trained in Japanese military academies where they learned what some have called the "Bushido spirit" or code of honor, duty, and courage of the traditional Japanese samurai. They stressed discipline and self-sacrifice, criticizing the cadets for any selfish or individualistic habits or actions. As commandant, Chiang Kai-shek played an active role at the Academy, delivering lectures, inspecting dormitories, and supervising the work of students and faculty. Chiang's speeches at the Academy emphasized proper attitude and behavior, demanding that faculty and cadets submit to the orders of the party, exhibit discipline and obedience, and be prepared to sacrifice their lives for the good of the nation. Instructors instilled in the cadets what would come to be known as the aggressive "Whampoa spirit," which stressed the importance of a willingness to take risks and to suffer substantial casualties in order to achieve victory in battle. This aggressive spirit of self-sacrifice played a prominent part in the training of cadets at Whampoa, as they would face numerically superior warlord armies and would require absolute unity of purpose, coordinated action, and proper strategy to defeat them. Chiang and the instructors believed that if properly led, motivated, and possessed of an appropriately aggressive strategy, the revolutionary forces could overcome any odds or obstacles. In general, the Whampoa cadets showed great discipline and a willingness to follow orders without question. Chiang reinforced this discipline by implementing the "Law of Joint Responsibility," which authorized the execution of those who retreated from battle without orders.[7]

By autumn 1924, the Academy had 1,000 cadets training to become professional military officers, all well-educated, capable, and completely dedicated to the revolution. The cadets proved their mettle in battle in October 1924 by defeating the Guangzhou Merchant Volunteer Corps, a private military force funded by local merchants who chafed under the taxation of Sun's revolutionary government. Chiang Kai-shek led the cadets against this force and confiscated part of a shipment of weapons it had purchased from Belgium. The Whampoa cadets faced a greater challenge in November when Sun Yat-sen traveled to Beijing at the invitation of northern warlords Duan Qirui, Zhang Zuolin, and Feng Yuxiang in order to discuss the problem of national unity. Guangdong warlord Chen Jiongming took this opportunity to prepare an attack on Guangzhou to oust Sun's revolutionary government. Chen commanded a collection of diverse military units numbering 50,000, spread across eastern Guangdong. Some of Sun's other warlord supporters did not offer assistance, forcing Chiang Kai-shek to rely on a hastily formed Whampoa military force to deal with Chen Jiongming's attack.[8] By December 1924, two regiments of 1,200 soldiers with officers drawn from the ranks of Whampoa officers and cadets prepared to undertake a campaign against Chen Jiongming to defend the revolutionary government's position in Guangdong, known as the Eastern Expedition of 1925. These two regiments performed well in the campaign, with key victories in two important battles at Danshui and Mianhu in February and March 1925, respectively. The successful campaigns of the Eastern Expedition not only drove Chen Jiongming into exile in Hong Kong and preserved the revolutionary government's position in Guangdong but also gave the Whampoa regiments valuable combat experience. Observers noted that although the Whampoa troops suffered from shortages of supplies and equipment, they displayed higher morale and better discipline than the soldiers of the warlord armies they faced and therefore proved popular with the local populace.[9]

The National Revolutionary Army

As the Whampoa troops won their initial battles in Guangdong, Sun Yat-sen fell gravely ill with liver cancer in Beijing, where he died in March 1925. Sun's death deprived the movement of its leader, but it did not derail the plan for national unifi-cation. Wang Jingwei and other senior leaders of the Guomindang continued to organize and build the political and military forces. The success of the Whampoa forces in eastern Guangdong gave them instant popularity and won new adherents to the Guomindang. Joined by supportive warlord troops from Yunnan and Guangxi, the Whampoa force became the NRA (National Revolutionary Army) in June 1925. A Military Affairs Council began to centralize command over the diverse units that made up the NRA, weeding out unfit soldiers, reorganizing the units, drawing up standard regulations, and appointing officers. At the same time, the leadership trans-formed Sun's revolutionary government in Guangzhou into a "national government," in opposition to the Beijing government of the northern warlords. Yet the loss of the most visible leader of the revolutionary movement and the man who authorized col-laboration with the Soviet Union and the Chinese Communists led to division within the ranks of the Guomindang leadership. Tension between "rightist" elements of the Guomindang, who opposed working with the Communists, and the Guomindang "leftists," who supported the united front, had been growing since the early days of the alliance. The Guomindang right suspected that the Communists intended to work their way into some of the most important offices of the government and take control of the party and government. Shortly after Sun's death, these elements began to express discomfort with the rise of Communists to important positions within the Guomindang. CCP membership had grown dramatically since the start of the united front, increasing ten fold, and many Communists had ascended to ranking positions in the Guomindang hierarchy. Such a rapid rise of Communist influence in the move-ment led a rightist group of Guomindang members, known as the "Western Hills Faction," to demand the expulsion of the Communists and all Soviet advisors from the Guomindang in December 1925.

While not necessarily associated with the Guomindang right wing, Chiang himself harbored strong doubts about the sincerity of the Chinese Communists and had long viewed the Soviet Union as a potential threat to China. His own experience in the Soviet Union as the leader of a military study mission had a lasting impact on his views of the Soviet advisors. The fact that the Soviet advisors did not support his plans for an early military expedition to unite China, preferring to wait until the military force had more training, increased Chiang's hostility toward them. By early 1926, Chiang came to believe that Wang Jingwei, the Guomindang leftists, and the Chinese Communists intended to remove him from power, as illustrated by the *Zhongshan* Incident. When the gunship *Zhongshan* unexpectedly anchored at Chiang's head-quarters at Whampoa on March 20, Chiang interpreted it as an attempt to kidnap him. Perhaps more a matter of miscommunication than a kidnapping plot, Chiang took no chances and immediately ordered his Whampoa cadets to arrest the captain, a Communist, and seize the vessel. He then declared martial law in Guangzhou and detained a number of Soviet advisors and Communist political officers. Chiang rele-nted only after negotiating an agreement with the Soviet advisors, which limited the activities of CCP members within the Guomindang. In May 1926, the Guomindang Central Executive Committee passed resolutions limiting Communists to no more than one-third of all committee memberships and prohibiting them from holding certain high ranking positions in the Guomindang. Moreover, Soviet advisors agreed to drop their insistence on delaying the military campaign against the northern warlords. The CCP members denounced this move but did not break with the Guomindang at this time. Soviet leader Josef Stalin, who directed the Chinese Communist movement from Moscow, advised the CCP to tolerate these resolutions and avoid an open split with the Guomindang until the Communist Party developed greater strength and support from the Guomindang left wing. Regardless, the incident revealed deep divisions within the Guomindang and the united front.

The Northern Expedition

In preparation for the military campaign against the warlords, the Whampoa forces that had fought well in the Eastern Expedition formed the First Army of the NRA under the command of He Yingqin, head of instruction at the Whampoa Military Academy. The other armies of the NRA included the forces of individual warlords who joined the movement, with Tan Yankai's Hunan forces forming the Second Army, Zhu Peide's Yunnan forces the Third Army, Li Jishen's Guangdong forces the Fourth Army, and Li Fulin's Fujian forces the Fifth Army. This loose alliance of Whampoa cadets and friendly warlord troops totaled 100,000 troops.

In July 1926, Commander-in-Chief Chiang Kai-shek and the NRA set out on the Northern Expedition, a campaign intended to unite the country by force of arms. To do so, the NRA would have to defeat the major warlord forces of Zhang Zuolin, Feng Yuxiang, Yan Xishan, Sun Chuanfang, and Wu Peifu. Their combined numbers far exceeded the NRA, but the warlords did not cooperate with each other, which allowed Chiang and the NRA to attack them individually. Chiang's strategy involved attacks through central China and along the eastern coast to seize control of financial and industrial centers and provincial capitals. The Expedition began with an attack on Wu Peifu's forces in Hunan Province, taking advantage of conflict between Wu and Feng Yuxiang. While Wu worried about an attack from the north by Feng's army, Chiang's NRA struck from the south. The defection of one of his generals, Tang Shengzhi, forced Wu Peifu to withdraw north across the Yangzi River as NRA forces captured Changsha, the capital of Hunan Province. A second column attacked Sun Chuanfang's forces to the east in Jiangxi Province. Heavy fighting through the months of October and November 1926 led to the capture of Nanchang, the capital of Jiangxi. This success came at great cost as NRA forces suffered approximately 20,000 casualties.

After protecting Guangdong against counterattack by Sun Chuanfang's troops, the First Army of the NRA moved up the coast into Fujian in a third column to attack Sun from the south. The disciplined and well-behaved NRA forces enjoyed support from the local population which provided information and supplies along the way. Outnumbered by as much as five to one, the First Army fought well, defeating Sun's forces and taking control of Fujian by the end of December. At the close of the year,

NRA forces occupied provincial capitals and major cities in Hunan, Hubei, Jiangxi, and Fujian.

As the NRA made progress in achieving its military goal of national unification, political and ideological disputes began to rise to the surface. Members of the CCP and the Guomindang left gathered around Wang Jingwei in Wuhan, the temporary headquarters of the Guomindang national government. They supported the efforts of the Communist labor organizers who encouraged strikes in major cities. The more conservative elements of the Guomindang did not trust members of the CCP and opposed the strikes as disruptive and counterproductive. They feared that a massive labor movement would not only alienate Westerners but might also lead Chinese elites to support the warlords who they felt would protect them from the radical policies advocated by the Communists. Rather than join Wang and the other Guomindang leftist leaders at Wuhan, Chiang marched on the major cities of Nanjing and Shanghai, consolidating his control over China's financial and industrial center. As Sun Chuanfang's forces collapsed with large numbers defecting to the NRA, Chiang's troops entered both cities in March 1927, setting up a separate government apparatus in Nanjing. The split between the Guomindang leaders in Wuhan, who tended to support the Soviet advisors and the CCP, and those Shanghai, who distrusted the Soviets and Communists, grew wider and threatened the military effectiveness of the NRA and the success of the Northern Expedition.

When Chiang's armies entered Shanghai, he gained the support of the commercial community which feared the policies of the Communists and urged Chiang to put down strikes and labor unrest. They offered him substantial financial support as incentive. Believing that the Guomindang leaders at Wuhan had conspired with the Communists, Chiang chose to break the united front and violently expel the Communists and their supporters from the Guomindang. On April 12, 1927, Chiang ordered a purge of all Communists in Shanghai, Nanjing, and other Guomindang-controlled cities. Chiang's paramilitary agents and plainclothes police rounded up known Communists and labor organizers, executing many in the streets. A series of attacks on the headquarters of all of Shanghai's major labor unions resulted in hundreds of arrests and executions. The next day, students and workers protested the violence and organized a demonstration against this purge. Chiang's troops opened fire on the crowd killing almost one hundred. The purge spread to other cities over the next several months and resulted in the deaths of as many as 30,000 people and the arrest of 25,000.[10]

The surviving Communists sought support from Wang Jingwei and the leftist members of the Guomindang at Wuhan, who initially refused to support Chiang's action. The Wuhan authorities expelled Chiang Kai-shek from the Party and relieved him of his command of the NRA, though they lacked the power to enforce these measures. Chiang remained in command of the NRA, supported by the majority of Whampoa Academy officers, and issued an ultimatum to the Wuhan leaders to acknowledge Nanjing's authority. In June, a Comintern agent revealed to the Wuhan leaders the contents of a secret telegram from Josef Stalin to the Chinese Communists ordering them to begin organizing the masses for large-scale seizures of property from Chinese landlords. Such aggressive actions alienated many of the Guomindang leftists, who then decided to follow Chiang's suit and expelled all Communists from the Guomindang and the NRA. Borodin left China shortly thereafter, ending the Guomindang's relations with Soviet advisors. With the Communists purged from his ranks, Chiang unified the remaining elements of the Guomindang around himself and continued his military campaign to the north.

The break with the Communists yielded rapid results for Chiang and his center-right Guomindang coalition. First, it removed the most important political rival to the Guomindang, the Chinese Communists and their Soviet advisors. Second, it made the anticommunist northern warlords more willing to consider joining the NRA, allowing Chiang to coopt them rather than face them on the field of battle. For example, Wang Jingwei and the Wuhan leaders had hoped Feng Yuxiang would support them, but instead he threw his support behind Chiang Kai-shek who promised Feng weapons and financial support. Finally, it encouraged Western powers to accept Chiang Kai-shek as the leader of the Guomindang and the legitimate government of China. Britain and France rejected overtures from the Wuhan leaders and extended formal recognition to Chiang's Nanjing government.[11]

Not all of Chiang's supporters approved of his policies which threatened to split the Guomindang, allowed the northern warlords to regroup, and jeopardized the success of the Northern Expedition. The immediate disruption caused by the split resulted in battlefield reverses as warlord forces pushed the NRA back in some areas. In the face of criticism from some of his leading subordinate officers, including He Yingqin, Li Zongren, and Bai Chongxi, Chiang resigned his position as commander-in-chief of the NRA in August 1927 and went to Japan. He expected that his officers would soon realize his value and ask him to return and resume command. In the meantime, Chiang married Song Meiling, the American educated daughter of a wealthy Chinese businessman and sister-in-law to Sun Yat-sen. After Chiang's resignation, Guomindang leaders from Wuhan and Nanjing continued the Northern Expedition in his absence, but Chiang's generals could not provide unified leadership. As a result, in December 1927, He Yingqin formally requested Chiang to return to his post as commander-in-chief. Chiang promised certain warlords command positions in the NRA, winning additional support for his return. When he resumed command in early 1928, he reorganized the NRA, which now totaled nearly one million soldiers including the newly incorporated warlord troops, taking personal command of the First Army of 290,000 troops. He appointed Feng Yuxiang and Yan Xishan commanders of the Second and Third Armies, respectively, and Li Zongren commander of the Fourth Army. This facilitated completion of the Northern Expedition and preserved Chiang's loyal Whampoa forces, but it also meant continued division and lack of unity for the ensuing decades as former warlords who accepted commands in Chiang's military did not always obey his directives.

As the NRA pressed northward, Chiang's troops moved into Shandong Province which had a significant Japanese population. The Japanese government feared for the safety of its citizens and sent a force of 2,000 troops to the city of Jinan to protect Japanese nationals and their property. In early May 1928, NRA forces clashed with

Japanese troops resulting in hundreds of casualties. Chiang ordered his forces out of the area, moving them north toward Beijing, but this "Jinan Incident" foreshadowed increasingly hostile and contentious relations between China and Japan. The Japanese Kwantung Army, stationed in Manchuria to guard Japanese interests such as the South Manchurian Railroad acquired in the war against Russia, had long been attempting to take control of Manchuria by forming an alliance with Manchurian warlord Zhang Zuolin. They offered military support against Chiang and the NRA, but Zhang would not commit to an alliance. In 1928, as Zhang withdrew from the Beijing area back to his Manchurian stronghold, Japanese soldiers assassinated him by blowing up his train, hoping that the ensuing chaos would offer an opportunity for the Kwantung Army to seize control of Manchuria in the name of protecting Japanese interests. The plan backfired when instead of chaos, Zhang Zuolin's son and heir, Zhang Xueliang, took over his father's troops and pledged support for Chiang's national government in late 1928.

In August 1928, Chiang Kai-shek arrived in Beijing, completing the Northern Expedition and at least nominally uniting China under a single government. On the surface, the gains of this period appeared impressive. China had risen from a state of military separatism in which independent warlords governed autonomous regions to military and political unity under Chiang Kai-shek. In reality, Chiang's decision to coopt warlords into the revolutionary army and government ensured continued division among various regional power figures and his purge of the CCP sowed the seeds of a civil war. Chiang emerged with control of the strongest military forces in the country, thanks to the loyalty of the Whampoa trained officers, but he also depended on the fragile support of regional warlords and business and financial leaders. His government had significant political, economic, and military problems which hindered his attempts to build a successful modern state over the next decade.

Nationalist and Communist Armies, 1927–1937

Having split violently with the Chinese Communists, defeated or coopted the major northern warlords, and completed the ostensible unification of China, Chiang Kai-shek established his capital at Nanjing. The Nanjing–Shanghai region, located in the industrially and agriculturally advanced Yangzi River valley, would serve as his base of power for the next 20 years. The former capital, Beijing, now took the name Beiping or "northern peace." The completion of the Northern Expedition and the nominal unification of China marked the completion of the first phase of Sun Yat-sen's three-stage plan. Although Chiang had not defeated all the warlords, he had at least temporarily won their cooperation and therefore set about building the new Republic of China. After the tumultuous and destructive events between the 1911 Revolution and the end of the Northern Expedition in 1928, many Chinese looked forward to the possibility of a strong and prosperous China under Chiang and the Guomindang. Meanwhile, the CCP began rebuilding after the 1927 purge, developing it own armed force in anticipation of a military struggle against Chiang's government.

Chiang Kai-shek and the Nationalist Government

Shortly after establishing the new "Nationalist" government in 1928, (so called because of the central role of the Guomindang or Chinese "Nationalist" Party) Chiang and the Guomindang Central Executive Committee adopted a provisional constitution called an "Outline of Political Tutelage." As Sun Yat-sen had envisioned, the government intended to instruct or tutor the Chinese people in democratic and constitutional practice. Chiang's Nationalist government and military would keep order and stability until the time when the Chinese people would hold national elections to produce a truly representative, democratic government. As commander of the NRA and hero of the Northern Expedition, Chiang Kai-shek dominated this new government, wielding great authority as a leading member of the Guomindang Executive Committee and commander-in-chief of the military. He always praised Sun Yat-sen's Three People's Principles which formed the basis for the Republic of China, but Chiang's top priority remained the creation of stable state with a strong military and the abolition of the unequal treaties with the West. He sought first and foremost to bring China to a position of strength and equality in the international community.

Chiang faced substantial challenges during the period from 1927 to 1937, known as the "Nanjing Decade," both from within the country and from outside of the country. He fought a series of military conflicts with the various warlords who had joined him in the Northern Expedition, continued his efforts to destroy the CCP, and had to deal with territorial aggression by the Japanese military. Those who hoped that the Nanjing Decade would bring peace and stability to China found instead factional struggle, civil war, and foreign invasion.

Perhaps the greatest problem that Chiang and his supporters faced in establishing a new national government stemmed from the problem of residual warlordism. Although the NRA had defeated some of the major warlords, others had joined the movement and proclaimed support for the Nationalist government at Nanjing. In his eagerness to achieve national unification, Chiang Kai-shek had negotiated with a number of powerful warlords to come to an accommodation, offering them appointments in the new government and army. These appointments allowed them to retain control of their own troops and their semiautonomous regional status, while paying mere lip service to Chiang Kai-shek and the Nationalist government. Some of these regional warlords had progressive and nationalist tendencies, but they tended to distrust Chiang and hesitated to submit their armies or regional bases to central control, cooperating with Chiang only so long as their interests did not conflict. If a warlord-turned–Nationalist general did not agree with the orders originating from Nanjing, he might subtly resist or even openly challenge Chiang's authority. As a result, the unification of China via the Northern Expedition proved more illusory than real as former warlords occasionally defied Chiang's attempts to assert central authority. Throughout the Nanjing Decade, certain parts of China remained beyond the effective control of the Nationalist authorities, neither contributing resources to the government nor receiving benefits from it.

From his base at Nanjing, Chiang had to deal with four major regional warlord forces, each of which posed potential problems for the Nationalist government: the so-called Guangxi Clique in the south under the command of Li Zongren, Bai Chongxi, and Li Jishen; Feng Yuxiang's forces in the north and northwest; Zhang Xueliang's forces to the northeast and in Manchuria; and Yan Xishan's forces in Shanxi Province. Each of these regional leaders received appointments in Chiang's Nationalist military but retained control of their own armed forces. The Northern Expedition could not have succeeded without their support, but as a result after 1928 Chiang had only partial control over the army that had swept him to power. Within the Nationalist military, Chiang relied heavily on his Central Army units, those commanded by graduates of the Whampoa Military Academy, which ranked among the finest and most loyal. The Whampoa Academy moved to Nanjing and became the Central Military Academy, which continued to produce well-trained and loyal officers for Chiang's Central Army. The other armies that made up the Nationalist military, troops commanded by former warlords Feng Yuxiang, Yan

Xishan, Zhang Xueliang, and Li Zongren, varied greatly in terms of quality and loyalty to Chiang, as did smaller provincial forces like those in Yunnan under Governor Long Yun. Chiang spent much of the Nanjing Decade in a protracted "chess match" with these regional leaders, constantly seeking ways to bring them under his central control. The regional leaders in turn sought ways to resist these attempts and tried to preserve their own independence and regional power. The problem of divided military commands continued to plague China, making it extremely difficult for Chiang and the Nationalist government to make progress toward the goal of building a strong and united China.

War of the Central Plains, 1930

One of Chiang's early plans for separating the former warlords from their armies and asserting greater central control over the entire Nationalist military involved a demobilization campaign. He met with individual army commanders to assess their loyalty and attitudes and then proposed a reduction and reorganization of the armed forces, designed to create a truly national army and reduce expenditures. The national army Chiang envisioned would have fifty to sixty divisions (600,000–720,000 men) on active duty with a substantial reserve force. The reorganization involved identifying the most capable officers for continued service, though often reassigned to a different unit, and the elimination of inferior or incompetent officers.[1]

The commanders of the regional armies recognized this as an attempt to deprive them of their bases of power and reacted against it. In February 1929, Li Zongren's troops revolted against Chiang's authority in Hunan, taking control of the provincial capital at Changsha and initiating a round of civil wars that would not end until 1931. Beyond the demobilization issue, the regional commanders clashed with Chiang Kai-shek over the issue of tax collection and how much they should remit to Nanjing. Chiang used bribes, popularly known as "silver bullets," to ensure that Feng Yuxiang did not support Li Zongren, and then attacked with force. In two months of heavy fighting, Chiang's Central Army troops defeated Li's Guangxi forces and expelled him from the Guomindang along with Bai Chongxi and Li Jishen, both of whom had supported Li. They returned to Guangxi but later rejoined Chiang's Nationalist government. The bribes Chiang paid to Feng Yuxiang secured only temporary inaction as within a few months Feng also revolted. Chiang managed to defeat Feng and force him to take refuge with Yan Xishan in Shanxi.

Chiang persisted with the demobilization until yet another revolt broke out in early 1930, this time pitting the combined forces of Feng Yuxiang, Yan Xishan, and Li Zongren against Chiang in the War of the Central Plains. This brief civil war involved over one million troops spread across several provinces in central China. Through a combination of military force, peace negotiations, and bribery, Chiang Kai-shek prevailed. With critical support from Zhang Xueliang, Chiang's forces attacked along the rail lines into Henan and Shandong, defeating his opponents and driving Feng Yuxiang into exile. Chiang broke Feng's army into small units and absorbed them into his own Central Army. Yan Xishan proved too deeply entrenched in Shanxi Province and remained in control of his army.

Although Chiang had put down the military revolt, he faced growing criticism from within the Guomindang and even calls for him to resign as president of the Republic. Chiang later did give up the office of president of the Executive Yuan in favor of Wang Jingwei, a veteran Guomindang leader, but retained the more important position of chairman of the Military Affairs Council, as his power in the Nationalist government derived from his control over the military more so than any political title. In fact, many of his orders went directly to the field headquarters of his armies, rather than through Nanjing where Wang Jingwei or another political rival might oppose or block them. By the beginning of 1931, Chiang had quelled the revolt and stabilized the Nationalist government, but pockets of China remained under the control of regional commanders. The loyalty of the Central Army officers who commanded the best trained and equipped units helped Chiang retain control of the Nationalist government and military, but the constant conflict with his own generals wasted valuable time and resources which hindered state-building plans. Moreover, it revealed the limits of his own military power and helped convince Chiang that his forces could not stand up to a powerful foreign army in the event of an attack. At the height of his power, Chiang never had firm control over more than perhaps two-thirds of the Chinese population.

Chiang Kai-shek and Military Modernization

Chiang believed that a strong and disciplined military could form the core of a modern state and serve as a model for the modernization of the Chinese nation as a whole. For example, in 1928 he considered plans for implementing compulsory military service for all Chinese men. Chiang believed that the recruitment of mercenaries and paid volunteers had led to the individual warlord armies that had divided China, but a universal conscription program supervised by central authority would create a truly national military force. Moreover, Chiang believed that such a program would also improve society by spreading military discipline and values to a larger segment of the population. According to the plan, draftees would serve two years of active duty, five years in the first-tier reserve, and ten years in the second-tier reserve. This conscription plan required careful registration of the population, which would be accomplished through the Baojia system of traditional China. A group of ten households formed a unit known as a Bao. Ten of these units formed a Jia, or 100 households. The Baojia system held each household responsible for its own members as well the other members of the unit. All healthy adult males had to register for military conscription, either for the Nationalist army or for the local militia. Though Chiang's government never succeeded in fully implementing this system of universal conscription, it illustrates his tendency to see the military as a critical component in the process of building a strong, modern state. For Chiang, a key part of modernization lay in militarization.[2]

Chiang's enthusiasm for military values and discipline as a vehicle for modernization is also evident in his 1934 New Life Movement. Believing that the same discipline, obedience, and moral code that molded cadets at the Whampoa Military Academy could be extended to Chinese society, Chiang inaugurated this national movement to revive traditional Confucian values and advocate modern order and hygiene. The New Life Movement sought to transform the nation and society by combining the Confucian virtues of propriety, justice, honesty, and benevolence, with modern values of discipline, self-sacrifice, and personal hygiene. As Chiang put it "By observing these virtues, it is hoped that social disorder and individual weakness will be remedied and that people will become more military-minded. If a country cannot defend itself, it has every chance of losing its existence.... Therefore, our people must have military training."[3] Chiang believed that the same military values and discipline that he demanded of his Central Army troops could benefit society as a whole. Although the New Life Movement did not have the desired effect, it clearly reveals Chiang's emphasis on militarization as the path to modernization.

In addition to seeing a disciplined, modern military force as critical to the development of a modern society, Chiang also believed that China needed a strong army in anticipation of a future conflict with Japan. Although he knew that his Nationalist military had not yet adequately prepared for such a conflict, he had little doubt that one day his armies would have to face the Japanese military on Chinese soil. In order to prepare for this conflict, Chiang employed German advisors to help him build his army, replacing the Soviet advisors who had left China shortly after the break with the CCP. A series of German advisors such as Max Bauer, Hans von Seeckt, and Alexander von Faulkenhausen, along with scores of subordinate advisors, offered Chiang advice on organization, strategy, and tactics over the course of the late 1920s and early 1930s. The Germans advocated three basic elements as the base for a modern Chinese army: a disciplined officer corps, elite forces that excelled in mobile warfare, and a domestic arms industry that could produce top quality weapons and ammunition. Chiang and his advisors planned to create and train a few initial elite divisions which would then serve as models for emulation by other units. The German government supplied equipment and industrial plans in return for raw materials and food exports. Under the guidance of his German advisors, Chiang created a general staff, a general headquarters, and a national defense council, all directly responsible to Chiang as commander-in-chief. Reflecting the German and Japanese militaries, the Chinese military enjoyed independence of command and remained under Chiang's personal control, rather than that of the government.[4]

The German emphasis on a disciplined and loyal officer corps appealed greatly to Chiang, whose own military training in Japan had introduced him to German-style military concepts and training. In building a new army after 1868, the leaders of Meiji Japan had borrowed heavily from the model of the German Imperial Army. Chiang Kai-shek hoped that the development of a professional officer corps to serve in all units of the Nationalist military would reduce his dependence on regional commanders of questionable loyalty and prepare China for a potential war with Japan. Chiang also appreciated the some of the political aspects of German fascism, which emphasized a single, strong leader, ultranationalism, and the militarization of society. This appreciation stemmed in part from his increasing frustration with democratic practice and the problem of dealing with constant political conflicts within the Guomindang. The rapid growth of the party that followed the creation of the united front and the completion of the Northern Expedition created new factions and incessant conflict among party members. Decision making tended to require coalition building which proved increasingly difficult and painstaking. Political factions arrived at occasional agreement on major policies only after extensive argument and compromise. Chiang felt that this constant political squabbling detracted from the stability of the Nationalist government and limited its ability to design and implement state-building measures. Even when the factions agreed and attempted to implement policy, the government often lacked the control and authority at the local level to enforce implementation in the provinces. Frustrated with the obstacles imposed by regional commanders and political factions within his own party, Chiang Kai-shek increasingly relied on his control of the military and used dictatorial means to enforce his political will.

Although Chiang and his German advisors worked to build a strong military force capable of defending China against internal revolt and external attack, they did not have time to prepare for the next round of foreign aggression against China. In September 1931, the Japanese Kwantung Army seized control of Manchuria, beginning the process of setting up a Japanese puppet state called Manchukuo (described in the next chapter). Large-scale anti-Japanese demonstrations erupted across China, and many demanded that Chiang take strong action to defend Chinese territory. Believing that Chinese military forces lacked the unity and strength required to meet the Japanese threat, Chiang instead chose to turn the matter over to the League of Nations in the hope of avoiding, or at least delaying, a full-scale war between China and Japan. Chiang had long anticipated a clash with Japan, but he felt that internal divisions of his government and army rendered it too weak to confront the powerful Japanese military. He insisted that China had to deal with internal problems, bringing the regional commanders and Chinese communists under control, before it could declare war on Japan. Chiang and his supporters described the Japanese as a superficial "disease of the skin," while the Chinese Communists represented a much more serious "disease of the heart."[5]

Despite the internal problems of the Nationalist government, its growing tensions with Japan, and increasing criticism of Chiang's authoritarian rule, he maintained his paramount position as head of the government and military. He relied heavily on the loyalty of his subordinate officers in the Central Army, which served as his principal base of support. Sun Yat-sen had envisioned a state in which the party would control the gun, but in some respects Chiang reversed this idea, using military power to control political authority. He appointed his own loyal military officers to important positions in the government, many of them graduates of the Whampoa Military Academy. By the early 1930s, Chiang came to believe that China needed not a liberal democracy, but rather a strong, nationalist, military leader. Like his views on the military, his political views combined the moral values of traditional Confucianism with the political characteristics of European fascism. Historian Frederic Wakeman has used the term "Confucian Fascism" to describe the combination of Chinese and Western principles that shaped Chiang's views. Chiang believed that in this time of crisis and national peril, China needed not division and debate, but strong leadership.[6]

His control of China's financial base in the Yangzi River valley also contributed to Chiang's dominant position in the government. Control of Shanghai and Nanjing meant access to revenue streams such as customs duties and lucrative taxes. Chiang pressured the Shanghai and Nanjing business communities for loans and "contributions," claiming that he protected them from the labor unrest and radical appropriations advocated by the Communists. His connections to the notorious Green Gang of the Shanghai underworld allowed him to use extortion and black mail to acquire additional funds from wealthy citizens who proved unwilling to contribute to his cause.[7]

The Communist Movement During the Nanjing Decade

As Chiang Kai-shek busied himself in Nanjing attempting to build a stable government and strong national military, Chinese Communist leader Mao Zedong began developing and implementing his own political and military policies that would lead to his rise to supreme power in his party and in the country. Such a rise seemed unlikely in the summer of 1927 as Mao and the CCP leadership sought to recover from the decimation of the "Shanghai Massacre" of the previous April, which reduced the CCP numbers to approximately 10,000 and forced it go underground. No longer able to operate openly for risk of arrest and perhaps execution at the hands of either Nationalist authorities or anticommunist regional officials, the CCP began furtively rebuilding its shattered organization. Although the Soviet policy of united front with the Guomindang had ultimately proved disastrous, in 1928 the CCP continued to look to the Soviet Union for aid and direction. Following the example of the 1917 Bolshevik Revolution, Stalin and the CCP Executive Committee prepared for armed insurrections, in which peasants and workers would launch spontaneous revolutionary struggles to establish urban "soviets" or local government councils of workers, peasants, and soldiers. They believed the conditions suited such a plan, as the Communists had been hoping to win new adherents among the left wing of the Guomindang. They also believed that a significant portion of the local population would support the Communists once they established control of major cities.

The Autumn Harvest Uprising, 1927

Although some members of the CCP doubted the advisability of Moscow's plan for armed insurrection so soon after the devastating purge just a few months earlier, in August 1927 CCP forces began a series of attacks on the provincial capitals of Nanchang in Jiangxi and Changsha in Hunan, collectively known as the Autumn

Harvest Uprising. Chinese Communists would later celebrate August 1, the anniversary of the 1927 attack on Nanchang, as the birthday of the Red Army. The attackers managed to seize control of Nanchang for a few days but ultimately withdrew in the face of superior Nationalist forces. The CCP leadership had limited military strength, and the attack failed to generate an uprising of the working classes as they had expected. Mao Zedong helped lead a September attack on Changsha, which yielded similar results.

Unlike more traditional Marxists who concentrated on organizing the urban working class, Mao believed that the Chinese peasantry could serve as a revolutionary force in place of a true proletariat class, which China lacked. Mao also saw tremendous potential for a peasant-based army to sweep the CCP to national power. He had spent time in his native Hunan Province in 1926, organizing peasant associations and drumming up support for the CCP among the peasantry. His investigation of the rural conditions in Hunan convinced him that the peasantry had great potential as a revolutionary class if properly led, but at the time the local CCP lacked the strength and preparation to undertake a major revolt. Moreover, he doubted the viability of Moscow's strategy of urban insurrection. Despite his doubts, Mao dutifully followed the orders of the Comintern and the top CCP leadership, and participated in the Autumn Harvest Uprising in Changsha, which ended in defeat.

After these successive defeats in the fall of 1927, Chinese Communist leaders had little choice but to temporarily abandon the policy of launching urban insurrections. They now formed separate base areas in which to regroup and prepare for the next attempt at seizing provincial, and ultimately national, power. Mao Zedong and remnants of his force that attacked Changsha withdrew to the countryside, finding sanctuary in a mountainous area of the Hunan–Jiangxi border called the Jinggang Mountains. Other CCP forces under military leaders Zhu De and Peng Dehuai joined him there. Far from the reach of Chiang Kai-shek's Nationalist forces, Mao, Zhu, and Peng formed a rural base with several thousand soldiers. Now convinced that the Comintern's policy of urban uprisings had been a failure, Mao began his own experiments in mobilizing the peasant masses as a substitute for urban-based revolution. His experience over the next few years convinced him that a strategy based on guerrilla and mobile warfare supported by a politically aware peasantry could bring the CCP to national power.

In 1929, Nationalist forces threatened his rural base, prompting Mao to move east across Jiangxi toward the Fujian border, where he settled in Ruijin in the southeast corner of Jiangxi Province. Operating from this rural base, Mao had little contact with the CCP leadership and a relative free hand in developing and implementing his own unorthodox policies. He also enjoyed a respite from Nationalist attacks, as Chiang Kai-shek concentrated on defeating the challenges posed by his own generals in the War of the Central Plains. Starting with only a few thousand poorly armed troops, Mao set about building a substantial rural base and separate government, building his initial force by incorporating local bandit gangs into his own Red Army. While other CCP leaders remained intent on winning control of urban areas, Mao pursued his strategy of building a rural base. By 1931, Mao's base had grown to the point that he declared it the "Chinese Soviet Republic" or "Jiangxi Soviet," a rival to Chiang's Nationalist government in Nanjing. His experiments in Jiangxi marked the beginning of his rise to political supremacy in the Chinese Communist movement, but for several years his activities in the countryside and among the peasants had little impact on the highest ranking CCP leaders who remained in Shanghai and other urban areas.

The Red Army and People's War

The defeats of 1927 left Mao with a strong appreciation for the importance of an effective military force. He drew on ancient principles of warfare outlined in Sun Zi's *The Art of War* to develop a military strategy known as "People's War." Specifically designed to use against a larger and better-equipped enemy, People's War had two core principles. First, it required the support of the rural masses which would not only provide peasant soldiers but also material supplies, intelligence, and help with logistics. As Mao famously described the relationship between the people and the guerrilla, "the former may be likened to the water, the latter to the fish who inhabit it. How may it be said that these two cannot exist together? It is only undisciplined troops who make the people their enemies and who, like the fish out of its native element, cannot live."[8] Second, Mao advocated an "active defense" which featured defense through decisive engagements. Rather than engage in large-scale battles with large Nationalist armies, Mao relied on speed, mobility, and maneuver to divide and attack small enemy units with decisive force. Both Zhu De and Peng Dehuai had greater military experience than Mao and favored more orthodox and professional military strategy and tactics, such as those taught the Whampoa Military Academy. Ultimately, Mao convinced them of the soundness of his "People's War" strategy of winning support from the local rural population and relying on peasant soldiers to engage in guerilla tactics and mobile warfare.

As he incorporated local peasants into the Communist Red Army in preparation to defend the rural base, Mao insisted that the military force do more than fight. He believed that it should also serve as a political tool to win the support of the peasantry. To this end, he imposed strict rules of conduct in dealing with the peasants, embodied by the "Three Rules and Eight Points of Conduct" which, in general, required Red Army soldiers to return everything they borrowed, to pay a fair price for anything they purchased, to pay compensation for anything they damaged, and to treat the local people with courtesy and honesty.[9] The Red Army conducted literacy programs to educate its soldiers, helped the local peasants with their farm work when possible, and trained them to serve in local militias. Exhibiting the communist spirit of egalitarianism, officers and enlisted men treated each other as equals, sharing the same uniforms, food, and accommodations. This provided a stark contrast with the conditions of traditional military service and offered an attractive opportunity to young peasant men. Such policies helped the Red Army grow from a few thousand in 1928 to perhaps 60,000 by the end of 1930. As had been the case at the Whampoa Military Academy under the supervision of Soviet advisors, political commissars played an important role in the army, attached to each unit down to the regimental level. They handled political indoctrination among the soldiers, mobilized support among the local population, and presided over logistical operations. As a result, the Red Army served as a tool to help Mao and the CCP win support from the peasants of the Jiangxi Soviet. The ranks of the party and the army swelled with new recruits, attracted by Mao's policies and the promise they held for China's future.

The Red Army organized these new recruits into three levels of military units. The first and lowest level, Red Defense Detachments or local militia, had only limited military training and took up local peacekeeping duties around their home villages. The second level, regional guerrilla forces, undertook formal military actions in their home area, but could also support other Red Army forces elsewhere for short periods of time. The third level, the Red Army main force, operated anywhere in the base area and served as a full-time professional military force. Men who performed well in the ranks of the local militia and regional guerilla forces could expect promotion to a Red Army main force unit. This provided the Red Army main force units with a steady supply of experienced soldiers from the lower levels.[10]

The Red Army also supported Mao's experiments in land reform. Mao's rural strategy depended upon winning the support of the local peasantry, without which his base could not survive. In order to win the support of the poor peasants, Mao sent work teams out across the Jiangxi Soviet to conduct a series of land reform campaigns. These work teams went to individual villages to analyze the class structure and to place the local people into categories such as landlords, rich peasants, middle peasants, and poor peasants, each determined in part on how much income one derived directly from one's own labor. In these campaigns, CCP officials, backed by the Red Army, confiscated land from landlords and sometimes rich peasants for redistribution to poor and middle peasants. Land reform campaigns occasionally turned violent and resulted in the deaths of landlords and rich peasants, but in most cases they helped win the support of the rural masses. In other cases, the CCP took advantage of whatever local tensions existed, siding with one group against another in order to win support. By implementing reforms that gave peasants immediate benefits, Mao built a self-sufficient rural base with an independent government and military that enjoyed the support of the local peasant population.

Despite the growth of the Jiangxi Soviet, Mao faced criticism from the Shanghai-based Central Committee of the CCP, which criticized him for having a "peasant mentality." Although Mao remained outwardly obedient to the party leadership, in his rural base he pursued his own strategy. The CCP leadership, collectively known as the "28 Bolsheviks" because they had spent time in Soviet Russia, rejected Mao's experiments with peasant revolutionaries in favor of the more orthodox Soviet approach which focused on the urban workers. They never approved of Mao's activities in the Jiangxi Soviet, even though the success of his rural strategy contrasted sharply with the failure of their strategy of urban uprising. In mid-1930, taking advantage of the War of the Central Plains, these leaders ordered another attempt at launching urban-based armed insurrections once again aimed at capturing provincial capitals Nanchang and Changsha. The failure of these attacks in August and September 1930 made it increasingly difficult to find fault with Mao's strategy of rural base building.

The Encirclement Campaigns, 1930–1934

Chiang Kai-shek faced several challenges in building his government at Nanjing, but he regarded the Chinese Communists as the greatest threat to China's unity and strength. In an attempt to crush Mao's Jiangxi Soviet, the largest of several CCP bases, Chiang launched five encirclement campaigns, which he called "bandit extermination" campaigns, between 1930 and 1934. Outnumbered and outgunned, Mao implemented his strategy of People's War, fighting only when reasonably assured of a quick and decisive victory. Rather than stand and defend the borders of his rural base in an attempt to prevent Chiang's forces from penetrating it, he preferred to withdraw and yield territory to the attackers, "luring the enemy deep" into terrain favorable to the Red Army. Once his forces drew the Nationalist troops into disadvantageous positions or separated them into smaller units, the Red Army then attacked them individually, concentrating overwhelming force on divided and isolated enemy units. Drawing on lessons of Sun Zi and other ancient military strategists, Mao organized his peasant soldiers for guerrilla fighting, emphasizing small ambushes and hit and run tactics. As Mao put it "the enemy advances, we retreat; the enemy camps, we harass; the enemy tires, we attack; the enemy retreats, we pursue."[11] Mao knew that he could not afford to fight conventional battles against Chiang's larger and better-equipped army. The Red Army had no arsenals and depended on captured weapons to supply its troops. As a result, Mao and his forces patiently waited for opportunities to outnumber and surround enemy forces. Mao understood that when his forces yielded territory without a fight, Nationalist forces sometimes abused the people who lived in the area and overturned the results of the CCP's land reform campaigns. He accepted this as a fact of life and even pointed out that abuses by the Nationalist forces might encourage the people to throw their support behind the CCP.

The first two encirclement campaigns, launched in December 1930 and February 1931, respectively, ended in immediate failure. The highly mobile guerilla forces of the Red Army made quick work of the 100,000–200,000 Nationalist troops, mostly provincial forces of questionable quality from Hunan and Jiangxi. Luring individual units into ambushes one at a time and moving quickly to strike in different areas, the Red Army concentrated first on the weakest and most vulnerable of the attacking forces. Rather than crushing the Jiangxi Soviet, the first two encirclement campaigns actually extended the area of CCP control, put thousands of captured weapons in the hands of Red Army soldiers, and increased their prestige in the eyes of the local peasantry. Chiang took personal command of the third encirclement campaign in June 1931, sending 130,000 troops in three columns against the Jiangxi Soviet. The Red Army allowed the Nationalist columns to penetrate the area, then harassed them as they drove toward the CCP base. Both sides suffered significant casualties before the campaign ended because of the Japanese invasion of Manchuria in September.

Mao had successfully defended his base three times, and his Red Army troops had gained valuable experience in the process. Yet during this period the Nationalists made a series of more successful raids against the mainstream leadership of the CCP, who remained in Shanghai and other urban areas. The threat of arrest by Nationalist authorities and the failure of earlier attempts at urban insurrection forced the 28 Bolsheviks to flee from the cities and take refuge at Mao's rural base. Although they found safety in the Jiangxi Soviet, they promptly criticized Mao for his "mistakes" and demoted him. As a result, the 28 Bolsheviks controlled the Jiangxi Soviet when in July 1932 Chiang launched a fourth encirclement campaign. This campaign involved 240,000 Nationalist troops, including 100,000 of Chiang's best Central Army troops. The 28 Bolsheviks, supported by other Communist leaders such as Lin Biao, Zhu De, and Zhou Enlai, rejected Mao's guerrilla strategy and tactics in favor of a more conventional attempt to defend the perimeter of the base. Rather than lure the enemy in and divide him into small units to be attacked individually, the new leaders sent Red Army units forward to aggressively engage Nationalist forces outside of the Jiangxi Soviet. This strategy succeeded, ending the fourth campaign in April 1933.

The success proved short-lived as Chiang and his German advisors carefully planned the fifth and best coordinated encirclement campaign, which featured a slow but thorough military encirclement and economic strangulation. Beginning in April 1934, 800,000 Nationalist troops advanced from several directions in separate columns. As they surrounded the Jiangxi Soviet, they erected a line of cement block-house fortifications with interlocking fields of fire. Slowly and with painstaking labor, the Nationalist forces sealed off the area around the mountain base and slowly closed the trap, preventing supplies from moving into the area around the base. Rather than rush in to meet the CCP forces and render themselves vulnerable to ambush, as they had done earlier, the Nationalist forces moved slowly with carefully coordinated movements. The Red Army engaged Chiang's troops from forward positions as they had in the fourth campaign, but with little success. They then fell back in an attempt to defend the territorial base using positional warfare as the Nationalists carefully cordoned off of the Jiangxi Soviet, slowly strangling the base.[12]

The Long March

There is no clear evidence that Mao's tactics would have succeeded and preserved the Jiangxi Soviet against the fifth and most formidable of the encirclement campaigns. Yet the 28 Bolsheviks had no effective strategy for dealing with it, which doomed the base to destruction. At best, Mao's strategy might have preserved Red Army strength for an attempt to break out of the encirclement. Trying to stand their ground against the superior numbers and firepower of the Nationalists, Red Army units suffered defeat after defeat. With the base in jeopardy, the CCP leadership decided to abandon the Jiangxi Soviet and retreat to the west. In October 1934, 85,000 soldiers, 15,000 government and party officials, and 35 women (mostly wives of CCP leaders) left the base on foot, beginning a year long, 6,000 mile retreat known as the Long March. They chose to break out in an area guarded by Guangdong regional troops, not Chiang's best, passing through the gaps in Nationalist units surrounding the base. A rear guard of 28,000 troops remained to cover the retreat of the larger group along with 20,000 wounded who could not march.

Moving first west into Hunan and then south into Guizhou, they intended to join with other CCP forces and form a new rural base. The participants of the Long March suffered greatly as they marched across difficult terrain, attempting to plot a course that weaved between Nationalist troops and other hostile forces. The retreat took the ragged and exhausted CCP forces through large forests, over raging rivers, and across great snow-capped mountains. In the mountains the thin air and bitter cold caused some to drop dead in their tracks, while others suffered from frostbite. Harassed by regional troops, ethnic minority villagers, and hounded by Chiang's small air force, the CCP Long Marchers made their way along a twisted path, feinting one way and then quickly changing their route in order to avoid contact with enemy forces. They eventually turned north and in October 1935, just over one year after leaving the rural base at Ruijin, a battered force of less than 10,000 of the original 100,000 inhabitants of the Jiangxi Soviet arrived at Yan'an in Shaanxi Province. The survivors of this tortuous march established another rural base here and continued the experiments in land reform and state-building they had begun in the Jiangxi Soviet.[13]

Although Mao's force had come close to complete destruction, the Long March thereafter loomed large in the minds of Chinese Communist leaders as evidence of their ability to survive against all odds. It also marked the emergence of Mao Zedong as the paramount leader of the CCP. In January 1935, the leadership stopped to assess what had happened and held a meeting in Zunyi, a small town in Guizhou Province. Mao criticized the 28 Bolsheviks for their decision to maintain a static defense, blamed them for losing the Jiangxi Soviet, and argued in favor of his mobile guerrilla strategy. A number of important CCP leaders, including Deng Xiaoping, Liu Shaoqi, and Zhou Enlai, supported Mao against the 28 Bolsheviks, marking his rise to the top of the CCP, a position he enjoyed until his death in 1976.

The period at Yan'an provided Mao and the CCP leadership with valuable time to restructure the Communist Party and Red Army, to organize the masses in support the CCP, and to develop new social, political, and economic institutions. At Yan'an, in complete control of the party and relatively free from Nationalist attacks, he continued his experiments and developed his version of Marxism–Leninism, which revolved around the concept of Voluntarism. Marx had based his ideology on the principles of materialism, believing that the forces of production and the economic structure of society determined the boundaries of human activity. Operating from a position of material weakness in a preindustrial country, Mao departed from this view by claiming that if properly motivated and led, people could overcome any material obstacle to accomplish their goals. Mao had great faith in the power of the human will and believed that if the people acted together and put forth their full effort, they could solve any problem or achieve any objective.

Mao's experience in the Long March and the miraculous survival of the CCP helped reinforce this concept. This idea informed much of Mao's thinking and his approach to all problems. In order to harness this great power of the people, Mao would later organize mass campaigns to mobilize the population for action. Mao's campaigns typically targeted specific problems such as corruption, correcting improper thought, or promoting collectivization of agriculture and often borrowed the language of the military to urge people to "make war" on the problem in question. The struggle against the Nationalists, the Long March, and Mao's military experience had a profound impact on his general thinking and approach to solving future problems.

Manchuria and the Sino-Japanese War, 1931–1945

Throughout the Nanjing Decade, China remained divided as both Chiang's Nationalist military and Mao's Red Army engaged in attempts at state-building from their respective capitals of Nanjing and Yan'an. At the same time, aggressive Japanese encroachments on Chinese territory posed a further obstacle to national unity and put China and Japan on a collision course. The 1931 Japanese military seizure of Manchuria ultimately led to the outbreak of full-scale war between China and Japan in 1937, which expanded into the Pacific War after 1941, and did not conclude until the Japanese surrender in 1945. The eight-year Sino-Japanese War interrupted the conflict between the Nationalists and Communists and had devastating consequences for the people of China.

The Manchurian Incident, 1931

Japanese interest in Manchuria dated back to the late nineteenth century and intensified after the Russo-Japanese War of 1904–1905. The economic and strategic factors that propelled Japan and Russia into armed conflict over Korea also led some Japanese to see Manchuria as essential to Japan's economic well-being and national security. In the early 1930s, as the impact of the Great Depression resulted in a dramatic decrease in Japanese exports, a sense of crisis and urgency intensified the belief among military officers that something had to be done to ensure that Japan had access to raw materials and markets in which to sell its exports. In 1931, a small group of officers of the Kwantung Army, a highly politicized unit of the Japanese Imperial Army stationed in Manchuria, hatched a plot to seize Manchuria from China.

On the night of September 18, 1931, Japanese soldiers from the Kwantung Army detonated an explosion along a section of tracks of the South Manchurian Railroad near the Chinese city of Shenyang, also known as Mukden. They blamed Chinese saboteurs and used the "attack" as a pretext to seize control of Shenyang. Japanese reinforcements quickly arrived from Korea and began a major offensive to take control of all of Manchuria. The Japanese government, in the hands of civilian party politicians since 1918, had no knowledge of the plot and tried to limit the scope of the incident through a peaceful settlement. This proved impossible as the Japanese military authorities generally supported the action and asserted the principle of "independence of supreme command," meaning that according to the 1890 Meiji Constitution, the Japanese military answered not to the government but only to the emperor. Despite the protests of successive prime ministers Wakatsuki Reijiro and Inukai Tsuyoshi, many in Japan applauded the actions of the Kwantung Army, including several cabinet members, numerous party politicians, and the general public.

Across China, people reacted to Japanese aggression in Manchuria by organizing boycotts of Japanese goods and menacing Japanese residents of China. The Japanese military dispatched marines to Shanghai to protect Japanese nationals from angry Chinese mobs, leading to clashes with Chinese troops in January 1932. The Japanese military responded with an aerial bombardment of a heavily populated area of Shanghai and sent an additional two army divisions in early March 1932, which drove Chinese forces out of the city. An armistice halted the fighting in early May, but the "Shanghai War," as Donald Jordan describes it, resulted in over 17,000 casualties among Chinese soldiers and civilians.[1]

Manchukuo, 1932

In March 1932, the Kwantung Army consolidated control over Manchuria by setting up a theoretically independent Manchurian state called Manchukuo. The new state of Manchukuo declared independence from Chinese rule and established a close economic and political relationship with Japan. The Japanese military placed several former Qing dynasty officials in important positions, including the last emperor Puyi who ascended the throne as emperor of Manchukuo. Despite the rhetoric of independence, most observers recognized it as a Japanese puppet, established for the economic and military benefit of Japan. The League of Nations appointed a five-member committee called the Lytton Commission to investigate the matter. Following an investigation lasting several months, the Lytton Commission reported to the League of Nations that the Japanese military action could not be considered legitimate self-defense nor did Manchukuo represent an independence movement of the Manchurian people. The League of Nations formally condemned Japan as an aggressor and adopted a policy of nonrecognition of Manchukuo. Japan promptly withdrew from the League of Nations in March 1933 and embarked on its own path outside of the international community.

The Japanese seizure of Chinese territory outraged Chiang Kai-shek, but he did not resort to military force to resist Japanese aggression. Chiang believed he needed more time to implement military reforms under the guidance of his German advisors before his military could stand up to the formidable Japanese Imperial Army. Only then, Chiang argued, could China confront the Japanese aggressors with any hope of success. He also maintained that the foreign crisis could not be solved until China had achieved a degree of domestic unity, especially with regard to the Communists who operated from a rival government in the hinterlands of Jiangxi. If Nationalist forces engaged the Japanese military before dealing with China's internal problems, Chiang declared, "certain unprincipled and divisive groups opposed to the Government would be sure to take advantage of the situation to create trouble."[2] In some respects, the Japanese invasion of Manchuria helped him in his struggle against regional commanders as the burden of dealing with the Japanese fell largely on Feng Yuxiang and Zhang Zuolin, whose armies occupied the northeast.

Unwilling to go to war and finding little meaningful support from the League of Nations, Chiang agreed to the Tanggu Truce in May 1933, which gave the Japanese military control over parts of north China and created a demilitarized zone between Beijing and the Great Wall. He then began preparations to continue his encirclement campaigns against the Jiangxi Soviet. Mao Zedong and the Chinese Communists took advantage of the rise in patriotic feelings after Japan's seizure of Manchuria, and Chiang's refusal to respond militarily, by calling for collaboration with all parties and armies in opposition Japanese aggression. Using slogans such as "Chinese must not fight Chinese," the CCP appealed to the nationalism of the Chinese people. Many students and young people in China responded to this patriotic call by demanding an end to civil war and calling for united action against the Japanese. This popular position, which required little real action, did much to boost the image of the CCP.

The Tanggu Truce did not solve the problem as the Japanese military continued with aggressive attempts to detach parts of north China, seeking to protect Manchukuo by creating a buffer zone separating it from China proper. In May 1935, the Japanese demanded that Chiang remove all Guomindang offices from north China and withdraw Nationalist military forces from the Beijing–Tianjin area. Still unwilling to go to war with Japan, Chiang authorized Minister of War He Yingqin to meet with Japanese General Umezu Yoshijiro and sign the He–Umezu Agreement in which Chiang's government agreed to remove all Guomindang offices and Nationalist troops from Hebei (formerly Zhili) Province and to stop all anti-Japanese activities. The Japanese Army moved again in November 1936, launching a full-scale invasion of part of Inner Mongolia, supported by planes and tanks. Nationalist troops in the area resisted, and Chinese civilians launched another round of anti-Japanese strikes and boycotts.

Although the voices of critics of his policy of avoiding confrontation grew louder, Chiang Kai-shek remained adamant that he must first unify the country before he could deal effectively with the Japanese military threat. He steadfastly refused calls for alliance with the CCP and immediate military action against Japan and cracked down heavily on his critics, jailing or even assassinating those who criticized his government.[3] The Communists had by this time completed the Long March and built a new rural base at Yan'an. Chiang ordered the Manchurian general Zhang Xueliang, whose father Zhang Zuolin the Japanese had assassinated 1928, to blockade Yan'an and lead a campaign to crush the Communists. Even as he followed Chiang's orders to prepare a campaign against Yan'an, the CCP's call for united action against the Japanese who occupied his Manchurian homeland struck a chord with Zhang. The CCP used effective propaganda, appealing to Zhang's Manchurian troops stationed far away from their homeland, urging them to join with the CCP and fight to recover Manchuria from Japanese control. In early 1936, Zhang Xueliang met with Zhou Enlai to discuss the possibility of concerted action against the Japanese. The desire to fight the Japanese swelled among some Nationalist officers and soldiers, but Chiang remained firm on the need to first deal with what he saw as the most dangerous opponent, the Communists.

Xi'an Incident, December 1936

In December 1936, Chiang Kai-shek flew to the city of Xi'an, south of Yan'an, in order to assess the situation and to prepare for a final campaign against the Communists. He assembled additional forces and bomber planes, intending to annihilate the CCP base at Yan'an. After discussions with the CCP leadership, Nationalist generals Zhang Xueliang and Yang Hucheng resolved that something had to be done to change Chiang's mind about national priorities. On the morning of December 12, 1936, Zhang's troops stormed Chiang Kai-shek's quarters at a hot springs resort outside of Xi'an. Most of Chiang's body-guards died in the assault, but Chiang fled over the back wall into the surrounding mountains. Zhang's men captured Chiang Kai-shek in a small cave on the mountainside. With Chiang in custody, Zhang Xueliang made a series of demands, including a reorganization of the Nationalist government to form a truly representative government, an end to civil war against the CCP, the release of all political prisoners, guaranteed political freedoms of assembly and speech, and the creation of a National Salvation Conference to discuss united military action against the Japanese.

Zhang Xueliang circulated the demands to top officers and officials of the Nationalist government and military. While most regional military commanders sat on the fence, waiting to see what would happen, Chiang's loyal Central Army officers threatened dire consequences if any harm came to Chiang. While some prepared to storm the city of Xi'an, Chiang's wife, Song Meiling, and brother-in-law, Song Ziwen, traveled to Xi'an to negotiate for his release. The Communists saw a great opportunity and sent Zhou Enlai to Xi'an to join the negotiations. Zhou supported Zhang's call for a coalition government and a united front against Japan, offering to submit the CCP Red Army to Chiang's command if he committed to a full-scale defense against Japanese aggression. Chiang stubbornly refused any kind of agreement and negotiations dragged on until Christmas day, when Chiang finally offered a verbal agreement that he would seriously consider the situation and promised to make changes. Zhang then released his commander-in-chief and the two men boarded a plane back to Nanjing. Cheering crowds welcomed them, but Zhang Xueliang faced a court martial for treason and spent most of the rest of his life under house arrest. Despite his verbal agreement at Xi'an, Chiang made no move to accept the CCP overture or to change his policies. Yet the mood in the nation made it difficult for Chiang to continue his policy of delaying military action against Japan. Increasing numbers of Chinese bristled at Chiang's reluctance to confront the Japanese, as nationalist and anti-Japanese sentiment swept the country. As a result, Chiang gradually began to pursue a policy of toleration in domestic affairs in order to fight together against Japan, leading to a second united front between the Guomindang and the CCP in September 1937. Like the first united front of 1924–1927, the union amounted to a marriage of convenience with neither side trusting the other.[4]

From the perspective of the Japanese military in Manchuria and north China, which preferred a weak and divided China that could not challenge Japan's position in Manchuria, the Xi'an Incident portended a possible united front between China's two prominent political parties and posed a potential threat to Japanese interests. The Japanese government adopted a conciliatory approach toward China emphasizing economic cooperation, but the Japanese military tended to see this as a direct threat to its goal of uniting Japan, Manchukuo, and northern China as an economic unit. Many young army officers serving in Manchuria felt a dire need to take complete control of north China in order to protect Manchuria. As Japanese troops in Manchuria grew restless, so did their Chinese counterparts. The Xi'an Incident and the change in Chiang's policy gave Chinese armies new confidence, leading to increased expressions of anti-Japanese nationalism and boycotts. Under such conditions, further military clashes seemed inevitable.

The Marco Polo Bridge Incident, 1937

Under the stipulations of the 1901 Boxer Protocol, Japan had the right to station its troops in north China along the Beijing–Tianjin corridor. Shortly before midnight on July 7, 1937, a Japanese regiment conducting training exercises near the Marco Polo Bridge, about fifteen miles west of Beijing, clashed with Chinese forces. The Japanese sustained no injuries during the brief fighting but claimed that one soldier had disappeared in the confusion. When Japanese officers demanded the right to search for this missing soldier in the nearby town of Wanping, Chinese authorities refused which led to more fighting until the two sides agreed to a cease-fire on July 9.

The exact details of this clash remain a mystery. Some claim that the Japanese instigated this incident as part of a plan to detach north China as a buffer zone between Manchukuo and Chiang Kai-shek's Nationalist government. There is ample evidence for this argument, as the case of the Manchurian Incident indicates that Japanese military officers occasionally acted without authorization from their superiors or the Japanese government. Yet at the time of the incident, the Chinese forces in the area outnumbered Japanese forces by ten to one, perhaps indicating the Japanese military had not made preparations to capitalize on this incident. Whatever the case, the incident precipitated a large-scale military struggle known to the Chinese as the Eight Year War of Resistance, or the Sino-Japanese War.[5]

Although the local Chinese commander, Song Zheyuan, agreed to remove his troops from Wanping, the Japanese and Chinese governments could not come to a satisfactory agreement over the issue. Chiang Kai-shek refused to negotiate until Japanese troops withdrew, insisting on a full restoration of Chinese control of north China. He reinforced his stand by sending several Nationalist divisions north to protect the Beijing–Tianjin corridor. The Japanese Army sent five divisions from Manchuria to reinforce Japanese forces in north China, which at the time had only 5,000 soldiers. This sparked another clash on July 25, in which the Japanese inflicted approximately 5,000 casualties on the Chinese. In the heat of the anti-Japanese movement, angry Chinese rioted and killed hundreds of Japanese civilians in north China. At this point, neither government showed interest in negotiation as both professed a determination to stand firm. Chiang Kai-shek announced his determination to wage all out resistance, declaring that "we have reached the point when we can endure it no longer; we will give way no more. The whole nation must rise as one man and fight these Japanese bandits until we have destroyed them."[6]

In the initial fighting in north China, heavily armed Japanese infantry routed Chinese forces and quickly took control of the Beijing–Tianjin region. As additional Japanese troops arrived in late July and early August 1937, Chiang reinforced his position around Shanghai, committing his best German-trained Central Army troops to defend the city. The Japanese responded by moving the battle from north China to the lower Yangzi River region. In some respects, this benefited Chiang as he had greater strength in this area than he did in north China, where generals of questionable allegiance commanded regional troops. For example, the officer who commanded Nationalist troops around Wanping, Song Zheyuan, had fought against Chiang in the War of the Central Plains in 1930. Another regional commander in Shandong allowed Japanese forces to land unopposed at the port city of Qingdao. In Shanghai, Chiang could rely on his Central Army troops. Moreover, the buildings of Shanghai might provide a measure of cover for his forces fighting against Japanese tanks and artillery, as opposed to the wide-open spaces of north China which left them vulnerable to superior Japanese firepower. Regardless, Chiang saw little choice but to stand and defend the Shanghai–Nanjing area, which constituted the power base of his army and government.

The Battle for Shanghai

The fighting at Shanghai began on August 13 with Japanese troops landing on the banks of the Huangpu River and warships bombarding Nationalist positions. Determined to hold his position at Shanghai, Chiang committed over 500,000 of his best troops to the battle, exhibiting the "Whampoa Spirit" of aggressive attack and self-sacrifice. Both sides poured in reinforcements, and casualties mounted as the fighting continued through to early November. In the end, Japanese air and naval firepower proved too much for the beleaguered Chinese defenders who suffered 270,000 casualties in three months of fighting. This included approximately 60 percent of Chiang's Central Army troops, a devastating loss at the outset of what would be a protracted war. After this point, Chiang would have to rely heavily on regional military forces whose commanders remained wary of Chiang's central authority. Moreover, the Japanese retained complete superiority in air and naval operations. Chiang attempted to use his own bombers to strike at the Japanese navy in the harbor which provided artillery protection for Japanese attacking troops. In an August 14 attack on the Japanese flagship *Izumo,* Nationalist bombers missed their targets and dropped bombs on Shanghai itself, killing hundreds of Chinese civilians. Despite the disadvantage in firepower, the Chinese fought tenaciously, inflicting 40,000 casualties on the Japanese. Fifteen new divisions of reinforcements reached China by the middle of September, bringing the total number of Japanese troops in and around Shanghai to 200,000.[7]

The Chinese suffered a severe blow on November 5, when three Japanese divisions made an amphibious landing near Hangzhou, southwest of Shanghai. These troops attacked the Chinese right flank, compelling Chiang's forces to fall back on Nanjing on November 11. Japanese troops captured the Shanghai–Nanjing rail line and wasted no time laying siege to Nanjing, the seat of the Nationalist government, in early December. After several days of artillery assault, Japanese troops entered the city on December 12, with Chiang's government and surviving troops making a rapid retreat up the Yangzi River. The Nanjing campaign proved one of the bloodiest of the war as Japanese troops committed horrific acts of violence against the civilian population. During the first month, Japanese troops raped an estimated 20,000 Chinese women, many attacks involving multiple attackers and ending with the cruel torture and murder of the victims. For a period of six weeks, Japanese soldiers moved through the streets of Nanjing indiscriminately killing men, women, and children, torturing, bayoneting, beheading, and machine gunning Chinese soldiers and civilians. Estimates of the number killed vary widely, from 50,000 to 200,000, but the savagery of the Japanese troops, who systematically butchered and raped the civilian population of Nanjing, shocked the world.[8]

The Japanese had no grand strategy for the war in China or ambitions to take direct control over all of its territory. Rather, the Japanese simply hoped to crush Chiang's government, forcing it to recognize Manchukuo's independence (and close relationship to the Japanese military) and accept regional economic, political, and military cooperation under Japanese direction. Japanese troops followed the rail lines in eastern and central China, pursuing Nationalist military forces, occupying major cities, and controlling the lines of transportation. Having put off military action against the Japanese for years, Chiang now refused negotiations and continued to resist. As a result, the Japanese government declared its intention to destroy Chiang's government as a part of the creation of a "New Order" in East Asia.

Although the Nationalist forces suffered defeats around the major cities of Beijing, Shanghai, and Nanjing, a victory against Japanese troops at Tai'erzhuang in April 1938 provided a much needed morale boost. As Japanese troops began a campaign against the city of Xuzhou in northwestern Jiangsu Province, Li Zongren's Guangxi troops lured the Japanese into a trap at Tai'erzhuang, just across the border in Shandong Province, sending 3,000 Chinese troops into the battle to drive the Japanese forces back. Over the next several days, the Nationalists reinforced with thousands of soldiers and some artillery to defend their positions against three counter-assaults on Tai'erzhuang. The Chinese enjoyed a rare logistical advantage in that they managed to cut Japanese supply lines to the city. As the two forces came together, the Japanese could not make effective use of artillery because so much of the combat took place in small units fighting at close range. Running low on ammunition, the Japanese withdrew leaving 16,000 dead and 100 tanks. Although one of only a few battles in which Chinese forces prevailed against the Japanese, it helped dispel any notions of the invincibility of the Japanese Imperial Army that might have arisen in the early stages of the war. Regardless, Japanese forces regrouped and captured Xuzhou in May.[9]

As Chiang's government and military retreated from Nanjing upriver to the interior of China, the Japanese continued to push westward toward Wuhan in pursuit. In order to delay the Japanese advance along the Longhai railroad, Chiang ordered the destruction of the Yellow River dikes near Zhengzhou, an important rail junction in central China. The Yellow River burst out of its bed, shifting violently to a southerly route and flooding large areas of Henan, Anhui, and Jiangsu provinces. This controversial move delayed the Japanese for several months but inflicted untold suffering upon Chinese civilians. The surging flood waters destroyed over 4,000 villages and left two million homeless, leading Chiang's critics to decry his lack of concern for the Chinese peasants.

The flooding slowed the Japanese but did not prevent them from eventually converging on Chiang's temporary capital at Wuhan, to which they laid siege in late August 1938 with tanks, planes, and artillery. Chiang, who again put up strong resistance, committed several hundred thousand Nationalist forces to the defense of Wuhan. The fighting raged for over five months, with hundreds of major and minor battles. To the south, a Japanese force made an amphibious landing near Guangzhou, capturing that city on October 21. Since the fall of Shanghai, most of China's imports entered the country through Guangzhou, the major port of south China. The fall of Guangzhou cut off a vital supply line and forced the Nationalists to withdraw from Wuhan on October 25, 1938.

Retreat to the Interior

Chiang had long feared that his Nationalist military could not match the discipline, mobility, and firepower of the Japanese Imperial Army, and so he had planned for an extended struggle. As the war began, the Nationalist government began moving important industrial facilities upriver beyond the range of effective Japanese occupation. Hundreds of factories, particularly those associated with military production, and tens of thousands of skilled workers packed up and moved along the Yangzi River, retreating from advancing Japanese troops. With the collapse of Chinese defenses at Shanghai, Nanjing, and Wuhan, Chiang's government followed the Yangzi River to Chongqing in Sichuan Province, which would serve as the wartime capital.

When the war began in 1937, on paper the Nationalist military included two million soldiers and only meager naval and air forces. Chiang Kai-shek exercised firm control over nearly thirty divisions of Central Army troops. After the devastating losses at Shanghai, the Central Army units recruited new soldiers and officers, but even though its numbers increased over prewar levels it never reached its earlier levels of effectiveness. The remaining provincial troops varied greatly in terms of their equipment, capability, loyalty to Chiang, and willingness to engage the Japanese. Chiang divided China in separate war zones, each under the command of a subordinate general. Some war zone commanders such as Li Zongren and Xue Yue demonstrated loyalty to Chiang and considerable skill as commanders. Others such as Yan Xishan, who came to an independent accommodation with the Japanese in late 1939, proved less reliable. Since he did not trust his regional commanders, Chiang tended to micromanage the war effort, insisting on personal supervision of operations in all war zones. He sometimes countermanded orders given by war zone commanders, leaving confused field officers to decide which set of orders to follow.

The Nationalist government had drawn up a plan for universal conscription to enlarge the army and create a substantial reserve force, but it remained on the drawing board leaving China with no reserves. As a result, Nationalist recruiting practices sometimes involved coercion, with peasants taken from the fields to training centers bound together by ropes to prevent escape. The scarcity of resources meant that recruits suffered from a lack of proper food and medical treatment. Lloyd Eastman has estimated that as many as one million Nationalist recruits died before they ever reached the training locations, often located in remote areas. The Japanese, by contrast, had seventeen divisions in China (each Japanese division had 20,000 soldiers as opposed to Chinese divisions of 10,000 soldiers), backed by an educated, trained, and well-equipped Japanese Imperial Army and a reserve force of approximately four million ready to enter service.[10]

Following fall of Wuhan and Guangzhou, Chiang shifted to a strategy that featured three basic principles. First, anticipating a long war of attrition, Chiang embraced the notion of "trading space for time," allowing Japanese troops to occupy areas of large population concentrations along the coast while the government and army withdrew into the vast interior of China. As the Japanese seized control of cities and industrial centers, Chiang hoped they would become bogged down in an extended struggle which would gradually sap Japanese strength. Second, having lost many of his Central Army troops, Chiang had no choice but to make greater use of regional forces against the Japanese. He sometimes used the distribution of resources and supplies as a tool for motivating the regional commanders. Third, Chiang sent many of his remaining Central Army units to the northwest to blockade the Communists at Yan'an, preserving his best troops for a later resumption of the civil war against the CCP.

By late 1938, the Japanese military had halted its advance into China's western provinces. The lengthening lines of supply and communication and threats of attack by Chinese guerrilla units made it impractical to continue. In control of large parts of north, central, and now southeastern China, the Japanese concentrated on consolidating their positions, conducting "mopping up" operations to eliminate pockets of resistance in the areas they occupied, and tightening the economic blockade of the Chinese coast. The Japanese government did not officially declare war on China, fearing that to do so would lead other powers cut off the flow of strategic goods that Japan needed for its industry and military. The Japanese instead referred to this conflict as the "China Incident." Indeed, the United States continued to sell Japan war

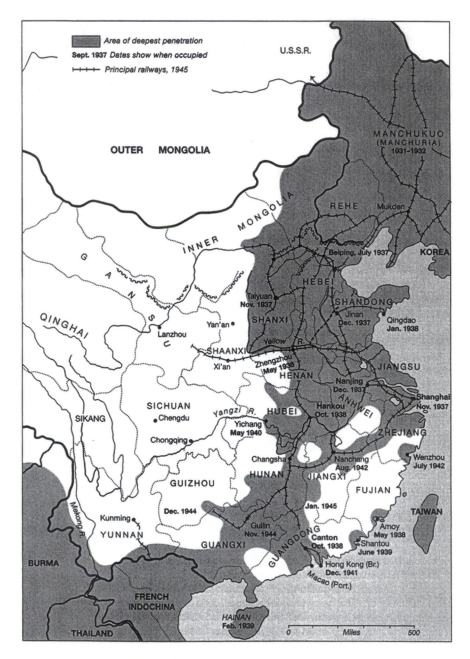

The Sino-Japanese War, 1937–1945. Schoppa, R. Keith, *Revolution and Its Past: Identities and Change in Modern Chinese History,* 2nd ed., ©2006, p. 265. Reprinted by permission of Pearson Education, Inc., Upper Saddle River, NJ.

materials without violating its Neutrality Acts, as Japan had not declared war on China.

With the fall of each major city or significant region, the Japanese hoped that Chiang's government would sue for peace. The Japanese also originally hoped to limit the number of Japanese troops in China to 250,000, but this proved an insufficient force to deal with the huge expanses of China. Well aware of its growing overextension, the Japanese military sought to avoid a long drawn out war in China which would leave Japan vulnerable to potential attack by the Soviet Union or the United States. As the war continued, Japan devoted more and more men and materials to the "China Incident" and inflicted horrific casualties on Chinese soldiers and civilians alike, yet with no sign that Chiang's government intended to accept Japanese terms for peace. As Edward Dreyer has noted, the Japanese Army found itself mired in a quagmire similar to the American experience in Vietnam, in which it won almost every major battle but eventually lost the war.[11]

Banished to the interior, Chiang Kai-shek waited for the international situation to change to his advantage. He had long believed that international politics would play an important role in the war, confident that Japan would eventually provoke war with either the Soviet Union or the United States, or both. During the initial phases of the war, Chiang and his representatives persistently sought the support of the Western powers. At the 1937 Brussels Conference, the Chinese delegates urged the Western powers to impose economic sanctions on Japan, to provide material aid to China, and to mediate the Sino-Japanese War. The Western states had no lack of sympathy for China's plight, but the United States, Great Britain, and the Soviet Union refused to forcefully challenge Japanese actions in China. The Soviet Union provided a small amount of aid to Chiang's government, hoping to block Japanese expansion in Asia by providing planes, advisors, and loans. The Japanese blockade of the China coast prevented the import of war materials, leaving the Burma Road, which connected China's Yunnan Province with India via Burma, as the only link between the Chinese government in Chongqing and the outside world. In 1938, the United States offered its first wartime aid to China in the form of a U.S. $25 million loan.

Chiang remained firm in his resolution to resist Japan while he waited for the Western powers to come to his aid, but another ranking official in the Nationalist government, Wang Jingwei, spoke out in favor of peace with Japan. Wang hoped to end the tremendous suffering of the Chinese civilian population by working with the Japanese rather than fighting against them. In December 1938, Wang broke with Chiang's government in Chongqing and slipped out through Hanoi to Nanjing, where in March 1940 he assumed leadership of a separate Chinese government "puppet" government supported by the Japanese. Realizing that it could not compel Chiang's government to capitulate, the Japanese military settled for "puppet" governments as an alternative. In order to lay the ground work for the creation of a Japanese-dominated East Asian economic bloc, the Japanese government announced a program of economic and military cooperation between Japan, Manchukuo, Wang Jingwei's regime at Nanjing, and other such "puppet regimes" the Japanese established in north China, eastern China, and Inner Mongolia. This would form the core of Japan's Greater East Asian Co-Prosperity Sphere, unveiled in the summer of 1940.

Throughout 1939, the Nationalist military conducted small and medium unit operations and guerrilla raids, taking advantage of opportunities to harass Japanese forces in rear areas despite shortages of weapons, ammunition, and equipment. Since Japanese troops generally moved by train, Chinese guerrillas could plan small attacks and ambushes along the tracks. In "trading space for time," Chiang hoped to tie down and wear out the enemy with a strategy well suited to China's weak position and inferior firepower. As a part of this essentially defensive strategy, Chinese forces did occasionally engage the Japanese in heavy fighting. In September 1939, as Hitler's army invaded Poland and ignited a European war, Chinese troops at Changsha forced a Japanese contingent of 120,000 soldiers to retreat hastily, leaving behind large quantities of arms and ammunition. Inspired by Nationalist victories at Tai'erzhuang and Changsha, Chiang planned a large-scale offensive across all war zones for the winter of 1939–1940. In the best-case scenario, Nationalist forces would drive Japanese forces back to the lower Yangzi River and retake Nanjing. At the very least, Chiang hoped to disrupt operations and inflict heavy losses on Japanese forces. Utilizing mobile warfare, the "Winter Offensive" targeted Japanese supply lines in an attempt to force the Japanese to abandon their positions. Chinese troops scored initial successes, recapturing several occupied towns in Jiangxi and Hubei provinces and inflicting significant casualties. The Japanese responded with an attack on Guangxi, thereby threatening Chongqing and entire southwest. Nationalist forces managed to regroup and block the thrust to the southwest, but the plan for driving the Japanese to the east failed. Nationalist forces suffered more than 50,000 casualties and thereafter refrained from large-scale offensives.

The United States and China

Prior to the Japanese attack on Pearl Harbor in December 1941, the United States had extended small amounts of aid to China but had remained preoccupied with events in Europe during the initial phases of the Sino-Japanese War. The September 1940 Tripartite Pact which allied Germany, Italy, and Japan and the Japanese military occupation of French Indochina in 1940 and 1941 indicated to American officials that Japan posed a significant threat and triggered a series of economic sanctions against Japan. When negotiations between American and Japanese diplomats yielded no results, the Japanese army and navy implemented a plan to simultaneously cripple the American Pacific Fleet through an attack on the naval base at Pearl Harbor and to seize the oil rich islands of the Dutch East Indies and other parts of Southeast Asia. With the American declaration of war on Japan in December 1941, the United States began to provide greater aid to China. American planners sought to ensure that China remained in the war, pinning down millions of Japanese troops which would otherwise be available for service in the Pacific against American forces.

In order to assist China in its war effort, President Franklin Roosevelt sent Lieutenant General Joseph Stilwell to China in 1942 to serve as Chiang Kai-shek's chief of allied staff and commander of the China–Burma–India Theater. Nicknamed "Vinegar Joe," Stilwell had substantial experience in China as a young officer in the 1920s, spoke Chinese, and seemed like an ideal officer to assist Chiang effectively prosecute the war against Japan. Blunt and outspoken, Stilwell clashed with Chiang over strategy and tactics. Stilwell argued in favor of training a force of Chinese soldiers to undertake a campaign to drive Japanese forces out of Burma in order to open up the Burma Road and increase the flow of supplies from India to Chongqing and southwest China. The Japanese occupation of Burma in early 1942 had closed the Burma Road and forced China to rely on air supply by planes flying "over the hump" of the Himalayan Mountains, a dangerous passage which dramatically reduced the flow of supplies. Although desirous of greater amounts of military aid, Chiang had little interest in sending some of his best remaining troops to fight in Burma. Now that China enjoyed the support of the United States and its allies, he intended to preserve his own armies for the upcoming battle with the CCP which would certainly resume following Japan's defeat. Yet he did not want to offend his new ally and therefore reluctantly agreed to contribute a CEF (Chinese Expeditionary Force) of 100,000 troops to take part in Stilwell's Burma operation.

The CEF's sound defeat in Burma at the hands of the Japanese in the spring of 1942 greatly strained relations between the two men and made future cooperation difficult at best. Stilwell followed this defeat in Burma with a plan to reorganize and retrain Chinese forces for aggressive action against the Japanese. This included purging the Nationalist ranks of officers he deemed incompetent or corrupt, some of whom enjoyed close personal relationships with Chiang. Chiang not only wanted to avoid risking his troops in large-scale battles against the Japanese, but he also feared that Stilwell's reorganization plans would undercut his control of the Nationalist military and the basis of his political authority. With regard to action against the Japanese, Chiang preferred a plan advocated by another American, Claire Chennault, who emphasized air power as opposed to Stilwell's ground strategy. Retired from the United States Air Force and employed as an advisor to the Chinese government, Chennault led the AVG (American Volunteer Group) or "Flying Tigers," which began flying bombing missions against Japanese positions in China in 1941. With a greater share of American supplies, Chennault claimed, he could destroy Japanese forces in China and even attack the home islands. Stilwell argued that such air raids would invite Japanese ground attacks on vulnerable air bases which the Nationalist forces could not protect. Chiang favored Chennault's plan, primarily because he believed it could be pursued at a lower cost to his own forces. In November 1943, planes from Chennault's AVG, now incorporated into the American military as the Fourteenth Air Force, conducted a successful bombing raid on a Japanese base on the island of Taiwan. Alarmed by this development, the Japanese military reacted, as Stilwell had predicted, by attacking air bases in Jiangxi and Zhejiang.

In mid-1944, the Japanese launched their largest campaign of the war, Operation Ichigo. Attempting to destroy Chinese air bases, inflict heavy losses on Nationalist forces, and to open a secure transportation corridor linking Beijing and Guangzhou, 200,000 Japanese troops attacked through central China and drove toward the southwest. Nationalist forces put up initial resistance but then collapsed in defeat suffering over 300,000 casualties. The disastrous impact of Operation Ichigo and the loss of airbases in Guangxi ended Chennault's strategy and triggered a final confrontation between Stilwell and Chiang. At Stilwell's insistence, American President Franklin Roosevelt requested that Chiang turn over command of all Chinese troops to Stilwell. Beyond the tremendous insult at the idea of turning over command of his armies to a foreign officer, to relinquish control of the Nationalist military would deprive Chiang of his power base. Moreover, even if he did turn over nominal command to Stilwell, Chiang's control over regional forces had limits and he could not turn over power he himself in many cases did not possess. Predictably, Chiang refused Stilwell's demand and insisted that President Roosevelt recall Stilwell and replace him with another officer. Roosevelt first dispatched a personal emissary named Patrick Hurley, a lawyer, former army officer, and diplomat, to mediate the dispute. Hurley advised Roosevelt that the two men could not work together and recommended Stilwell's recall. Otherwise, Hurley feared, Chiang Kai-shek might pull out of the war and make a separate peace with Japan, which would have disastrous consequences for the American effort in the Pacific. Roosevelt approved Stilwell's recall in October 1944, replacing him with General Albert Wedemeyer. Hurley stayed on in China to mediate between the CCP and the Nationalists in order to put forth a united war effort.[12]

The Red Army in the Sino-Japanese War

Another source of friction between Chiang and Stilwell revolved around the issue of relations with the Chinese Communists. Stilwell felt that the United States should explore relations with the CCP with an eye toward providing material aid to the Red Army in order to assist in operations against the Japanese. The CCP had long called for a united front against the Japanese and in the wake of the Xi'an Incident agreed to ally itself with Chiang's Guomindang for a second time. In September 1937, the Communist Party agreed to end its revolt against Chiang's government, to halt its expropriation of land from wealthy landlords, and place its armed forces under Chiang's command. In 1937, the Red Army had approximately 30,000 main force troops which it reorganized into the Eighth Route Army. A second force of some 12,000 soldiers who had stayed behind at the beginning of the Long March formed the New Fourth Army. Both accepted Nationalist authority, but retained their own officers and connections to regional and local guerrilla forces which normally supported the main force Red Army units. Mao refused Chiang's demand that these units accept Nationalist staff officers, but he agreed to abolish the post of political commissar. Most of the commissars simply assumed new titles as "deputy commanders."[13]

Over the course of the war, the Communist forces grew dramatically and by 1945 reached nearly one million. This growth resulted partly from practical policies that appealed to the peasantry and partly because of public expressions of patriotism and desire to fight the Japanese. Operating from several base areas in north China, the CCP spent the early years of the war expanding these bases and recruiting new troops. In 1939, Chiang grew so concerned with CCP expansion that he sent hundreds of thousands of his best troops to blockade Yan'an. The Second United Front did not result in close cooperation between Communist and Nationalist units, which occasionally clashed despite the nominal alliance. In December 1940, Chiang's suspicions that the New Fourth Army intended to establish a new base area in central China led him to order all CCP forces to withdraw back to the north of the Yangzi River. The Communist commanders complied with the order but did not make Chiang's deadline for completion of the withdrawal, which led to a bloody clash in January 1941 known as the New Fourth Army Incident. Guomindang forces surrounded and fired on the New Fourth Army as it moved north across the Yangzi River, inflicting 4,000 casualties on CCP forces. This marked the end of any form of cooperation between the Communists and Guomindang for the remainder of the war.[14]

As the war progressed, the Communist forces continued to concentrate on expanding the area under their control. They operated from five major rural bases, with Yan'an (the Shaanxi–Gansu–Ningxia base) the largest, the size of the state of Ohio and home to 1.4 million people. At the same time Communist military forces concentrated on a combination of guerrilla attacks and small or medium unit mobile operations to harass the Japanese units on the fringes of the occupied areas or scattered outposts. Attacks on small Japanese units or their Chinese "puppet" troops slowly helped drain Japanese strength and increased CCP stocks of weapons and ammunition. Occasionally, the Communists launched larger attacks, such as the Hundred Regiments Offensive of August 1940, a large-scale campaign across north China designed to attack Japanese lines of supply and communication. The campaign resulted in tens of thousands of Japanese casualties and boosted morale among the Communists, but it also incited the Japanese to react in savage fashion with a "Three All Policy" in north China—kill all, burn all, loot all. The Chinese civilian population suffered greatly under this brutal policy as the Japanese tried to punish the local population for supporting the Communists. After the Hundred Regiments Offensive, the CCP armed forces returned to small- and medium-sized actions and guerrilla tactics rather than risk large operations.

In the summer of 1944, a group of American military officers, informally called the "Dixie Mission" because they headed into "rebel territory," traveled to Yan'an to observe the CCP and assess the Communists' potential for fighting against the Japanese. The Dixie Mission reported favorably on the CCP, describing it as the most cohesive and efficient fighting force in China, superior to most of Chiang's Nationalist armies. The report from the Dixie Mission even indicated that the CCP might be in a better position to fight the Japanese and to rule China after the war. This supported the view of some American officials who advocated a coalition between the CCP and Nationalists. Chiang, of course, staunchly opposed the distribution of any American aid to the Communists and refused to consider cooperation. Patrick Hurley attempted to mediate between the two parties, flying to Yan'an to talk with Mao Zedong and other CCP leaders in November 1944. The CCP leaders impressed Hurley, who then drew up a plan for a coalition government with CCP representation in the Nationalist government, civil and political freedoms, legal status for the CCP, and the unification of armed forces. Mao approved of this plan and signed off on it, but Chiang demanded that the CCP turn over all of its military forces to the Nationalist command before creating a coalition government. Unwilling to trust Chiang, Mao refused to give up control of his military forces until the formation of a coalition government. Unable to bring the two sides together, Hurley recommended continued support for Chiang and his Nationalist government. Some members of Hurley's staff disagreed and sent messages to Washington in which they described the Nationalists as corrupt and the CCP as a more promising candidate for leadership in China. Franklin Roosevelt sided with Hurley, and the United States continued to support Chiang and his government.

Events in late 1944 and early 1945 clearly indicated the approaching defeat of Japan. The American island hopping campaigns resulted in the capture of Okinawa and opened the door to sustained bombing attacks on the Japanese home islands. The German surrender in May 1945 freed resources from the European Theater for use in the Pacific. In July the leaders of the Allied powers met at Potsdam and demanded Japan's unconditional surrender. On August 6 and 8, the United States dropped two atomic bombs on Hiroshima and Nagasaki, bringing the war to a close for all intents and purposes. Soviet forces attacked Japanese positions in Manchuria on August 8. Less than a week later, the Japanese emperor announced Japan's surrender, ending the military conflict between China and Japan that began in Manchuria in September 1931.

The ultimate victory over Japan came as an allied effort in which the Chinese contribution played a substantial role. From 1937 to 1941, China fought alone against hundreds of thousands of better trained and equipped Japanese troops. Including those troops stationed in Manchuria, approximately half of the more than two million Japanese troops in the field at the end of the war occupied some part of China. China and its people had suffered greatly during the war, sustaining over three million military casualties and perhaps as many as eighteen million civilian deaths. The war destroyed much of the nation's limited infrastructure ruined the economy. At the end of the eight years of bitter warfare, the Chinese people suffered both physical and material exhaustion.

The Chinese Civil War, 1945–1949

In August 1945, the Chinese Communists and Nationalists again faced each other in a civil war that had been interrupted in 1931 when the Japanese military seized control of Manchuria. The outbreak of full-scale war with Japan in 1937 led to a second united front between these two rivals, but as the New Fourth Army Incident of January 1941 indicated, tensions and hostilities lay just below the surface. Both sides had spent the latter years of the war against Japan marshaling their forces for the resumption of the civil war once the Japanese surrendered. The end of the war came much sooner than many had expected, catching Chiang Kai-shek and his exhausted Nationalist government unprepared for the immediate consequences of the Japanese surrender. With over one million Japanese soldiers in China laying down their weapons and Soviet troops occupying Manchuria, both the CCP and the Nationalists turned their attention to the task of recovering as much territory as possible in order to improve their own position in the coming struggle for control of China.

Nationalist and Communist Armies in 1945

Despite the massive casualties suffered during the war, Chiang's Nationalist army totaled approximately three million men in August 1945. His Central Army forces had suffered substantial losses during the early years of the war and had not returned to prewar effectiveness. The bulk of the Nationalist military still came from regional armies of varying quality and questionable loyalty to central authority. At the end of the war, perhaps as many as 250,000 former "puppet" troops who had served the Japanese quietly joined Chiang's Nationalist military. The switch to a strategy of "trading space for time" after 1938 had placed more of the burden of fighting on regional commanders, allowing Chiang to preserve what remained of his Central Army units and weaken those regional commanders he distrusted. A reorganization campaign in early 1946, designed to further weaken the regional commanders and reaffirm central control of the military, demobilized the weakest and most unreliable units and brought the total down to 2.7 million soldiers. Chiang's forces enjoyed a significant advantage over the CCP in terms of firepower and equipment, due primarily to American material assistance during the war, including an air force of 1,000 aircraft. Yet the Nationalists had neither effective maintenance systems for their equipment nor an adequate transportation system to move men and supplies. Moreover, eight years of bitter struggle against the Japanese left Nationalist armies with little appetite for further fighting.

The Communists experienced tremendous growth during the war years, though their numbers fell far short of equaling the Nationalist forces. Spread out across eighteen "liberated areas" in north and central China, the CCP controlled territory that included nearly 100 million people from which to draw recruits. During the latter years of the war against Japan, Mao and the CCP leaders at Yan'an had concentrated on building a strong, modern military force that could stand up to Chiang's Nationalist armies in large-scale battles. Red Army main force units improved and modernized by adding specialists in engineering, artillery, and communications. Despite a willingness to rely on guerrilla tactics at times, Lin Biao, Zhu De, Peng Dehuai, and other Red Army commanders, all professional military men, built a formidable force capable of engaging in conventional warfare. By mid-1946, the Communists had approximately 1.2 million soldiers in Red Army main force units, organized into five field armies and armed with weapons captured from the Japanese or Nationalist forces. Mao and other members of the MAC (Military Affairs Committee) decided to seize towns, cities, and centers of communications and transport as soon as the Japanese surrendered, but individual commanders of the five field armies enjoyed considerable freedom with regard to operations. Even before the surrender, Lin Biao's Fourth Field Army began moving against Japanese positions in north China and Manchuria in preparation for the resumption of civil war, significantly expanding the amount of territory under CCP control.

Chiang Kai-shek had no intention of letting his control of China slip away after having survived the war against Japan. He directed the defeated Japanese to surrender only to Nationalist troops and ordered Chinese Communist forces to remain in place. The Nationalist forces, originating from a disadvantageous position in southwestern China and along various battlefronts, found themselves unable to effectively reoccupy the major cities of the east that had fallen under Japanese occupation. General Albert Wedemeyer, Commander of United States Forces in the China Theater, arranged for American transport planes to fly hundreds of thousands of Chiang's troops from the interior to major cities such as Beijing, Tianjin, Shanghai, and Nanjing, so they could immediately restore Nationalist authority in these areas. He also dispatched 60,000 United States Marines to assist in occupation duties. With American support, the Nationalist government reoccupied many of the cities of south, central, and eastern China, but the Communists benefited from the Soviet presence in Manchuria. As arranged at the Yalta Conference of February 1945, the Soviet Red Army had joined the war against Japan and invaded Manchuria in early August 1945. Orders regarding the Japanese surrender in China did not apply to Manchuria where Soviet troops handled the task of disarming over 700,000 surrendering Japanese soldiers. The Soviet presence facilitated CCP movement into Manchuria and offered the Communists substantial amounts of captured Japanese arms.

Patrick Hurley, originally Franklin Roosevelt's personal emissary and in 1945 the United States ambassador, remained in China after the Sino-Japanese War in an attempt to prevent a civil war by facilitating an alliance between the Communists and Nationalists. He presided over negotiations in late August, inviting Mao to Chongqing for talks with Chiang Kai-shek. The talks continued for several weeks, as American aircraft carried Nationalist troops to important cities on the east coast, but ended in October with meager results. The two leaders smiled and toasted each other before the cameras and agreed on certain political matters, such the pursuit of Sun Yat-sen's Three People's Principles; the protection of individual freedoms of speech, press, and association; and the need to implement free elections. They had less success on the issue of military unification. Mao and the Red Army had fought hard to expand the territory under Communist control during and immediately after the war, and had no intention of surrendering CCP territory or command of Red Army forces to Chiang until the creation of a genuine coalition government. Chiang insisted that he first retake complete control of Manchuria and that Communist armed forces submit to his command as a precondition for coalition government. Neither trusted the other enough to take the initial steps necessary for a peaceful settlement. Mao left Chongqing in October, ending the negotiations.

The Marshall Mission

As the peace talks failed, Communist and Nationalist forces clashed in Manchuria. Patrick Hurley resigned as ambassador in November 1945, but President Harry Truman still hoped to preserve peace in China and sent General George Marshall, a former chairman of the Joint Chiefs of Staff, to act as a special emissary. Like Hurley, Marshall sought to bring the two sides together in the hope of forming a united and democratic government in China. Marshall attempted to take a neutral position between the combatants, but this proved impossible as the Truman Administration and the American Congress continued to provide aid to Chiang's Nationalist government alone. Marshall hoped to make it clear to Chiang that continued American financial support for his government depended upon realistic steps toward a meaningful peace agreement and the creation of a government of national unity. Reports of corruption and ineptitude in Chiang's government and military made some in Washington wary of continuing support for a regime that seemed incapable of governing. Yet even as Marshall explained these concerns to Chiang Kai-shek, the United States sent a shipment of military aid to outfit thirty-nine infantry divisions and a number of air squadrons, undercutting Marshall's threats.

Marshall began his mission by establishing three points as a basis for negotiations: a cease-fire in the civil war, a conference to discuss coalition government, and the integration of the Communist and Nationalist forces into a single, national military force. Both sides overtly welcomed Marshall's mediation, but each refused to take the necessary steps to secure an agreement. Chiang's army enjoyed a numerical superiority over the Communists, and he remained confident of his ability to crush the CCP forces on the field of battle. He showed little flexibility in negotiations and authorized his supporters to begin marginalizing members of the Guomindang who favored cooperation with the Communists. Mao and the CCP leadership saw little incentive to make substantial concessions and believed that the issue would be decided on the battlefield. Having survived the five encirclement campaigns, the Long March, and the Sino-Japanese War, Mao believed that his Red Army could succeed even if outnumbered and outgunned. While the negotiations dragged on, both sides prepared to settle their differences through military means.[1]

Marshall's efforts to mediate the dispute met with initial success as he arranged a cease-fire beginning on January 10, 1946, and convened a multiparty conference called the PCC (People's Consultative Conference) to discuss coalition government. The conference brought together delegates from multiple political groups, but no general agreement emerged as representatives from the CCP and the Democratic League, another prominent critic of Chiang's regime, rejected stipulations that reaffirmed Chiang's dominant position in the government. Chiang demanded that the Communists surrender control of their armed forces prior to the establishment of a coalition government and once again the CCP insisted that this take place after the establishment of a coalition government. CCP representatives eventually left the PCC, dooming it to failure. When Marshall briefly returned to the United States in March 1946, hostilities resumed between Nationalist and Communist forces.

Chiang's unwillingness to form a genuine coalition government with Communists stemmed both from his own anticommunist views and his confidence that he could use force to destroy the CCP in short order. In early 1946, Chiang believed he operated from a position of strength, commanding a substantial military force and enjoying the material support of the United States. He remained confident that the United States would continue to support his government, despite warnings from Hurley and Marshall that American material aid depended upon his willingness to form a genuine coalition government. Such warnings had little impact on Chiang who believed American material support would continue as long as he opposed the Chinese Communists. With neither side showing genuine interest in a peaceful settlement, the negotiations collapsed and military clashes resumed.

Chiang took the initiative in the fighting of early 1946, sending his forces to reoccupy major cities in central Manchuria, such as Shenyang and Changchun, along with parts of Inner Mongolia. Back in August 1945, 100,000 Communists troops under the command of Lin Biao, a veteran of the Whampoa Military Academy, had moved quietly into Manchuria and received Japanese weapons from Soviet troops. By the time Soviet troops began withdrawing from Manchuria in March 1946, Lin Biao's Communist troops had acquired enough weapons to put up strong resistance at Changchun before eventually withdrawing from the city. George Marshall returned to China to try to stop the fighting and managed a second cease-fire agreement in June. The peace did not last and by January of 1947 he realized that his mission had failed and that China was headed for civil war. As Marshall prepared to depart from China, Chiang told him that Nationalist armies would use force to take control of the rail lines of north China and then crush the Communists who, like a "ripe apple, would fall into our laps."[2] Marshall criticized both parties for their failure to cooperate and compromise.

People's War

Mao showed no more inclination to compromise than did Chiang Kai-shek and deserves equal responsibility for the failure to reach a negotiated settlement. He understood that the Nationalist forces enjoyed advantages in numbers and firepower, but always believed that superior strategy and motivation would allow his forces to surmount material obstacles. The experience of the Long March provided evidence of the CCP's ability to adapt and overcome despite great hardship and adversity. In dealing with Chiang's larger army, Mao returned to his strategy of People's War emphasizing support of the rural population, the use of appropriate guerrilla tactics as a part of an overall protracted struggle, and the eventual use of larger, more conventional attacks with concentrated force on the enemy's weak points. Mao envisioned the civil war taking place in three stages, beginning with a withdrawal from contested areas in order to preserve his forces while "luring the enemy deep," dispersing Chiang's forces and stretching his supply lines. During this first stage, CCP forces would limit their actions to guerilla and small unit mobile attacks on isolated enemy units and supply lines, in order to preserve CCP strength while slowly weakening the Nationalists. When Chiang's forces and position had been undermined and CCP strength had grown to the point at which the two sides had more or less equal numbers, CCP forces would move to stage two of People's War which would involve larger unit mobile warfare concentrated against enemy weak points, designed to inflict greater damage on the enemy, further weakening his position and sapping his strength. Once Mao's forces enjoyed numerical superiority and clear advantage, the third stage would begin featuring large-scale conventional attacks as part of a general offensive designed to crush the enemy with coordinated campaigns.

As Chiang's Nationalist forces went on the offensive in early 1946, Mao ordered the CCP military, now formally titled the PLA (People's Liberation Army), to take the defensive. In the first stage of the renewed fighting, PLA forces allowed Nationalist troops to move into north China and Manchuria to occupy the cities and industrial centers, such as Jinzhou, Siping, Jilin, Shenyang, and Changchun. The PLA avoided battle, preserved its strength, and extended its control over rural areas of Manchuria and north China, while abandoning urban areas it could not defend. From July to December 1946, the Nationalists attacked aggressively, capturing major cities and hundreds of smaller towns from the CCP. In March 1947, the Nationalists conducted a large-scale attack on the Communist base at Yan'an. Over 150,000 troops and dozens of aircraft participated in this symbolic assault which drove Mao and the Communist leadership out of Yan'an and yielded 10,000 prisoners. A force of 20,000 PLA troops covered Mao's retreat, allowing him to move across north China and eventually to Xibaipo in southern Hebei Province, which would become his new headquarters.

While this activity gave the impression of Nationalist success, the CCP had deliberately yielded much of this territory, preferring to wait for the Nationalist offensive to lose steam. Once the Nationalist forces had spread themselves out across north China and Manchuria, the PLA would begin small offensive operations against Nationalist outposts that guarded the major rail networks, which connected the major cities. By wresting control of the rail lines across north China and Manchuria, the PLA hoped to prevent Chiang from moving his troops by train which would nullify the Nationalist numerical advantage. Meanwhile, CCP recruitment continued, increasing the number of soldiers in PLA main force units, regional guerrilla units, and local militia forces.

In mid-1947, after a series of Nationalist victories, the tide of the battle began to turn. Despite success in capturing Yan'an and driving the PLA from urban areas, the Nationalist forces could not maintain the momentum because of overextension. Moreover, like the Japanese, Chiang's Nationalist forces occupied the major cities of the north and northeast, and controlled the rail lines connecting them, which left them vulnerable to guerrilla attacks and sabotage along the lines of communication and transportation. As the Nationalist forces spread themselves thinly across north China and southern Manchuria, the PLA launched guerrilla attacks on isolated Nationalist outposts and supply trains, which yielded additional weapons and supplies for the Communist forces.

The PLA in Manchuria

Manchuria lay at the heart of CCP strategy in the civil war. Only in Manchuria, where they acquired Japanese weapons from Soviet troops, could PLA forces compete with Chiang's forces in terms of firepower. Chiang attached great symbolic value to Manchuria, the scene of Japan's initial invasion of China in 1931, and dispatched large numbers of troops to drive Communist forces from its cities. With the exception of a few battles, the PLA did not contest for control of these urban areas and withdrew to the countryside, where it used its traditional techniques to win support from the peasantry. Successfully filling the void left after the defeat of the Japanese, the CCP provided law and order for the peasants of Manchuria. They conducted land reform as they had elsewhere, although land conditions in Manchuria did not resemble those of more populated areas of north China. In every area they controlled, the Communists organized the local peasantry into local militia to support CCP operations and to train for later service in PLA main force units. Manchuria, as Steven Levine describes it, became the CCP's "Anvil of Victory."[3]

The PLA began offensive operations in late 1946, but not always with great success. In early 1947, Lin Biao led his Fourth Field Army south across the Songhua (Sungari) River in a series of attacks against Nationalist forces in central Manchuria at Siping, Jilin, and Changchun. Nationalist forces under the command Du Yuming, a Whampoa Academy man, defended Siping and prepared to protect nearby Shenyang with air support from American-supplied planes. After suffering nearly 40,000 casualties in Nationalist counterattacks, Lin Biao pulled his troops back north of the Songhua River. In another campaign against Siping in the fall of 1947, Lin Biao's forces concentrated on severing the rail lines that connected Siping with Changchun and Shenyang. It proved much easier for the Communists to attack and destroy railroad tracks than for the Nationalists to defend or repair them. Although in November he again withdrew to the north bank of the Songhua River, Lin Biao succeeded in isolating the Nationalists by cutting their lines of supply and reinforcement.

By late 1947, Nationalist forces had not only failed to crush the CCP in Manchuria but also found themselves entrenched in isolated cities in central Manchuria, incapable of effectively supporting each other and unable to withdraw south of the Great Wall. Chiang used his American-supplied air force to resupply Nationalist troops, but this tactic proved ineffective because of administrative corruption and an unwillingness of pilots to fly at appropriately low altitudes for fear of Communist antiaircraft artillery fire. Many of the supplies dropped from Nationalist planes at high altitudes missed the intended target and fell into the hands of the PLA. While the Nationalists held the cities, the Communists controlled the countryside and ground transportation links between cities, effectively cutting Manchuria off from the Nationalist forces in north China. The overextended Nationalist troops in Manchuria gradually fell back into a triangular region around the cities of Shenyang, Changchun, and Jinzhou.

As Lin Biao slowly isolated and surrounded Nationalist troops in Manchuria, Communist forces in north and central China did the same, striking at vulnerable Nationalist positions. With Chiang committing hundreds of thousands of his best troops to Manchuria, the remainder of his forces stretched thinly across the major cities of north and central China. PLA soldiers relied on speed and mobility, attacking railroad lines to isolate enemy positions and make reinforcement difficult. Beginning in August 1947, a PLA force under the command of Liu Bocheng scored a series of successes against Nationalist forces along the Yellow River, isolating and destroying entire units. Liu's forces cut off traffic along the Yellow River and crushed Nationalist units guarding the Longhai (east–west) and Pinghan (north–south) railroads, preventing troop movements in support of threatened positions. This not only boosted CCP morale but also revealed the vulnerability of Chiang's forces in north China, encouraging the CCP to go on the offensive elsewhere. Conditions proved especially ripe in central China where desperately poor peasants joined the CCP in large numbers, swelling the ranks of the PLA. Communist troops went on the offensive, scoring a series of victories in Manchuria and north China, including the recapture of the former CCP base at Yan'an. With each victory, PLA strength and capabilities increased with captured Nationalist weapons and supplies. At the same time, the Nationalist military began to disintegrate and morale plummeted. Large-scale defections, sometimes involving entire units and their officers, bolstered the CCP position by adding new and battle ready forces to the PLA. In this manner the CCP slowly whittled away the Nationalist positions in Manchuria and north China.

The 1947 defeats in central and north China forced Chiang Kai-shek to reevaluate his strategy. When the fighting began in 1946, he had been willing to commit so many troops to Manchuria in part because he believed he had firm control of China south of the Great Wall. The CCP victories along the Yellow River indicated that he needed additional troops to consolidate his hold on central and north China. Some of Chiang's subordinate officers recommended recalling units from Manchuria to positions south of the Great Wall. Major General David Barr, head of the United States Military Advisory Group, warned that the Nationalist forces had overextended themselves and recommended pulling troops back from Manchuria where they could regroup, secure control of north China, and then slowly retake Manchuria through carefully coordinated movements. Chiang refused this advice, intent upon reasserting his government's control over Manchuria.[4]

In the fall of 1947 Chiang attempted to rectify the situation by removing Du Yuming from command of Nationalist troops in Manchuria and replacing him with Chen Cheng, another trusted officer from the Whampoa Academy. Chen advocated a more aggressive approach in Manchuria which required even larger numbers of troops to divide the CCP forces into two groups and destroy them in separate battles. Chiang agreed and gave Chen command of 500,000 troops supplied with new American weapons and equipment to accomplish this goal. In response, Lin Biao returned to the familiar Communist strategy of avoiding large-scale battles while concentrating on disrupting communications and transportation lines that connected the Nationalist forces. Attacking railroad tracks that linked the major cities of Shenyang, Changchun, and Jilin, Lin prevented Chen from implementing his plan by moving his troops with great speed, separating and isolating Nationalist forces so he could attack them individually. As the Nationalist position slowly eroded over the winter of 1947–1948, defections to the Communists became more common, swinging the balance of numbers toward the CCP.

Chiang Kai-shek flew to Shenyang in January 1948 to personally observe Chen Cheng's operations against the CCP. Lin Biao's attacks on supply and transportation lines disrupted Chen's plans and left his troops isolated. Chiang then relieved Chen of his command, replacing him with Li Weihong. Meanwhile, PLA forces captured the port city of Yingkou in February and Jilin and Siping in March. By the early spring of 1948, the Nationalist position in Manchuria had reached the point of desperation as Chiang's forces held on to only a few urban centers while the CCP controlled the countryside and ground routes in and out of Manchuria. Li Weihong asked for reinforcements to protect Shenyang, but few troops could be spared from north China where Nationalist forces faced similar problems. Chiang's air force supported the beleaguered Nationalist forces in Manchuria by bombing and strafing PLA positions, but they proved ineffective and often inflicted more damage on civilians than on the Communists.[5]

In the summer of 1948, Mao announced that the PLA would go on the offensive, emphasizing larger unit mobile warfare, rather than the small and medium unit operations that they had employed up to this point. This marked the beginning of the third stage of the war in which the CCP forces would begin full-scale conventional assaults on Nationalist positions. Having grown in number to some two million soldiers, the PLA slowly closed in on and strangled the isolated Nationalist

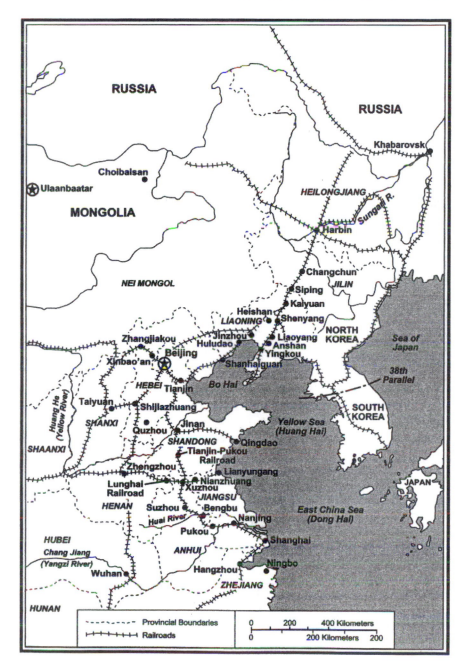

Northeastern China During the Civil War, 1945–1949. From *Chinese Warfighting: The PLA Experience Since 1949,* ed. Mark A. Ryan, David M. Finkelstein, and Michael A. McDevitt (Armonk, NY: M.E. Sharpe, 2003). Copyright © 2003 by the CNA Corporation. Reprinted with permission of M.E. Sharpe, Inc.

units in Manchuria, which depended on air supply for their survival. With dwindling support from an increasingly disillusioned American government, Chiang attempted to reinforce his position in Manchuria with a massive airlift of men and supplies.

Three Final Campaigns

Sensing that the tide had turned in their favor, in the summer of 1948 Mao and the CCP leadership planned a series of major campaigns that would crush Chiang's forces and end the war. In the early stages of the war, the PLA had operated with a degree of decentralized decision-making in which individual commanders enjoyed flexibility in planning their attacks in carrying out Mao's general strategy of People's War. In late 1948 and early 1949, Mao and the MAC asserted greater central control and co-ordination in planning and conducting large-scale campaigns. The weakening of the Nationalists and growth of its own forces meant that the PLA now enjoyed numerical superiority in some battles, allowing for larger operations involving divisions and entire armies. Beginning with a concentrated attempt to conquer Manchuria, taking the last major cities held by the Nationalists in October and November of 1948, the CCP launched three successive campaigns that broke the back of the Nationalist military and resulted in a victory for the Chinese Communists. The Liaoning–Shenyang, Huai–Hai, and Beijing–Tianjin campaigns paved the way for the end of the civil war and the establishment of a new Communist government in China.

The first of these final campaigns, the Liaoning–Shenyang Campaign, began in western Liaoning Province in Manchuria in September 1948. Following up on the momentum from victories in late 1947 and 1948, 700,000 PLA troops attacked the remaining major cities in Manchuria in order to bring it under complete control. First isolating each city before attacking, PLA forces captured Jinzhou and Changchun in mid-October, defended by 120,000 and 80,000 Nationalist troops, respectively. In early November, PLA forces attacked and took control of Shenyang, defeating or taking the surrender of 230,000 defenders. Having cut off all supply lines and ground transportation, the besieged Nationalist forces could not retreat overland to north China nor could they evacuate by air. When they managed to briefly recapture the port at Yingkou in October and gain access to the ocean passage to north China, rather than attempt to evacuate troops from Shenyang the Nationalists concentrated on defending their positions. The conquest of these cities put hundreds of thousands of Nationalist forces out of commission, many of which joined the PLA and contributed massive amounts of American-made weapons and ammunition to Communist stockpiles. It also freed PLA troops in Manchuria to move south of the Great Wall to participate in campaigns against Nationalist-held cities in northern and central China. Chiang quickly shifted his attention to regrouping and holding on to north China in preparation for the next CCP campaign. The loss of so many of Chiang Kai-shek's best troops in Manchuria represented a dramatic reversal of fortune for the Nationalists. Just eighteen months earlier Chiang seemed poised for victory as his forces captured the Communist capital at Yan'an and put Mao to flight. The devastating and demoralizing loss of Manchuria set off a chain of military defeats that spelled the end of Nationalist rule on the Chinese mainland.

The Huai–Hai Campaign, the largest and most decisive of the three final campaigns, began in November 1948 and continued through early January 1949. Under the command of General Su Yu, the PLA followed similar tactics employed in Manchuria, moving with great speed, surrounding and isolating individual Nationalist forces, and then applying concentrated force in order to drive them south of the Yangzi River. The Communists identified Chiang Kai-shek's headquarters at the city of Xuzhou, located at the junction of critical north–south and east–west rail lines, as a key objective which would give them control of the railroads north of the Yangzi River. Utilizing the labor of hundreds of thousands of peasants who assisted with transportation and supplies and employing heavy artillery captured from the Nationalists, PLA forces defeated Nationalist armies under the command of Du Yuming and Liu Zhi. Typically, the Nationalists remained in static positions, defending cities or rail lines, which rendered them vulnerable to the mobile tactics of the PLA. While artillery pounded the center of Nationalist positions, the Second and Third Field Armies of the PLA spread out to the flanks cutting off retreat and pushing the enemy forces into the shelling at the center. Chiang had not expected the CCP to launch a second campaign so quickly on the heels of the conquest of Manchuria and had little time to prepare. PLA forces captured Xuzhou in January 1949. The Huai–Hai Campaign ultimately cost Chiang more than 400,000 Nationalist troops, crippling his military capabilities. He offered to negotiate a settlement with the CCP, which rejected his offer and demanded his unconditional surrender. Chiang resigned as president of the Republic of China on January 10, 1949, turning the reins of government over to his vice-president Li Zongren.

Before the conclusion of the Huai–Hai Campaign, the CCP leadership prepared another campaign in north China designed to take control of the major cities that the CCP forces had bypassed on the way to Xuzhou. This third and final Beijing–Tianjin Campaign prevented Chiang from regrouping in north China and secured control of Beijing, Tianjin, Zhangjiakou, and the entire north China plain. The campaign began in November and ran through January, with PLA troops pouring into north China from Manchuria to capture these major cities, killing, wounding, or capturing of hundreds of thousands of Nationalist troops.

The combined impact of the Liaoning–Shenyang, Huai–Hai, and Beijing–Tianjin campaigns destroyed Nationalist power in north China and forced Chiang's armies to fall back in disarray. Still facing the internal divisions which had plagued the Nationalist military since the end of the Northern Expedition, Chiang refused to delegate authority to others and continued to micromanage the war effort. He distrusted some of his more capable commanders, such as Li Zongren, Bai Chongxi, and Xue Yue, who did not belong to his Central Army. Moreover, some regional commanders refused to come to the aid of others when needed. Low morale in Nationalist units can be tied in part to economic problems. Chiang's government could not control inflation, which meant that soldiers could not support their families and officers saw their savings disappear overnight. This eroded confidence in the ability of Chiang's government to lead the nation, prompting demoralized Nationalist troops to surrender or desert in large numbers. The Communists dealt effectively with the inflation problem by issuing pay to the soldiers in the form of everyday goods and sundries. Moreover, when Nationalist troops surrendered or defected, the CCP welcomed them with open arm and treated them well. After a brief political indoctrination, surrendered Nationalist soldiers commonly had the choice of joining the PLA or simply returning home with a promise to fight no more.

In control of Manchuria and north China, the Communists regrouped in early 1949 to prepare for an assault on southern China. PLA armies marched west and south, rapidly taking control of large cities and mopping up remaining Nationalist forces. In May, several important cities in the lower Yangzi River region fell to Communist forces, including Nanjing, Shanghai, and Hangzhou, with only token resistance from the rapidly collapsing Nationalist military. Chiang Kai-shek withdrew from Shanghai to Guangzhou and from there prepared to evacuate to the island of Taiwan. Anticipating rapid victory, the CCP formed what it called a democratic coalition government, dominated by the CCP but including representatives of other smaller political parties. Mao Zedong served as chairman of the new government which designated Beijing as the capital, restoring that city's earlier name. On October 1, 1949, Mao announced the establishment of the PRC (People's Republic of China), initiating a new phase of China's history with Communist rule on the Chinese mainland. Chiang and thousands of his followers fled to the island of Taiwan, which had been prepared as a last retreat in case of emergency. PLA forces attempted to pursue the Nationalists and take control of Taiwan, but the lack of adequate naval forces and failed attempts to take offshore islands convinced Mao and the CCP leadership to shelve plans for attacking Taiwan. PLA forces instead marched west to Xinjiang and Tibet, bringing both under Communist control. Chiang's Nationalist regime remained in power on Taiwan for the next several decades.

The rapid collapse of the Nationalist military and government and the Communist victory in the civil war can be attributed to a combination forces. One might point to the economic problems that plagued the Nationalist government in the final years of the war against Japan and throughout the postwar conflict with the CCP. Inflation, already rampant during the war with Japan, spiraled out of control after 1945. Partly the result of the Nationalist practice of printing massive amounts of new money to meet its needs, inflation and financial mismanagement prolonged the suffering of the Chinese people even after victory over Japan and rendered millions of Chinese impoverished and disillusioned.[6] Misconduct and corruption among Nationalist officials also undermined Chiang's government. In restoring Nationalist authority to areas that had been occupied by the Japanese during the war, Nationalist officials acted as returning conquerors and "carpet baggers." Using their authority to enrich themselves rather than to see to the needs of those who had lived under Japanese rule, some Nationalist officials manipulated exchange rates to amass personal fortunes. Others seized property from the Japanese and sold it off to the highest bidder rather than returning it to the rightful prewar owners. Showing little concern for the common people who had lived through eight years of war and occupation, Nationalist officials did much to alienate the residents of the major cities of the east and north. This eroded confidence in Chiang's government and led many to seriously consider political alternatives to the Nationalists. The regime acted with a heavy hand against critics, labeling them Communist sympathizers, further contributing to the discontent among the people.[7]

In contrast to Nationalist weaknesses, one can point to the effectiveness of the CCP to explain the Communist victory. The CCP won the support of rural Chinese, an essential element of Mao's strategy of People's War, and created large peasant armies by advocating and implementing land reform. In areas it controlled during the Sino-Japanese War and after, the CCP targeted the poor peasants and farm workers who had received nothing from the Nationalist government and promised to improve their lives through a land reform campaign or educational opportunities. This group formed the base of support that carried the CCP to power in the civil war. CCP cadres showed a great degree of flexibility and a willingness to adjust policy according to local conditions in order to win support in areas not afflicted by high rates of tenancy or in urban areas where residents had a different set of priorities and grievances. By positioning itself as the protector local interests, whatever they might be, against what it described as a predatory Nationalist regime, the CCP won far broader support than its agrarian policies would have achieved on their own.[8] The Communist military also proved itself more disciplined than the Nationalist military which offered a promise of effective government under the Communists. When entering new cities or reoccupying areas after the Japanese surrender, the CCP did not act as conquerors or carpetbaggers but rather made a concerted effort to win the support of the local people. The discipline and good behavior of the Communists compared favorably with the poor discipline and corruption of the Nationalists.

Such socioeconomic factors influenced the course of the civil war and help explain the position of each combatant, but did not necessarily determine the outcome of the war. In 1945, Chiang's Nationalist government and military enjoyed a substantial advantage over Mao and the CCP. The Nationalist military stood at more than twice the size of the Communist Red Army and enjoyed the material support of the United States which provided substantial amounts of weapons, ammunition, equipment, and even an air force. Chiang's government also had domestic and international legitimacy and access to the majority of the Chinese population for purposes of taxation and conscription. As Odd Arne Westad has argued, the Nationalist defeat in the civil war stemmed primarily from a series of poor decisions and tactical errors.[9] For example, Chiang insisted on a military campaign to subdue the CCP in 1946 even though his government and military had not yet recovered sufficiently from the ravages of the war with Japan. The Nationalist military may have enjoyed greater numbers and better equipment than the Communist troops, but the eight years of brutal combat with Japanese forces left them exhausted, war-weary, and unprepared to quickly deploy for a renewed civil war.

The Communists, on the other hand, had vastly expanded and modernized their main force military units during the war with Japan, and PLA soldiers showed greater motivation and morale. Moreover, Chiang's decision to commit large numbers of troops to Manchuria before consolidating his control of China south of the Great Wall rendered his force vulnerable to the guerrilla attacks and mobile operations at which the Communist forces excelled. The loss of Manchuria in 1948, along with hundreds of thousands of Nationalist troops, dealt Chiang and his supporters a blow from which they could not recover. Finally, the CCP showed greater flexibility in both military and political activities which allowed it to take advantage of Nationalist mistakes. Using guerrilla tactics where appropriate and eventually transitioning into large-scale conventional attacks, the PLA attacked Nationalist weak points, offsetting its superior numbers and firepower.

CHAPTER 11

China and the Korean War, 1950–1953

In the months following establishment of the PRC in October 1949, PLA units pushed to the south and west in order to "mop up" remaining Nationalist forces. Chinese troops invaded Tibet in October 1950, pressuring the Dalai Lama to accept Chinese sovereignty over the region, which brought the approximate borders of the former Qing dynasty under Communist control, with the notable exceptions of Taiwan and Mongolia. Mao and the CCP leaders busied themselves extending their control across the length and breadth of China, preparing for a nationwide land reform campaign, a reorganization of China's industrial sector, and generally attempting to rebuild China after over a decade of war. Events in Korea, however, led the PRC to put its reconstruction efforts on hold and again concentrate on military affairs.

Mao's "Lean to One Side"

With regard to foreign policy, Mao had made it clear that the PRC would "lean to one side," supporting the Soviet Union in the emerging Cold War. From the CCP perspective, American military and economic aid to Chiang Kai-shek's regime during the civil war, totaling US $2 billion from 1945 to 1949, clearly indicated a hostile attitude toward the PRC as did Washington's refusal to recognize Mao's new government. From the American perspective, Mao's bellicose statements about American imperialism, his visit to the Soviet Union in December 1949 to meet with Josef Stalin, the resulting Sino-Soviet Treaty of 1950, and formal recognition of the PRC by the Soviet bloc countries placed China squarely in the enemy camp.

Despite Mao's statements of Sino-Soviet solidarity, the relationship between these two Communist leaders showed signs of strain. While in Moscow, his first time outside of China, Mao appealed to Stalin for economic and military support for reconstruction and completing the unification of China, including planes with which to attack Taiwan. Stalin expressed support for PRC plans with regard to Taiwan and after several weeks of discussion agreed to a security treaty that obligated the Soviet Union to protect China in the event of an attack and provided modest economic support in the form of a US $300 million loan. The Soviets also promised to evacuate Lushun and Dalian by 1952, the last vestiges of the old Russian concessions in

Liaodong, returning these ports to Chinese sovereignty. In return, Mao had to recognize the independence of the Mongolian People's Republic, which remained firmly under Soviet influence. Mao had hoped for greater generosity from Stalin, but he accepted the treaty and returned to China to continue building a new socialist state.

Taiwan posed a difficult problem for the new government, as Chiang's Nationalist regime continued to claim its place as the legitimate government of all of China and threatened to recapture the mainland. Mao and the CCP had every intention of "liberating" Taiwan and completing the revolution, but delayed an immediate attack. PLA commanders at the time did not believe their troops could mount a successful armed invasion of Taiwan because of logistical problems and a lack of air and naval capabilities. Earlier assaults on offshore islands, including Jinmen off the coast of Fujian and Dengbu near the Zhejiang coast, resulted in defeat and convinced CCP leaders to exercise caution with regard to Taiwan. Chiang's government had consolidated control over the island, with nearly one million men under arms. Mao moved PLA units into Fujian Province opposite to Taiwan but made no immediate move to attack the island. The fact that the United States continued to support Chiang Kai-shek complicated the issue and indicated to the PRC leaders that the United States posed the greatest threat to China's national security. Despite some initial hope on both sides that a working relationship might develop between the United States and the PRC, mutual distrust and deep suspicion made this difficult as the Cold War spread from its origins in Europe into a global struggle. Regardless, the outbreak of fighting in Korea in June 1950 destroyed any chance of normal relations between the United States and the PRC and alienated the two states for decades.[1]

Origins of the Korean War

The origins of the war in Korea go back to Japan's colonization of Korea in 1910 which made it part of the Japanese empire until the end of the Pacific War in August 1945. During the period of Japanese rule, a Korean nationalist movement emerged and set up a government-in-exile in northeastern China under Syngman Rhee, a Western-educated Korean nationalist who served as president. In the 1920s, Koreans living in Russia organized a Korean Communist Party, which enjoyed economic and political support from the Soviet Union and eventually began operating in northwestern Korea. In the last days of the Pacific War, Soviet troops invaded Manchuria and pushed across the border into northern Korea. According to the hastily arranged occupation agreement, a line drawn across the 38th parallel divided Korea into two zones. Soviet forces accepted the surrender of Japanese soldiers in Korea north of the 38th parallel and American troops did the same to the south. Never intended to permanently divide the country, the division of Korea would become a lasting boundary.

At the Yalta Conference in February 1945, Franklin Roosevelt and Josef Stalin discussed plans for postwar Korea, including the possibility of a trusteeship to prepare it for independence after Japan's defeat. Yet almost immediately after assuming postwar occupation duty both powers began to take steps away from unification of the peninsula. American forces controlled southern Korea through a pro-Western Korean government while the Soviets governed northern Korea through Korean "People's Committees." The two zones increasingly acted as separate entities, widening the gulf between them and in effect creating two Korean states. Soviet and American negotiators failed to agree on how to unify the two zones to create an independent Korean government. As a result of the rise of Cold War tensions in the early postwar years, neither the Americans nor Soviets would accept the government sponsored by the other. In 1947, the United Nations took up the issue of Korean independence, creating a commission to supervise elections for a national assembly and a single national government. According to the UN plan, both American and Soviet forces would withdraw once the new government took power. The Soviets and their Korean allies in the north boycotted the UN commission, but the Americans went forward with elections in the southern zone in May 1948. A "national" assembly and a new government called the ROK (Republic of Korea) emerged, with Syngman Rhee as president. In retaliation, the Soviet Union sponsored elections in the northern zone, which established a separate "national" government, the DPRK (Democratic People's Republic of Korea) under Korean Communist leader Kim Il-sung. Shortly thereafter, the Soviets withdrew from North Korea, followed by an American withdrawal from the south in June of 1949. Both the United States and the Soviet Union left behind millions of dollars worth of military equipment.

By January 1950, American leaders had come to see Mao and the PRC as a part of the Soviet Union's plan for aggressive expansion of communist ideology. Fearful of the consequences of the spread of communist influence in Asia and the successful testing of an atomic weapon in the Soviet Union, President Harry Truman directed the Secretaries of State and Defense to assess the long-term goals of American foreign policy vis-a-vis the Soviet Union and its allies. The resulting document, National Security Council Memorandum Number 68 or NSC-68, served as a guiding light for U.S. national security policy. It characterized the Soviet Union, and its ally the PRC, as part of monolithic communist bloc intent upon territorial expansion and called for substantial increases in U.S. military spending to meet this threat. As the United States government grew increasingly concerned with Soviet and Chinese intentions, Mao Zedong and the leaders of the PRC worried about American involvement in three key areas on China's periphery. American support for Chiang Kai-shek's government on Taiwan, for the French attempt at colonial restoration in Indochina, and for the Republic of Korea aroused Chinese fears of encirclement by the United States and its allies. Mutual fear and suspicion created a security dilemma in which each side perceived the other as a potential threat and contributed to the international crisis that arose with the June 1950 outbreak of the Korean War.

North Korean Attack

Kim Il-sung had been planning a military action against the ROK since 1949 and had met with Stalin in April 1950 to secure Soviet support. After consultations with Stalin, Kim visited Beijing in May and briefed Mao Zedong on his plans for the attack, omitting most of the details. Mao valued the DPRK leader as an important comrade, as Kim Il-sung had a long association with the Chinese Communists, had participated in military operations against the Japanese in Manchuria, and even spoke Chinese. Mao did not express great enthusiasm for the plan, doubting its chances for success, but he nonetheless extended moral support for the attack. Kim did not ask for Chinese participation in the attack, convinced that Soviet material support would be sufficient. Neither Kim nor Mao believed that the United States would send troops to Korea and even if it did, Kim believed his forces would crush the ROK military in a matter of weeks, before the Americans could organize a defense of the south.[2]

Mao's doubts about Kim's plan reflect his preoccupation with domestic affairs and concern that war in neighboring Korea might disrupt his attempts to build a strong, socialist China. PRC leaders had been busy crafting the new Agrarian Reform Law of June 1950 which outlined a massive program to confiscate land and property from China's "landlord" class and redistribute it to the masses of landless peasants. Clearly, Mao had been concentrating on the economic reorganization of China rather than resolving the Korean issue by force. That Mao had no intention of waging war in Korea is supported by the fact that in the spring of 1950 the CCP leadership decided to begin a massive demobilization campaign within the PLA which would reduce its numbers by 1.4 million soldiers. This would not only alleviate the expense of supporting these troops but also free them up for service in other areas. With the exception of Kim's briefing in May 1950, PRC leaders had little detailed knowledge of the situation in the DPRK. The Chinese ambassador to Pyongyang did not even reach his post until August, over one month after the war began.[3]

On the early morning of June 25, 1950, more than 100,000 troops of the KPA (Korean People's Army) charged south across the demilitarized zone at the 38th parallel supported by heavily armored Russian tanks, attacking along a 150 mile-wide front. ROK troops broke under the impact of the assault and withdrew southward. Drawing comparisons between the Korean, Chinese, and Soviet Communists and earlier European fascists Benito Mussolini and Adolf Hitler, President Harry Truman viewed this attack in the context of German aggression in Europe and World War II. He concluded that failure to respond would be tantamount to appeasement and would have adverse consequences for the United States and its allies in Asia. Assuming that the USSR had been the true driving force behind the attack, he interpreted the DPRK assault as a test of American willingness to stand by its allies.[4]

Truman quickly brought the issue to the UN Security Council which on June 27 passed a resolution condemning the attack and declaring that the DPRK had breached the peace. As a permanent member of the Security Council, the Soviet Union could have used its veto power to prevent this resolution, but it had no representative at the meeting because of its boycott of the United Nations over its refusal to offer China's seat on the Security Council to the PRC. Chiang's government on Taiwan still held China's UN seat and would continue to do so until 1971. The Security Council urged member nations to furnish assistance to the ROK to help fend off the attack. The ROK government appealed directly to the United States for help, and Truman promptly authorized General Douglas MacArthur, Supreme Commander of Allied Powers in command of the occupation force in Japan, to use American air and naval forces to attack KPA forces south of the 38th parallel. Truman also ordered the Seventh Fleet of the United States Navy to take up a position in the Straits of Taiwan, fearing that the PRC might take advantage of the situation to launch an attack on Taiwan. MacArthur quickly assessed the situation and told Truman that he required American ground forces to stop the KPA advance into South Korea. Truman agreed and authorized the use of American ground forces stationed in Japan, ordered American pilots to bomb locations inside the DPRK, and established a naval blockade of the Korean coast. Although he did not seek formal Congressional approval for a declaration of war, Truman met with Congressional leaders who offered bipartisan support. Many members of the Truman administration and the U.S. Congress shared the view that the DPRK attack challenged American ability to support its allies and felt that a failure to respond to this challenge would damage American credibility.

On July 7, the UN Security Council passed a resolution recommending a unified command under the United States to direct military actions and to restore peace on the Korean peninsula. As commander of the combined UN forces in Korea, General MacArthur commanded troops from sixteen member nations which dispatched armed forces to South Korea, though American and ROK troops constituted 90 percent of the combat forces. The first American troops to reach Korea fell back before the well-organized communist assault, but the KPA offensive soon ran out of steam as its troops tired and outran their supply lines. In early August, UN forces established a defensive perimeter around the port of Pusan at the southeastern tip of the Korean peninsula while American bombers pounded KPA forces and supply lines.

When the war began, the PLA had only one army of approximately 50,000 soldiers along the Yalu River, which forms the border between the PRC and DPRK. Alarmed by the rapid reaction of the United States and the United Nations in defense of the ROK, in July Mao began moving PLA armies from locations in southern China to the northeast and reorganized them as a NEBDA (Northeast Border Defense Army) under the command of General Su Yu. Most of these troops came from the elite Fourth Field Army which had done much of the critical fighting in the Chinese civil war. PLA commanders did their best to conceal the troop movements, keeping these forces hidden from American reconnaissance flights. By the end of July, nearly 225,000 PLA troops had moved to the PRC–DPRK border along with stockpiles of weapons, ammunition, and supplies, as PRC leaders kept a close eye on developments in Korea.

The Inchon Landing

A turning point in the war came on September 15, 1950, when American forces launched an amphibious assault at Inchon, on the west coast of the ROK near the 38th parallel. A difficult operation because of complicated tides and mud flats, American troops went ashore hundreds of miles behind KPA lines and severed lines

of supply and retreat. Although the Soviets and Chinese had warned Kim Il-sung of
the likelihood of such an attack, it caught all parties by surprise as American troops
moved across the peninsula, cutting off KPA troops in the south from those north
of the 38th parallel. Thousands of KPA troops surrendered while those that could
withdrew back north of the 38th parallel.

At this point the PRC leadership began to openly criticize the United States
and its allies for "imperialist aggression" in Korea, claiming that "North Korea's
defense is our defense" which suggested that China might defend North Korea.
Although Mao had not been involved in the planning for the attack, he believed
that under the circumstances the PRC must provide support to the DPRK and be
prepared to send Chinese troops to Korea should Kim Il-sung make a request for
help. The likelihood that Chinese troops would have to fight in Korea increased dramatically in late September when Truman ordered MacArthur to send American
forces north of the 38th parallel, exceeding the original objective of defending the
ROK and raising the possibility of overthrowing the DPRK, uniting the Korean
peninsula, and "rolling back" the spread of Communism in Asia. In late September
and early October 1950, ROK and American forces crossed the 38th parallel and
began pushing toward the DPRK capital at Pyongyang. PRC leaders watched as
American forces advanced across the 38th parallel and the U.S. Seventh Fleet
protected Taiwan, forcing them to shelve any ideas of attacking Chiang's government
in the near future. Chinese officials would debate how to respond this development,
but Mao believed strongly that they should support the DPRK. In fact, a PLA
advance team crossed the border into the DPRK on September 20, scouting the
terrain in preparation for possible military operations.

The Inchon landing had dramatically reversed the military situation and placed
the KPA squarely on the defensive. As a result, on October 1 Kim Il-sung sent a telegram to Mao Zedong asking him to send Chinese troops to the DPRK to support
the KPA. The next day Mao convened a meeting of the Politburo at which the top
leaders of the PRC discussed the situation and the advisability of direct participation
in the fighting. Several prominent political and military leaders expressed concerns
about engaging the United States in a military conflict so soon after establishing
the new Chinese state. Lin Biao, commander of the Fourth Field Army and hero
of the Manchurian campaigns of the civil war, and Gao Gang, chairman of the
northeastern region, argued that the PRC had not yet the strength to fight a successful war against the United States. American technology and firepower, including the
possible use of atomic bombs, put the PLA at a distinct disadvantage. Carrying
mostly small arms and unable to match American artillery and airpower, they
believed that the PLA should remain in Manchuria while the CCP leadership
concentrated on economic reconstruction.[5]

Although the meeting entertained such dissenting views, Mao favored intervention
and carried the day. He acknowledged the concerns raised by Lin, Gang, and others,
but pointed out that China enjoyed certain advantages as well. The UN force in
Korea totaled 440,000 troops, but the ROK contingent accounted for almost half
of this force. Mao believed that the number of troops the United States could send

to Korea had limits and that Chinese forces would therefore enjoy numerical superiority in head-to-head combat. Nor did he worry about the potential use of atomic weapons against China, arguing that China's vast size and population would limit their effect. Finally, he argued that the Americans had a larger plan of aggression in East Asia and that the PRC would eventually have to go to war against the United States. Why not fight in Korea where the terrain favored the Chinese style of fighting, the PLA supply lines would be short, and the American logistical chain long and complicated?

Beyond the practical issues of numerical superiority and terrain, Mao had more fundamental geopolitical and ideological reasons for wanting to send Chinese troops to support the DRPK. First, the presence of American military forces on the border posed a direct threat to China's national security. If successful in Korea, Mao believed the United States would then attack the PRC. Manchuria, with its important deposits of iron and coal and home to nearly 80 percent of China's industry at the time, had to be protected. Second, Mao believed that the PRC had an obligation to support fraternal communist parties seeking to carry out their own revolutions. Ironically, just as many in the U.S. government saw Korea as a test of American resolve and willingness to support allies, Mao had his own version of a "domino theory" in which a loss for the "revolutionary camp" would lead to greater attacks from the "reactionary camp" led by the United States. Third, Mao believed that his own revolution in China still faced many challenges and an American victory in Korea might incite the forces of "counterrevolution" in China, pro-Guomindang or anticommunist elements, to rise up against Mao's government. The new PRC government, according to Mao, had to demonstrate to its people that it could protect China from external and internal threats. Mao also used the Korean crisis to mobilize the masses for continuing the revolution in China and making the transition to socialism. In August 1950, huge rallies took place across China as part of a mass campaign to "Resist America, Support Korea" designed to energize the Chinese people in support of the DPRK, but also to engage in socialist construction at home, such as land reform and collectivization. Finally, from the Chinese perspective, American aggression provided the root cause of the conflict and the PRC occupied the moral high ground on this issue. After UN forces crossed the 38th parallel and entered the DPRK, Chinese soldiers would not be attacking the ROK but rather defending the DPRK.[6]

Although convinced that the PRC must fight in Korea, Mao would not commit Chinese troops until Kim Il-song specifically requested help. Kim hoped to win the war on his own, but the rapid response of the U.S. and UN forces and the American landing at Inchon forced him to turn to Mao for help. At the October 2 meeting, the CCP Politburo agreed with Mao's arguments and authorized intervention. Foreign minister Zhou Enlai denounced the United States as China's most dangerous enemy and sent warnings to American leaders through speeches and indirect messages via the Indian ambassador to the PRC, declaring that China would not tolerate aggression against its neighbors. Such warning presaged Chinese intervention in Korea, but few Americans took these signs seriously. Observers in Washington tended to view such statements as bravado designed to conceal the fact that the PRC forces had poor weapons and equipment, no air support, and continued to deal with the monumental problem of economic reconstruction. Both Truman and MacArthur discounted the Chinese threat as U.S. and UN troops advanced north toward the Yalu River. Meanwhile, the PLA moved additional troops to Manchuria and the DPRK–PRC border.

In preparation for action in Korea, General Peng Dehuai, a CCP military leader dating back to the days at the Jiangxi Soviet, assumed overall command of the NEBDA. Two other prominent generals, Lin Biao and Su Yu, had declined command because of poor health. In order to avoid a formal state of war with the United States, which might invite an attack on the PRC and drag the Soviet Union into a conflict that could result in World War III, Mao made no declaration of war. Since the appearance of PLA forces in Korea could be construed as an act of war, NEBDA forces took the name "Chinese People's Volunteers" (CPV), implying that Chinese soldiers fighting in Korea had all volunteered to support a neighboring state. This title also reflected the Chinese view of the moral justness of their cause. In reality, all CPV came from PLA units and retained the same officers, enlisted men, and organization. They simply removed all PLA insignias from their uniforms, including the red star on their military caps.[7]

Chinese Intervention

In early October, Mao gave the final order for Chinese troops to hasten preparations for joining the war and to begin crossing the border. On October 19, the first of 260,000 CPV troops stationed on the border at Andong began crossing the Yalu River on pontoon bridges, moving only at night to avoid detection. Mao had hoped for a brief conventional struggle in which, with Soviet air support, the CPV would destroy U.S. and UN forces and solve the Korean issue in favor of Kim Il-sung's DPRK. Yet in early October Stalin retracted an earlier promise to provide air support for Chinese troops, forcing Mao to alter his strategy. The new strategy called for the CPV to establish a defensive base of operations in the area just across the border in North Korea. In the face of superior firepower and mechanization, Mao returned to the basic strategy and tactics that had brought success in earlier conflicts against the Nationalists and the Japanese. Rather than take up static positions and try to hold them, the CPV would allow the UN forces to advance toward the Yalu River, "luring them deep" in preparation for attacks on their flanks and rear areas, applying concentrated power to the enemy's weak points. Mao again advocated an "active defense," relying on speed and mobility to launch decisive operations against specific targets as a part of an overall defensive strategy. Mao sought not to capture and retain control of territory so much as to inflict significant casualties on the U.S. and UN forces, gradually weakening the Americans to the point at which they could not continue the war.[8]

On October 25, Chinese troops suddenly appeared in battle against ROK troops at Unsan, wiping out a battalion and driving the survivors southward before withdrawing back toward the Yalu River. CPV forces again attacked on October 28, defeating ROK units near Onjong. Although Chinese commanders feared that these engagements would alert the Americans to the presence of Chinese troops in Korea and eliminate the element of surprise, MacArthur still believed that the Chinese would not join the fighting. He knew that PRC had massed troops on the border and that some Chinese soldiers had been taken prisoner by ROK troops, but he still believed that the Chinese would limit themselves to defending their own territory and would not commit large numbers of troops to battle in Korea. As a result, American forces continued to march north in two columns as MacArthur planned an offensive to end the war and unify the peninsula, expressing confidence that "the boys" would be "home for Christmas." The Eighth Army under General Walton Walker advanced on the western side of the peninsula through Pyongyang and toward Unsan, while the U.S. Marine X Corps under General Edward Almond did the same in the east, from Wonsan north toward the Changjin (Chosin) Reservoir. The mountainous terrain of the north separated the two forces, putting more than fifty miles of difficult ground between them.

Once again using the strategy of "luring the enemy deep" before launching decisive attacks, Peng Dehuai moved additional CPV units across the border to take a favorable position in the area north of the Changjin Reservoir in preparation for a second offensive. At the same time, he intentionally released a number of ROK and U.S. prisoners, hoping that they would return to their own lines believing that the Chinese intended to withdraw to the border. On November 25, over 200,000 Chinese troops poured out of the mountains to attack unsuspecting U.S. troops. Taking advantage of the terrain which divided the American forces, the CPV attacked the Eighth Army and X Corps individually, catching them unprepared for such a massive assault. The outnumbered U.S. and ROK forces fell back from the Changjin Reservoir in a bloody retreat over miles of frozen ground. By the middle of December, CPV and KPA forces had retaken Pyongyang and driven all U.S. and UN forces south of the 38th parallel.

Chinese troops had won impressive victories in their first two campaigns of the war, but they faced significant logistical problems which rendered further offensive action difficult. CPV soldiers carried mostly small arms, had little artillery, and had no air support. Ammunition and food had to move along a tortuously slow route supply route which proved inadequate for keeping the soldiers properly provisioned. A severe shortage of trucks, which could travel only at night with all lights off, meant that supplies moved primarily by animal and human transport, covering at best twenty miles per night. After reneging on his initial promise to provide air support for Chinese forces, in November 1950 Stalin ultimately authorized Soviet MiG planes and pilots to fly limited missions within thirty miles of the PRC–DPRK border. Yet Soviet pilots did not support CPV campaigns nor did they protect the long supply lines which remained vulnerable to American bombing.[9] Having rapidly advanced hundreds of miles down the peninsula by the end of December, CPV soldiers grew increasingly weary and hungry, but their supplies met only 25–30 percent of their needs.[10] Moreover, the cotton-padded uniforms of the Chinese soldiers provided little protection against the subzero temperatures of the Korean winter. The lack of warm gloves, caps, and boots left soldiers vulnerable to illness which incapacitated large numbers of

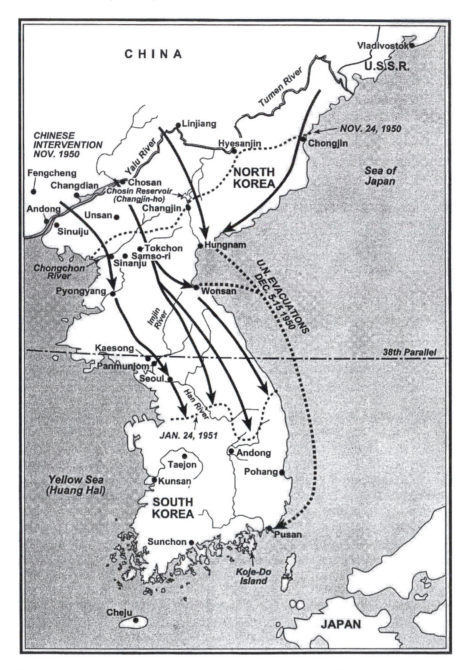

The Korean War. From *Chinese Warfighting: The PLA Experience Since 1949,* ed. Mark A. Ryan, David M. Finkelstein, and Michael A. McDevitt (Armonk, NY: M.E. Sharpe, 2003). Copyright © 2003 by the CNA Corporation. Reprinted with permission of M.E. Sharpe, Inc.

troops. One Chinese captain recalled that his division lost 700 soldiers to frostbite in its first week of action in November 1950.[11] Unlike earlier conflicts fought inside China, Chinese soldiers could not depend on local villagers to support them nor could they live off the land. In some cases they had to trade valuable supplies to local Korean peasants for small amounts of food.

Under these conditions, Peng Dehuai recommended waiting before beginning a third campaign in order to allow the troops to rest, recuperate, and resupply. Back in Beijing, Mao learned of the successes of the first two campaigns and overestimated the capabilities of Chinese forces in Korea. Having long held the view that the power of the human will could overcome material obstacles, Mao ordered Peng to continue with another offensive operation. The Chinese soldier, Mao believed, with greater numbers and higher morale could triumph over American firepower and material strength. Peng warned Mao of the logistical problems and fatigue of the troops, but reluctantly agreed to launch another campaign. He chose December 31, the night of a full moon and an American holiday, to launch the third campaign in which CPV forces crossed the 38th parallel and drove U.S. and UN forces out of Seoul, the ROK capital. Peng halted the advance of the weary CPV soldiers in early January 1951.

The capture of Seoul proved a fleeting victory as UN forces made a swift counter-attack in late January, catching the Chinese troops unprepared. Again, Peng advocated withdrawal in order to preserve Chinese strength, falling back on more easily defendable positions, while Mao again ordered an attack. Mao still hoped that aggressive CPV action could destroy U.S. and UN forces and reunify the Korean peninsula. Kim Il-sung and KPA generals agreed with Mao and criticized Peng Dehuai for hesitating. The fourth CPV campaign illustrated the validity of Peng's warnings as exhausted and ill-equipped Chinese forces withered in the face of vastly superior firepower. U.S. and UN forces pushed the lines of battle back toward the north, inflicting horrific casualties on Chinese troops. In February, Peng returned to Beijing to meet with Mao and other leaders in order to convince them of the need to delay further campaigns until the troops had a chance to prepare properly. His sobering assessment of the situation had some effect, as two months past before the fifth and final CPV offensive campaign of the war. In the meantime, the UN tried to arrange a ceasefire and peace talks, but Mao refused to engage in talks prior to the removal of all foreign troops from Korea. Instead, the UN General Assembly condemned China as an aggressor on February 1, 1951.

After two months of preparations, the Chinese launched their largest offensive of the war, involving 700,000 CPV and KPA troops. This fifth campaign began in April 1951 and lasted for over a month, but again the superior firepower of the U.S. and UN forces wreaked havoc on the Chinese, forcing an end to the campaign in May. U.S. troops had halted the Chinese offensive just below the 38th parallel. The failure of the fifth campaign forced Mao to reconsider his strategy and abandon his goal of unifying the Korean peninsula under DPRK rule. Unable to destroy his enemy, Mao abandoned large campaigns of annihilation in favor of small-scale attacks designed to gradually weaken U.S. and UN forces. CPV forces dug in at the 38th parallel and erected defensive fortifications for positional defense and smaller unit attacks. Mao now hoped that the mounting toll of casualties and stalemated battlefront would convince American leaders to negotiate a peace settlement on Beijing's terms.

Stalemate and Armistice

Despite earlier pleas for caution, Peng Dehuai still hoped to break the stalemate at the 38th parallel and made tentative plans for a sixth campaign for the fall of 1951. Peng and Mao eventually shelved the plan when it became clear that the costs would be too great. By this time, important changes in the American war effort had already taken place. General MacArthur claimed that victory in Korea required bombing targets inside China as well the use of Chiang Kai-shek's forces from Taiwan in diversionary attacks on the China coast. His statements about employing nuclear weapons and "unleashing Chiang Kai-shek" irritated Truman and others who feared that such action would bring the Soviet Union into the struggle and possibly precipitate World War III. MacArthur eventually went public with his disagreement with Truman, openly criticizing U.S. foreign policy. For example, on March 24, 1951, as Truman tried to arrange for a ceasefire in Korea, MacArthur issued a statement in which he advocated an attack on the PRC and threatened the use of atomic weapons. In April, Truman relieved MacArthur of his command, replacing him with General Matthew Ridgway.

Mao had earlier rejected an invitation to negotiations, but in June 1951 he agreed to participate in ceasefire talks proposed by the Soviet Union. His willingness to begin peace talks came after he concluded that CPV forces could not break the stalemate and that the successful defense of the DPRK allowed China to proclaim victory in the war. Mao hoped for a settlement in a matter of weeks, but the negotiations dragged on for two years. Disagreements over the agenda, such as whether to discuss an exclusive ceasefire or to include the removal of all foreign troops from Korea and where to set the line of demarcation between the DPRK and ROK, prevented a rapid agreement. Meanwhile, sporadic fighting continued around the 38th parallel. Talks broke off in August and resumed in October, yet with little progress. The issue of repatriation of Chinese prisoners of war emerged as one of the most important issues in the peace talks. The United States questioned Chinese lists of American prisoners, which included only a fraction of those American officials believed had been taken prisoner in the fighting. The PRC objected to American demands that the repatriation take place on a voluntary basis, believing the U.S. forces wanted to prevent the return of large numbers of CPV prisoners. The PRC also accused the United States of engaging in biological warfare in Korea, intentionally spreading infectious diseases among CPV and KPA soldiers. Although Chinese leaders may have been convinced of the validity of these accusations, there is no credible evidence to support them.[12]

The prolonged fighting and tedious negotiations dragged on into 1953, until both Chinese and American leaders agreed to terms. The July 27 armistice agreement ended hostilities, set the line of demarcation at the 38th parallel, and called for the voluntary repatriation of all prisoners of war. Some scholars have suggested that threats to use atomic weapons by new American president Dwight Eisenhower and his Secretary of State John Foster Dulles, relayed to the Chinese through Indian diplomats, helped break the deadlock, and convinced Mao and the PRC leadership to come to terms. More recent research in Soviet archives has suggested that the death of Josef Stalin led the new collective Soviet leadership to encourage the Chinese to end the fighting.[13] After consultations with Soviet leaders and Kim Il-sung, Mao authorized Peng Dehuai to sign the armistice agreement.

China's participation in the war proved extremely costly in both men and material. Counting both combat and noncombat servicemen, more than two million "volunteers" served in Korea, totaling nearly 73 percent of PLA forces. According to Chinese sources, in just under three years of combat CPV forces suffered 390,000 casualties, including 148,400 killed, though some have suggested that Chinese casualties may have reached as high as 900,000. Among the dead lay Mao's own son, Mao Anying, who died in a U.S. air raid in November 1950. The staggering losses suffered in the face of devastating U.S. firepower led some Chinese military leaders to advocate a program of military modernization after the war. Peng Dehuai in particular argued that China must develop a modern, technologically advanced army like that of the USSR if it were to confront the United States on the field of battle in the future. At the same time CPV success in the war reaffirmed Mao's belief in the power of human will and spirit to overcome material obstacles. Unable to match American technology and overwhelming firepower, Chinese soldiers employed the Maoist strategy of "luring the enemy deep," separating and isolating the enemy, and concentrating superior force against enemy weak points to achieve significant results in the first two campaigns of late 1950. Even though subsequent campaigns revealed the limits Chinese military capabilities in Korea, Mao believed that this experience supported his view that if properly motivated and led, the Chinese people could accomplish any goal no matter how ambitious. The Korean War, along with the experience of the Sino-Japanese and civil wars, helped shape Mao's later domestic campaigns such as the Great Leap Forward of 1958–1960, which he compared to a military conflict, urging the Chinese people to do "battle" with the "Western imperialists" in order to "achieve victory" by surpassing Western countries in terms of industrial production.

Despite the costs, many Chinese felt the war experience brought significant benefits. Rather than view the war as a stalemate without a victor, Chinese leaders and citizens alike declared the fighting in Korea a glorious victory and a source of pride. The Chinese troops who fought in difficult conditions and bitter cold against the overwhelmingly superior firepower of the U.S. and UN forces to defend China's borders deeply impressed many Chinese. The Chinese also took pride in China's resolute support for a neighboring and fraternal communist state, the DPRK. With this victory and the death of Stalin, Mao believed that the mantle of leadership of the world communist movement had passed to him. PRC leaders would tend to see China, rather than the USSR, as the appropriate model for the poor and oppressed nations of Asia, Africa, and Latin America. This had important consequences for China's relationship with the USSR, where Soviet leaders continued to view Mao and the PRC as subordinates in the world communist hierarchy.

Above all, the war in Korea had significant ramifications on China's relations with the United States by reinforcing Chinese perceptions of the United States as an aggressive imperialist state and the greatest danger to China's national security and world revolution. Mao and his colleagues interpreted the war as clear evidence of American ambition to act as the dominant power in Asia and its hostility toward the PRC and the Chinese people. The United States refused to recognize the PRC, allowing Chiang Kai-shek and the Guomindang regime on Taiwan to continue to represent China in the United Nations. The animosity derived from the Korean War would characterize Sino-American relations for two decades.

CHAPTER 12

Border Conflicts: Jinmen, India, and the USSR, 1958–1969

In the two decades after the Korean War armistice, the PRC did not participate in major conflicts comparable to the Sino-Japanese War, the Chinese civil war, or the fighting in Korea. Mao and the CCP leadership gave primary attention to economic reconstruction and building a new socialist state. Yet the PLA did see sporadic action in a series of brief conflicts on the borders of the PRC. In 1958, PLA forces initiated a bombardment of Nationalist-held islands off the southeastern coast; in 1962 the PLA fought a brief border war with India; and in 1969 PLA troops exchanged fire with Soviet troops in two bloody incidents on the Wusuli (Ussuri) River. None of these military engagements lasted longer than a month or two, but each revealed the degree to which the PRC relied upon military force to defend its territory and to influence the behavior or policies of China's neighbors. Moreover, each of these brief conflicts reflected the deteriorating relationship between China and the Soviet Union, which would lead to a dramatic change in China's foreign policy by 1970.

Sino-Soviet Relations

After 1949, the leaders of the PRC and the USSR tended to project a unified image of close relations and proletarian solidarity. In reality, serious tensions plagued the Sino-Soviet relationship from the earliest days of the PRC. In fact, the first two decades of the PRC saw a marked deterioration of relations between these two communist states that culminated in the border clashes of 1969. The roots of the Sino-Soviet split go back to the early period of the Chinese Communist movement. As a CCP leader, Mao had never enjoyed a particularly strong attachment to the Soviet Union or its representatives, who tended to scorn his approach to the Chinese revolution which focused on the peasant and the countryside rather than the proletariat and urban areas. Josef Stalin had consistently favored other Chinese Communist leaders who had studied in the Soviet Union, such as the "28 Bolsheviks" of the Jiangxi Soviet era, overlooking Mao and his "heterodox" strategy. Even after the Zunyi Conference of January 1935, which marked Mao's emergence as the dominant leader of the CCP, Stalin remained reluctant to accept his leadership. For his part, Mao distrusted Soviet advice after the devastating experience of April 1927, when

Chiang Kai-shek ordered the violent break with the Chinese Communists. Despite signs of the impending split, Stalin had ordered the CCP to maintain its united front with the Guomindang in part because of his domestic rivalry with Leon Trotsky. Mao rightly feared that Soviet domestic politics could adversely influence Moscow's views of the Chinese Communist movement and he doubted Stalin's ability to direct the CCP from thousands of miles away in Moscow. Mao did not believe that Stalin had an adequate understanding of Chinese society and had little confidence in his ability to serve as a political and military strategist for the Chinese revolution. Mao felt that only a Chinese who understood the sinification of Marxism could lead the revolution and that the CCP ultimately succeeded in spite of, rather than because of, Moscow's support.

As a result of these tensions, Mao maintained cordial relations with Stalin but sought opportunities to secure political and economic aid elsewhere. In January 1945, he sent a request to Franklin Roosevelt, relayed through Patrick Hurley, to send a CCP delegation to Washington to discuss coalition government with the Nationalists and to explore the possibilities for U.S. support for the CCP. Hurley passed on the request along with his opinion that recognition of the CCP as a legitimate political entity would not be in the interests of American objectives in China. Roosevelt rejected the request, but it suggests that Mao had concerns about exclusive reliance on the Soviet Union for material aid. Mao's concerns seemed validated when the Soviet Union signed a treaty with Chiang Kai-shek's Nationalist government in August 1945. In the treaty, Stalin pledged to continue to recognize Chiang's government as the legitimate government of China in return for Chiang's recognition of Soviet control of Outer Mongolia and Soviet interests in Manchuria. Stalin also made attempts to coax Xinjiang Province into declaring independence under Soviet protection in 1949, backing a Turkic regime which resisted incorporation into the PRC.

Nonetheless, as the civil war ended, Mao clearly announced that the PRC would "lean to one side," following the Soviet Union in foreign policy and supporting Moscow in the unfolding global Cold War. Rather than an indication of close Sino-Soviet relations, Mao's stance likely reflected the fact that the CCP viewed the United States as the greatest threat to the PRC. In December 1949, shortly after the CCP victory, Mao traveled to Moscow to meet with Stalin, seeking support for his new government and plans to "liberate" Taiwan. Stalin offered support and material aid, but not quite as much as Mao had hoped. In the end, the two leaders signed a treaty of friendship, alliance, and mutual assistance in February 1950. The Soviets extended a modest loan of $300 million to the PRC, but Mao had to acknowledge Soviet control of Outer Mongolia and agreed to joint control of the resources and railroads of Manchuria. When the fighting in Korea began in June 1950, Stalin first promised to provide air support for Chinese troops, then withdrew his promise, only to later agree to provide limited air support near the Yalu River border. While Chinese "volunteers" suffered hundreds of thousands of casualties in Korea, including one of Mao' sons, the Soviets offered equipment and supplies for which they insisted that the Chinese pay.

Despite these tensions, Mao and the CCP needed material support and technical expertise which necessitated a close relationship with the Soviet Union. Thousands of Soviet economic and technical advisors traveled to the PRC in the 1950s, and the Chinese sent thousands of students to the USSR for technical training. During the First Five Year Plan, which began in 1953, the USSR and its Eastern European allies accounted for 75 percent of the PRC's foreign trade. Despite a degree of mutual mistrust between Mao and Stalin, the alliance with the Soviets remained the most important pillar of PRC foreign policy in its first two decades.

After Stalin's death in 1953, the Sino-Soviet alliance showed signs of increased strain. In early 1956 the new Soviet leader Nikita Khrushchev addressed the Twentieth Congress of the Communist Party of the Soviet Union (CPSU) and bitterly criticized Josef Stalin, his policies, and his leadership. This "Secret Speech" signaled Khrushchev's intention to deviate from Stalinist practice, which produced a dramatic response in Beijing. Mao had no advance warning that Khrushchev intended to openly vilify Stalin, whom Mao had consistently praised, and found that some of Khrushchev's criticisms of Stalin could apply to Mao as well. For example, Khrushchev excoriated Stalin for creating a "cult of personality" in which he presented himself as an all knowing and infallible leader. Mao would not reach the peak of his "cult of personality" until the Cultural Revolution of the late 1960s, but in 1956 he enjoyed tremendous prestige and wielded great authority in China, which led him to take Khrushchev's comments personally. Furthermore, Mao believed that Stalin's death left Mao, not Nikita Khrushchev, as the leader of the international Communist movement. The CCP regarded Mao as a great Marxist–Leninist thinker and claimed that China's experience should serve as a model for revolutionary movements in poor countries in Asia, Africa, and Latin America. Soviet leaders clung to their positions as leaders of the world's first Communist revolution and the world revolutionary movement. Nikita Khrushchev had no interest in Mao's innovations and continued to view Mao and the PRC as secondary leaders of the world Communist movement. Mao had little respect for Khrushchev's attempts to take the USSR in a different, and from Mao's perspective erroneous, direction.

Mao and Khrushchev also disagreed on fundamental issues such as the nature of the relationship between the communist and capitalist worlds. Mao claimed that the "East Wind prevails over the West Wind," implying that communist world and the combined strength of the USSR and the PRC would triumph over the capitalist West in a military conflict. From Mao's perspective, the United States and the Western capitalist powers posed a significant threat, having deployed their forces all around China in places like Vietnam, Korea, and Taiwan. Khrushchev, on the other hand, sought to reduce tension between the capitalist and communist camps through a policy of "Peaceful Coexistence." Anxious to avoid a larger war with the capitalist West which might lead to a nuclear war, Khrushchev believed that the Soviet Union would triumph in the Cold War through peaceful means, because of the superiority of the Soviet system of organization and production. Mao rejected this view, believing that he could not avoid war with the capitalist West and that it might actually help bring about further Marxist revolutions in other countries, as had been the case in

Russia in World War I and China in World War II. In public, Mao claimed that he did not fear atomic weapons, referring to them as "Paper Tigers" and claiming that people determine the outcome of wars, not weapons.[1] In the event of an atomic attack, Mao believed that the Chinese people could retreat to the interior and that China's huge population could absorb the loss of hundreds of millions of people and still continue fighting. Even if his private views differed, the Soviet leadership found such reckless talk alarming and provocative. Despite these disagreements, Chinese and Soviet leaders did their best to maintain a façade of unity and to mask over their internal disputes before the international community. Since Mao needed Soviet support for a future military campaign against Chiang's forces on Taiwan, he muted his public criticism of Khrushchev and the Soviet Union.

The Jinmen Bombardment of 1958

The Korean War and the presence of the U.S. Navy's Seventh Fleet in the Straits had forced Mao to temporarily shelve his plans for a campaign against Taiwan, but it remained an important piece of unfinished business. As long as Chiang's regime remained active on Taiwan, Mao could not consider the unification of China complete. Since the Nationalist regime on Taiwan enjoyed the military support of the United States, Mao could not undertake a full-fledged attack without Soviet support. During his visit to Moscow in 1949–1950, Mao found Stalin receptive to the idea of a Taiwan campaign, but the DPRK attack in June 1950 prevented serious planning for any such operation. With the Korean armistice and Stalin's death in 1953, Mao hoped to revive plans for the "liberation" of Taiwan, but discovered that Khrushchev and the new Soviet leaders preferred to avoid any action that might provoke a military response from the United States.

Regardless of Soviet wishes, in the spring of 1954, Mao ordered the PLA to conduct an artillery bombardment of Nationalist forces on small islands off the coast of Zhejiang Province. The Nationalist forces on these islands and others occasionally launched small guerrilla attacks against the mainland and threatened PRC shipping along the coast. Mao needed Soviet support for an attack on Taiwan to offset American support for Chiang Kai-shek, but he did not want to delay military action against Taiwan too long. He feared that the international community would grow accustomed to the idea of a divided China, as it had to the separate regimes in Korea. In the fall of the same year, Mao decided to keep up the military pressure on Taiwan by ordering another PLA artillery bombardment, this time on the Jinmen and Mazu islands which lay off the coast of Fujian Province. The barrage inflicted casualties on the Nationalist forces protecting the islands but did not result in their withdrawal. Instead, it helped produce closer relations between the United States and Taiwan via a mutual security treaty in December 1954, which bound the United States to defend Taiwan in the event of a PRC attack.[2]

From Beijing's perspective, the Taiwan issue fell into the realm of domestic affairs and had nothing to do with international relations. American support for Chiang's government on Taiwan amounted to foreign interference in China's domestic affairs.

As Mao continued military action against the offshore islands, the PRC began a foreign policy drive to win support for its position on the Taiwan issue by forging alliances with Asian and African nations. Designed in particular to emphasize China's friendly relations with its Asian neighbors, this foreign policy stressed China's peaceful intentions in Asia and its willingness to resolve the Taiwan issue through negotiation. At the April 1955 Asian-African Conference in Bandung, Indonesia, PRC premier Zhou Enlai showcased China's willingness to adhere to the principles of mutual nonaggression and respect for territorial integrity in its relations with other states, with the clear implication that other states should support China's position on Taiwan as a domestic rather than foreign policy issue. Meanwhile, PLA amphibious operations drove Nationalist forces from islands off the Zhejiang coast, bringing them under PRC control. Other PLA units concentrated on building airfields in Fujian Province in anticipation of an amphibious operation against Taiwan.

In 1958, Mao again directed PLA artillery batteries to shell Jinmen. He had several reasons for doing so, beyond simply capturing Nationalist-held territories. First, the shelling allowed Mao to assess the strength of the Nationalist commitment to the defense of these islands and the United States' willingness to support Chiang Kai-shek. Second, it is likely that Mao intended to use conflict in the Taiwan Straits to generate domestic support for his Great Leap Forward, a radical plan for dramatic increases in agricultural and industrial production that began in the summer of 1958.[3] In addition, the barrage would test the limits of Soviet support for Chinese military action against Taiwan, to see if Khrushchev would stand firm in the face of conflict with the United States. The shelling began in August, just weeks after Nikita Khrushchev had visited Beijing for talks with Chinese leaders.

Jinmen Island lies approximately two miles off the coast of Xiamen and 140 miles from Taiwan. The 80,000 Nationalist troops defending the island relied completely on supplies from Taiwan. The initial shelling concentrated on docks, warehouses, and artillery posts, inflicting hundreds of casualties and threatening to cut Jinmen off from all reinforcements and provisions. American President Dwight Eisenhower immediately ordered the U.S. Navy's Seventh Fleet and additional ships into the region, and American aircraft began transporting Nationalist troops to Jinmen. In early September, American ships began escorting Nationalist supply ships, daring PLA batteries to fire on them. Mao ordered the PLA to continue shelling but only to hit Nationalist vessels and avoid the Americans. Luckily for the PLA, American escorts remained back several miles off the coast of Jinmen, avoiding a direct Sino-American incident. Still, Nationalist fighter planes with U.S.-supplied air to air missiles shot down several PLA fighter planes.[4]

The barrage continued intermittently and in late October the PLA began shelling only on alternate days, but the Nationalist troops showed no sign of withdrawing from Jinmen. Mao called off the shelling in December, preferring to leave the islands in Nationalist hands. He believed that he could continue the barrage at a later date if he wished to increase tension in the Straits and that this might drive a wedge between

Taiwan and the United States, which wanted to avoid being dragged into a war with the PRC. Yet the Taiwan Straits Crisis indicated strong commitments on the part of the Nationalists and Americans to the defense of Taiwan and its offshore islands. This further delayed PRC plans for a Taiwan campaign and fueled the mutual suspicion and hostility between the United States and China.

Of perhaps even greater consequence, the shelling had a chilling effect on Sino-Soviet relations. PRC leaders had given Nikita Khrushchev no indication that they intended to shell Jinmen when he visited Beijing, an act he considered reckless and ill-advised. Mao's willingness to provoke the United States at a time when Khrushchev and the Soviets sought to reduce international tension between the Cold War adversaries struck the Soviets as a deliberate challenge to their policies. In 1957, Khrushchev had agreed to give the PRC a sample atomic bomb and to provide technical assistance so that China could build its own nuclear weapons. In light of what he regarded as Mao's irresponsible actions in the Taiwan Strait, Khrushchev canceled the agreement. Soviet criticism of Mao's socioeconomic policy during the Great Leap Forward also contributed to the souring of Sino-Soviet relations. Rather than producing dramatic increases in production, the Great Leap Forward exhausted the Chinese people and created a famine that resulted in the death of as many as 25 million people. In the summer of 1960, the USSR declared its intention to remove all 1,390 experts and advisors working in China. They returned to the USSR in September, leaving their project incomplete and taking their blueprints with them.

The Sino-Indian Border War

As Sino-Soviet relations deteriorated, Mao and the PRC leaders attempted to secure friendly relations with the nations of Asia and Africa. Since they were both newly established Asian states, the PRC and the Republic of India found common ground for establishing friendly relations. One of the first noncommunist governments to recognize the PRC, the Indian government established full ambassadorial relations with Mao's China in 1950. India offered its services as a mediator between the PRC and the United Nations during the Korean War and in 1954 sided with the PRC in the international arena, supporting the PRC bid for a seat at the United Nations and lobbying for Chinese participation at the Geneva Conference. Chinese leaders responded with overtures of friendship and mutual respect. In 1954, China and India signed an agreement in which each agreed to abide by the "Five Principles of Coexistence," including mutual respect for territorial sovereignty, nonaggression, and noninterference in the domestic affairs of the other. A year later at the 1955 Asian-African Conference in Bandung, Indonesia, Chinese Foreign Minister Zhou Enlai met with Indian Prime Minister Jawaharlal Nehru, repeating China's desire for peaceful relations with neighboring states, including India. The two leaders subsequently exchanged state visits and spoke of the relationship between their two countries in the Hindi expression *Hindi-Chini Bhai Bhai* or "Chinese and Indians are Brothers."[5]

Despite these public expressions of friendship, territorial disputes on the Sino-Indian border made amicable relations difficult. The dispute centered on two areas, one in the western sector of the India–Tibet border near the Indian territory of Ladakh and the other in the eastern sector of the border on the southern slope of the Himalaya Mountains. In each sector, Chinese and Indian maps differed, putting tens of thousands of square miles in dispute. The Chinese claimed that the boundaries had never been clearly marked and agreed upon. The Indians countered that a 1914 agreement with the Tibetan government had determined the boundaries which the PRC must now respect. The dispute remained a minor issue between the two states until 1958 when the Chinese announced that the PLA had built a major road linking the Xinjiang and Tibetan Autonomous Regions. The road cut across the Aksai Chin Plateau, which fell into the disputed territory of the western sector. New Delhi protested this action, but the PRC refused to relinquish control of this territory or the road, which facilitated the movement of men and supplies and ensured PLA control over Tibet.[6]

The border dispute revealed differences of opinion between Beijing and New Delhi, but the issue of Tibet provided the context for the 1962 military clash. Mao placed a high priority on securing the borders of his new state and prepared to send PLA units to "liberate" Tibet in 1949. The PLA easily subdued Tibetan forces in the eastern region bordering Sichuan Province and then appealed to the Dalai Lama, the spiritual and political head of Tibet, for a negotiated settlement. Despite concerns about submitting to PRC authority, in 1951 the Dalai Lama agreed to support a 17 Point Agreement negotiated by Chinese and Tibetan representatives. This agreement acknowledged Tibet's place as a part of the PRC but preserved its cultural traditions and provided for a certain degree of autonomy. Mao moved carefully to avoid any disruption of this agreement, but it proved increasingly difficult to reconcile the goals of Chinese officials who sought to bring socialist transformation to Tibet and Tibetan nationalists who sought greater autonomy. Sino-Tibetan relations took a turn for the worse in 1957 when Mao learned that the United States had trained and equipped Tibetan exiles in the United States and infiltrated them back into Tibet to conduct guerrilla resistance against the PRC. An armed uprising against Chinese rule in the spring of 1959 precipitated a violent crackdown by the PLA and prompted the Dalai Lama to flee to India where he set up a government-in-exile.[7]

India's reaction to events in Tibet complicated the border dispute with China. Long sympathetic to the Tibetans with whom the Indians had cultural ties, New Delhi criticized Beijing's handling of Tibetan affairs and provided sanctuary for the Dalai Lama and his followers. PRC leaders resented Indian support for the Tibetan government-in-exile and the fact that the Indian government had facilitated American CIA operations in support of Tibetan anticommunist guerrillas. In the eastern sector, Chinese attempts to block mountain passes and prevent the infiltration of Tibetan guerrillas from India led to a few brief exchanges of fire between Indian and Chinese forces in 1959, adding to the mounting tension. A simple matter of boundary markings in remote frontiers would not likely have led to war between China and India, yet by 1960 Mao had come to believe that the Indian government had colluded with the United States to foment revolt in an attempt to detach Tibet from the PRC in order to make it a base for further attacks on Chinese territory. The border issue took on great importance only so much as it related to the PLA's ability to protect and control Tibet, raising a minor border dispute to the status of a national security issue in the minds of China's leaders.[8]

Zhou Enlai visited New Delhi in April 1960, hoping to negotiate a satisfactory settlement to the border issue. He met with Nehru and proposed an exchange of territories in which China would recognize the boundary indicated on Indian maps in the eastern sector, the McMahon Line of 1913, and in return the Indian government would recognize Chinese control of the Aksai Chin Plateau in the western sector. This arrangement would secure for China the critical road link between Xinjiang and Tibet and for India the southern slope of the Himalayas to protect northeastern India. The Indian government rejected this proposal, demanding as a precondition for talks that the Chinese withdraw from all territory claimed on Indian maps, including the Aksai Chin Plateau. Strategic and national security concerns prevented the Chinese from seriously considering such a withdrawal, and Indian nationalism prevented the acceptance of a compromise, setting the stage for a military clash in the disputed areas. Meanwhile, the PLA continued to build roads and border outposts in the disputed zones. Hoping to block what he viewed as Chinese territorial expansion at India's expense, in 1961 Nehru authorized a new "Forward Policy" whereby Indian military forces and border guards advanced into the disputed territories to build outposts and establish effective occupation.

In 1962 Indian patrols pushed deeper into the disputed territories in both the eastern and western sectors, prompting China to condemn these "provocations" and to call again for negotiations to settle the issue. In the summer and fall, Indian troops began crossing the McMahon Line in the eastern sector, occupying territory that clearly fell under Chinese sovereignty on Indian maps. Occasional exchanges of fire took place as each side remained determined to hold its ground. As PRC leaders called for negotiations, PLA forces began preparations for possible military action in both sectors. With a total force of nearly 150,000 troops in Tibet, the PLA assembled forces of 10,000 and 6,000 in the disputed eastern and western sectors, respectively. Indian troops had greater numbers in the eastern sector, perhaps 16,000, but in the western sector only matched Chinese strength at 6,000. PLA forces had much better equipment, including heavy-padded uniforms to protect them against the bitter cold. Having learned hard lessons about the importance of logistical operations in difficult terrain and extreme weather from its experience in Korea, the PLA built roads to ensure a steady flow of men and supplies to the disputed areas. Moreover, having operated in Tibet for over a decade, Chinese troops had experience in these remote areas and had acclimated to life at high altitudes. Indian troops which pushed forward into the disputed regions had less experience and found resupply and reinforcement difficult, mostly by air drop.

Unable to compel the Indian government to settle the issue through negotiations, Chinese leaders planned to secure the disputed territory by force. On October 20, 1962, PLA forces began simultaneous attacks in both disputed areas. In the eastern

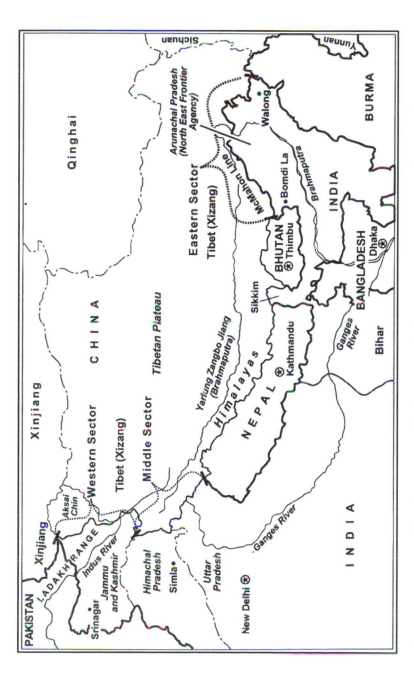

The China–India Border, 1962. From *Chinese Warfighting: The PLA Experience Since 1949*, ed. Mark A. Ryan, David M. Finkelstein, and Michael A. McDevitt (Armonk, NY: M.E. Sharpe, 2003). Copyright © 2003 by the CNA Corporation. Reprinted with permission of M.E. Sharpe, Inc.

sector, the attack began with a brief but devastatingly accurate artillery barrage on Indian outposts followed by infantry assault. Chinese troops quickly overran isolated Indian positions which fell too far apart to support each other. An attack in the western sector yielded similar results. Both sides reinforced their positions, but the Chinese maintained a clear advantage in firepower, supply, and position, often attacking downhill. The PLA planned a second attack for mid-November, but had to swing into action early to meet an Indian counteroffensive. PLA forces blunted the Indian attack and on November 16 launched their second offensive in the western sector, crushing Indian troops and inflicting significant casualties. Two days later, the PLA attacked in the eastern sector, occupying territory south of the McMahon Line. On November 20, the PRC announced a unilateral ceasefire and withdrew its armed forces from the newly occupied areas to the original borders it had claimed prior to the fighting. This left India in control of territory south of the McMahon Line in the east, but placed the strategic Aksai Chin Plateau in the west securely in Chinese hands, roughly the same exchange Zhou Enlai had proposed in 1960. Having driven Indian troops off territory claimed on Chinese maps, the PLA took no further offensive action.

The war lasted only one month, but it proved costly for India which suffered over 3,000 casualties and almost 4,000 prisoners of war, all of whom the PRC promptly repatriated. The Chinese have not released their own casualty figures, but their losses were certainly well below these levels. The PLA showed great skill in this limited war, demonstrating the traditional tactics of massing overwhelming force against isolated enemy positions. It also exhibited significant improvement in logistics, despite the challenges of fighting in remote, mountainous areas. The war demonstrated to the world that China took seriously issues of territorial integrity and national security but also showed that it could exercise restraint. PRC leaders only resorted to armed force after multiple attempts to solve the issue through diplomacy and once committed to military action PLA troops took control of only that territory that China claimed prior to the fighting. Yet this restraint drew little praise for Beijing as the governments of India and the United States took the border war as evidence of Chinese territorial ambitions and its willingness to use force against its neighbors. Moreover, the war led Mao to once again question Soviet support for the PRC in international affairs. Moscow provoked even great consternation in Beijing when it not only failed to offer strong support for the Chinese in the dispute but also provided India with economic assistance and military equipment, including transport planes and high-altitude helicopters.[9]

The PLA in the Cultural Revolution

The PLA's strong performance in the brief border war with India reflected some of the changes that had taken place since the Korean War. Minister of Defense Peng Dehuai's emphasis on professionalism and modernization had produced a smaller but more effective military. Peng relied on the model of the Soviet Red Army to remold China's traditional forces, which relied heavily on regional and militia forces, into a professional military force with greater emphasis on the training and equipping of PLA main force units. In 1955, the PLA took a step away from its egalitarian traditions by adopting a Soviet style system of ranks and uniform insignia, with progressive pay grades. The total PLA force dropped from five million in 1953 to roughly half that number in 1957. The new Military Affairs Commission (MAC) abolished the old regional Field Armies, replacing them with Army Corps of three divisions, and divided the state into thirteen military regions in which any unit could serve.

Peng's emphasis on Soviet style professionalization and training contributed to the PLA's success on the Sino-Indian border, but it also helped end his career as minister of defense. Beginning in 1958, Mao's Great Leap Forward consumed the Chinese people in a collective effort to make a tremendous "leap forward" in agricultural and industrial production. Huge collective farms known as People's Communes stretched across the countryside and backyard furnaces for producing steel lit up the night sky as the population threw itself into an around the clock effort to catch up with the Western powers in terms of industrial production. The resulting damage to the economy and people stunned Peng Dehuai, who penned a letter criticizing the Great Leap and pointing out that all leaders, including Mao, bore responsibility for its consequences. Mao bore a grudge against Peng because his attempts to professionalize the PLA rejected Mao's notions of an egalitarian Red Army. As a result, Mao took Peng's words as a personal attack and launched his own tirade against Peng, accusing him of "right opportunism" and of leaking false information to the Soviet leaders who then used it to criticize the PRC. Mao arranged Peng's dismissal as minister of defense in 1959, replacing him with Lin Biao.

As minister of defense, Lin Biao supported Mao by emphasizing political ideology alongside military training. He reasserted the authority of the political commissars who had seen their role reduced under Peng Dehuai. In 1965, Lin took a significant step away from Peng's professionalization of the PLA by abolishing all ranks and insignia from uniforms in a return to Maoist egalitarianism of the Yan'an days. This change reflected Mao's complaints that the officer corps had set itself up as an elite and privileged group, aloof from the common soldiers and masses. Lin also supervised the publication of a book of selected quotations from Chairman Mao to reinforce Mao's thought among the rank and file of the military. This would later become the infamous "Little Red Book," studied and revered by millions of Red Guards during the Cultural Revolution. Under Lin's guidance the PLA also became an instrument for promoting Mao's thought within Chinese society as a whole. In 1963, the PLA began a campaign to "Study Lei Feng," a young soldier who had died in an unfortunate accident. His "diary," actually the creation of PLA propaganda writers, contained numerous stories of his selfless service to others and dedication to the study of Chairman Mao's words. Posters appeared across China urging the people to "Study Lei Feng" and emulate his devotion to the chairman. Mao expanded the movement by directing the entire population not only to study Lei Feng but also to "Learn from the PLA." Along with Lin's revival of ideology and the study of Mao Zedong Thought in the ranks of the military, the PLA continued to pursue technological advancements. Since the Soviet Union retracted it promise to share a sample atomic bomb with China in 1959, PRC scientists worked diligently on their own nuclear program. In 1964, the Chinese successfully tested their first atomic bomb and in 1967 they followed with a successful hydrogen bomb.

The failure of the Great Leap Forward and Peng's criticism led Mao to question the dedication of many CCP members and to begin planning for another campaign, this one designed to cleanse the CCP of those Mao believed sought to restore capitalism and to set the nation on the proper path toward Communism. When Mao launched his Great Proletarian Cultural Revolution in 1966, he called upon the young people of China to identify and eliminate corrupt and counterrevolutionary officials who had taken the "capitalist road." In doing so, he unleashed incredibly destructive forces that would require the services of the PLA to restore order. As Red Guards across China attacked authority figures and engaged each other in sometimes violent struggle, Mao quickly realized that matters had spun out of control and in January 1967 he directed the PLA into the fray to establish order with the ambiguous directive to "support the leftists" or true supporters of Chairman Mao. Since all Red Guards claimed to support Mao and accused others of opposing him, the PLA tended to impose order by moving against the most radical activists. After several months of fighting and chaos in many provinces, PLA forces managed to quell the worst of the violence and establish a semblance of order. The purge of so many political officials created a void that Mao filled in part by giving military officers a greater role in political affairs. PLA officials would occupy a greater number of political posts for the next several years.

Sino-Soviet Territorial Dispute

The Cultural Revolution emboldened many Chinese to openly attack those whom they viewed as enemies of the PRC, both at home and abroad. Red Guards targeted not only "Capitalist Roaders" within China but also those who supported "Soviet Socialist Revisionism." The war with India had helped remind the Chinese of their resentment over Sino-Soviet territorial issues that dated back to treaties signed between the Russian Czarist government and the Qing court. PRC leaders had long emphasized the need to end China's "century of humiliation" at the hands of foreign imperialists and to restore China's historical territorial boundaries. In the nineteenth century, Czarist Russia pressured the Qing court to sign treaties in 1858 (Treaty of Aigun) and 1860 (Beijing Convention) which gave Russia some 133,000 square miles south and east of the Wusuli River which became the Russian maritime province. As the Chinese saw it, these territorial concessions resulted from "unequal treaties" and therefore they should revert to Chinese sovereignty. Beijing began to assert these claims shortly after the border war with India, publishing a list of "lost territories" which included parts of Siberia, the maritime province, and hundreds of thousands of square miles of territory. These assertions called into question the legitimacy of the Sino-Soviet border which the Chinese claimed resulted from imperialist aggression. Moscow rejected these claims and refused to engage in negotiations on the subject.

Small-scale border skirmishes took place as early as 1959, typically caused by the Chinese who periodically crossed the Wusuli River to erect outposts on the Soviet bank. As the aggressive rhetoric of Chinese Red Guards experiencing the Cultural Revolution identified the Soviet Union as a "Revisionist" and "Socialist Imperialist" state, Soviet border guards increased their patrols and vigilance along the river. In 1967, frontier incidents began to occur with increasing frequency. According to the Chinese, the Soviets violated the Chinese border 4,000 times between 1964 and 1969. This trend culminated in two major clashes in March 1969. The clashes took place on Zhenbao Island (Damansky Island to the Russians), located in the Wusuli River. The island measures one mile in length and a third of a mile wide, is located in the middle of the river with substantial channels on each side, and forms the boundary line between the PRC and the Soviet Union. Uninhabited except by occasional fishermen, the island has little strategic value. The Chinese viewed the island as Chinese territory in part because they claimed it had originally been part of the Chinese bank and only became an island due to erosion. The Soviets likewise claimed it as part of Soviet territory. The border had not been clearly defined since the 1860 Treaty between the Qing court and Russian Czarist government, which set the border at the Heilong and Wusuli rivers.

After 1967, as China conducted its Cultural Revolution, the Chinese government grew increasingly strident on the border issue, condemning the Soviet Union for alleged border violations. In truth, both sides violated the border, briefly occupying disputed islands or making limited ventures across the river. Initially, the two sides found ways to defuse the tension along the border. For example, Chinese soldiers occasionally dropped their pants and collectively "mooned" their Soviet counterparts across the river. Soviet troops eventually retaliated by holding up pictures of Chairman Mao, redirecting the insult at the "Great Teacher and Helmsmen" of the Chinese people. During the Cultural Revolution, such harmless juvenile behavior likely proved a source of serious aggravation for the Chinese troops.[10]

The March Border Clashes

The Chinese typically kept greater numbers of PLA troops along the eastern part of the border with the Soviet Union than on the western border in Inner Mongolia and Xinjiang. In March 1969, the PLA stationed 380,000–480,000 soldiers along or near the border, supported by 30,000–40,000 border patrol guards. The Soviets deployed the bulk of their troops on the border to the west but had 250,000–300,000 troops along the Heilong and Wusuli rivers which formed the border with Manchuria. Although outnumbered, the Soviets enjoyed a substantial advantage in firepower and equipment, along with a superior logistical system.[11]

On the night of March 1–2, 1969, three hundred Chinese soldiers and border guards walked across the frozen river to Zhenbao Island where they prepared an ambush by digging fox holes in a wooded area and laying down phone wire for communication. Early the next morning, a row of twenty apparently unarmed Chinese soldiers walked across the island toward the Soviet bank of the river, loudly repeating quotations from Chairman Mao as they marched. From nearby outposts, Soviet border guards observed the Chinese and sent a force in APCs (armored personnel carriers) and trucks to meet them. The Soviets marched out toward the Chinese, ordering them back to their own bank of the river and linking their arms to block the Chinese advance. When the Chinese reached within twenty feet of the Soviets, the first line scattered to reveal a second row armed with automatic weapons that opened fire, killing several Soviet border guards. At the same time, the 300 Chinese soldiers waiting in ambush began lobbing mortar shells on Soviet positions. Additional Soviet border guards rushed to the scene and Chinese troops charged their positions, leading to hand-to-hand combat lasting two hours. Both sides withdrew from the island, each claiming victory. The Chinese took nineteen prisoners but executed them all.

Both sides rushed troops to the area to prepare for a possible second clash, patrolling the river banks and the island, but making no attempt to occupy it. The tension mounted, setting the stage for a larger clash that took place on March 15. While the evidence indicates that Chinese troops initiated the hostilities in the first clash, it is by no means clear which side began the second, as each maintains that the other fired first. On the morning of March 15, 2,000 PLA troops crossed the ice onto Zhenbao Island under the support of mortar fire. The Soviets enjoyed a substantial advantage in firepower, pounding Chinese positions with artillery and tank fire before launching infantry assaults. The Chinese used recoilless rifles against the Soviet tanks with some success. After several hours of fighting, the Chinese withdrew to their side of the river. Casualties are difficult to estimate but could range from a few dozen to 140. Once again, both sides claimed victory and blamed the other for starting the clash. Tensions remained high on the border until September when high-level meetings took place between Zhou Enlai and Alexei Kosygin, brought together for Ho Chi Minh's funeral. They reached an understanding that there should be no additional clashes and maintenance of the status quo border situation.

In order to understand this border clash, it is important to note that it came in the wake of the Soviet invasion of Czechoslovakia. In August 1968, Soviet leader Leonid Brezhnev ordered Soviet Red Army tanks to crush a liberalization movement in Prague, justifying his actions with what came to be called the "Brezhnev Doctrine." This doctrine stated that the Soviet Union reserved the right to intervene in any communist country in which elements hostile to Communism emerged. Chinese leaders believed that the Soviets might use this doctrine to launch an attack on China. Manchuria, home to China's greatest industrial centers and location of important resources, lay within reasonable striking distance for Soviet forces on the border.

The bloody clashes of 1969 revealed to the world the severity of the Sino-Soviet split and shattered the idea of a communist "monolith" once and for all. It also marked the beginning of a dramatic change in Chinese foreign policy, as the PRC now concentrated on improving relations with the United States. The invasion of Czechoslovakia in 1968, the Brezhnev Doctrine, and the Sino-Soviet border clashes of 1969 convinced PRC leaders that the greatest threat to China's national security came not from American capitalists but rather from the "socialist imperialists" of the USSR. Thomas Robinson, who has devoted years to the study of the Sino-Soviet border clash, has examined new Chinese evidence which indicates that Mao intentionally ordered the initial ambush of Soviet forces on March 2, 1969, as a part of his plan to break with the Soviet Union and cultivate better relations with the United States.[12] If true, this amounted to an extremely dangerous way to reorient Chinese foreign policy by risking war with the Soviet Union. Regardless, Mao and the PRC leadership expressed an interest in improving relations with the United States, which culminated in Richard Nixon's historic 1972 visit to Beijing. Arriving in Beijing in February 1972, Nixon and Secretary of State Henry Kissinger met with Mao and other Chinese leaders. At a state banquet, Zhou Enlai called for the normalization of relations between China and the United States, and Nixon responded by stating that he saw no reason why China and the United States should be enemies. At the end of the visit, the two sides issued a joint communiqué at Shanghai, in which both sides promised to work together peacefully, not to seek the hegemony in Asia and to facilitate economic, technical, and cultural exchange. The Shanghai Communiqué also dealt with the most important issue in Sino-American relations, the status of Taiwan. Nixon acknowledged that "there is but one China and Taiwan is a part of China" and promised to gradually remove American forces and military installations from Taiwan. The Chinese accepted this general statement and agreed that reunification between mainland China and Taiwan should take place peacefully and should be settled by the Chinese themselves.

Even before Nixon's visit, the PRC began enjoying the benefits of a new relationship with the United States. In October 1971, the PRC took its seat at the United Nations, replacing Taiwan as the legitimate representative of China. For the first time in its history, the PRC now had access to American technology along with industrial and agricultural products that could help China modernize all sectors of the state, including the military. This reorientation of Chinese foreign policy helped pave the way for dramatic changes to the PRC after Mao's death in 1976.

CHAPTER 13

China, Indochina, and the 1979 Sino-Vietnamese War

Since its establishment, the PRC has attached great importance to Vietnam because of its geographical proximity to the southern border and its extensive cultural and historical ties to China. Vietnam, "the Smaller Dragon," has borrowed heavily from Chinese social, cultural, and political traditions, but it has also suffered long periods of Chinese occupation and rule. The result is a "love–hate" relationship between the Chinese and Vietnamese, which has had a profound impact on their policies toward each other. As Vietnam became a flash point in the Cold War, Beijing paid keen attention to events in Indochina and played an active role in the military conflicts in that region, making significant contributions to Vietnam's war efforts against both France and the United States. Despite this aid, mutual distrust developed in the 1960s and 1970s that led to a bitter conflict between the two communist states and a brief war in early 1979.

China and the First Indochina War

Shortly after defeating Chiang Kai-shek and the Nationalists, Mao and the PRC extended moral and material support to Ho Chi Minh's DRV (Democratic of Vietnam) in its war against a restoration of French colonial rule. Even before Chinese material aid began to flow across the border, Ho Chi Minh and Vo Nguyen Giap, commander of the anti-French Viet Minh forces, had embraced Maoist military theory by practicing their own version of People's War against the French from 1946 to 1950. Unable to match French troop levels or firepower in the initial stages of the fighting, the Viet Minh abandoned urban centers and withdrew to the country-side. In the remote, mountainous regions of northern Vietnam, the Viet Minh moved freely among the peasantry, explaining their goals of national liberation and land reform, and recruiting new supporters and soldiers. French forces and colonial troops pursued them in these remote areas, occupying various strategic outposts and stretching French lines of supply and communication. The Viet Minh restricted their attacks to small unit guerrilla attacks, battalion level and below, designed not to inflict massive damage on French forces but rather to gradually weaken them by dispersing their forces, attacking their weak points, and continuing to develop Viet Minh strength and capabilities. This closely resembles the first stage of People's War as Mao employed it against Chiang and the Nationalists in 1946–1947.

The CCP victory in the Chinese civil war and the arrival of PLA forces on the Sino-Vietnamese border marked an important turning point in the war as the Viet Minh now had access to Chinese advice and assistance. Mao extended formal diplomatic recognition to the DRV in January 1950 and hosted Ho Chi Minh and other Vietnamese leaders in Beijing. Mao proved eager to assist Ho and promised to commit substantial resources to the war effort. As had been the case in the Korean War, Mao believed that he had an obligation to support another communist leader in a time of crisis and viewed the PRC as a champion of revolutionary movements in Asia. Mao also saw the necessity of guarding China's border with Indochina which he identified as one of three areas likely to support an American attack on the PRC. He quickly organized a group of military advisors under the name CMAG (Chinese Military Advisory Group), commanded by General Wei Guoqing, to cross the border to meet with Vietnamese leaders. Many of the CMAG advisors drew upon their experiences in Korea and played a central role in Viet Minh military planning. The PRC also supplied material aid including small arms and ammunition, artillery pieces and shells, motorized vehicles, and food supplies.

The first demonstration of new Viet Minh capabilities as a result of PRC aid came with an offensive against French positions along the Sino-Vietnamese border in the fall of 1950. Using tactics that had proven successful for PLA forces in the Chinese civil war and in the early campaigns in Korea, Viet Minh troops attacked and captured isolated French outposts at Cao Bang, Dong Khe, and Lang Son. These attacks drew relief columns from other outposts, which the Viet Minh attacked in ambushes, yielding additional weapons and ammunition. This offensive secured the border region, ensured a steady flow of supplies from China, and also gave the Viet Minh a new sense of greater capabilities.[1]

Following the successful border offensive, the CMAG supported larger Viet Minh attacks on targets in and around the Red River delta, such as Vinh Yen and Hoa Binh in 1951. These attacks proved costly as French firepower inflicted tremendous casualties on the Viet Minh attackers. Mao made it clear that the PRC would not provide ground troops to fight against the French and instead urged a return to smaller attacks and a strategy of protracted war. In 1952, the CMAG advocated a campaign to take control of French outposts in the northwestern part of Vietnam and to create a separate base area in neighboring Laos. French General Henri Navarre attempted to block Viet Minh access to Laos by establishing a fortified base at the remote border village of Dien Bien Phu in the autumn of 1953. With the Korean armistice, the PRC could provide even greater amounts of weapons and equipment to the DRV, increasing its capabilities. CMAG chief Wei Guoqing helped General Giap and Ho Chi Minh plan the siege of Dien Bien Phu using a strategy of attacking isolated artillery posts to the north of the main base and airstrip rather than a direct attack on the center. China provided hundreds of artillery pieces and tens of thousands shells which the Viet Minh managed to conceal in the mountains surrounding the base. The attack began on March 13, 1954, and lasted for almost two months before the base fell as Viet Minh troops overwhelmed the dazed and exhausted defenders. This defeat broke the back of the French military effort in Vietnam as Ho Chi Minh's forces now held a distinct military advantage and controlled approximately 80 percent of the country.

Prior to the siege of Dien Bien Phu, the major powers agreed to send representatives to a conference at Geneva in May 1954 to discuss certain international issues, including the situation in Indochina. The delegates began their discussions on Indochina the day after the base at Dien Bien Phu fell, giving the DRV representative Prime Minister Pham Van Dong a strong bargaining position. Yet Chinese Foreign Minister Zhou Enlai pressed Dong and the DRV leaders to limit their demands in order to avoid the risk of American intervention. Although President Dwight Eisenhower had declined French requests for American air support at Dien Bien Phu, his administration had offered substantial support to the French, funding as much as 80 percent of the war effort. Zhou sought a peaceful environment in which the PRC could concentrate on economic construction and the transition to socialism without an American military presence on its southern border. Lacking strong support from the Chinese or the Soviets, Dong had little choice but to agree to scale back his demands and settle for a temporary division of Vietnam at the 17th parallel with national elections scheduled for 1956. The Geneva Accords of 1954 extended international recognition to the DRV, but it also sowed the seeds of discontent between Chinese and Vietnamese Communists. Decades later Vietnamese officials would accuse the PRC of colluding with French imperialists to work out a peace agreement that benefited China and France at the expense of Vietnam.[2]

China and the Second Indochina War

The outcome of the 1954 Geneva Conference may have planted seeds of a later rift between Chinese and Vietnamese Communists, but in the immediate years that followed the PRC continued to provide generous material and military aid to the DRV. Ho Chi Minh visited Beijing in 1955, where Mao received him warmly and pledged continuing support. When it became clear that the new RVN (Republic of Vietnam) under President Ngo Dinh Diem in South Vietnam would not agree to hold the elections stipulated by the Geneva Accords, Mao urged the DRV leaders to be patient, to refrain from military action against the south, and to concentrate on economic reconstruction in the north. The DRV leaders agreed, but communist agents who remained in the south found themselves hounded by Diem's military, the ARVN (Army of the Republic of Vietnam), and security forces. They began small attacks on ARVN forces and assassinations of RVN officials in the countryside. As the level of violence in the south increased in the late 1950s, DRV leaders gradually moved to a position of supporting armed struggle against the Diem's government. The 1960 founding of the NLF (National Liberation Front for South Vietnam), a southern united front organization under communist direction aimed at the overthrow of Ngo Dinh Diem's American-supported government, marked the resumption of open war in South Vietnam. President John Kennedy took office in January 1961 and began a dramatic increase in the amount of U.S. military aid and the number of advisors to Diem's government, prompting Mao to follow suit with additional material support for the DRV and NLF. As always, Mao felt an obligation to support national liberation movements in Asia, but he also used this aid to strengthen Sino-Vietnamese relations in the context of the growing Sino-Soviet rift. Moreover, Chinese leaders saw benefits in strengthening the DRV as a buffer against the growing American presence in South Vietnam. Having failed in Taiwan and Korea, Mao believed that the United States now sought to use Vietnam as a base to attack China.[3]

The 1964 Tonkin Gulf Incident and the subsequent American decisions to bomb the DRV and send American ground forces to South Vietnam forced PRC leaders to confront the possibility of an attack on southern China. Mao declared that he would only dispatch Chinese combat troops to Vietnam in the event of an American ground attack on the DRV but promised Ho Chi Minh all the material support China could provide. While Mao did not send combat troops, he did send PLA engineers to build roads and defensive works and antiaircraft artillery pieces and crews to protect DRV cities and strategic targets against American bombers. Between 1964 and 1969, 320,000 Chinese soldiers served in the DRV in these capacities.[4]

Despite the seemingly close relationship, the war strained relations between PRC and DRV leaders as disagreements arose over military strategy and the DRV's relations with the Soviet Union. In the war against France, Chinese military advisors played an important role in developing and implementing strategy. In contrast, during the war against the Americans, DRV leaders kept Mao and the Chinese informed but maintained complete control of the decision-making process. Advocating a strategy of protracted war, Mao urged the DRV to use small- and medium-sized operations to slowly sap American strength and will to fight. He also opposed negotiations, preferring that Hanoi continue the fight with single-minded determination. The DRV leaders embraced Mao's general military strategy but added their own innovations. For example, they followed the basic premises of People's War, but favored occasional larger operations designed to test American resolve and trigger a general uprising among the people of the south. The Tet Offensive of 1968 reflects this thinking, which the Chinese regarded as reckless and ill-advised. When the DRV agreed to peace talks in 1968 as a part of its strategy of "fighting while talking," Mao bristled at the rejection of his advice not to negotiate. In addition, Mao wanted Hanoi to demonstrate its gratitude for Chinese aid by supporting the PRC in its growing dispute with the USSR. Ho Chi Minh had always walked a careful line between these two communist giants, hoping to preserve friendly relations and material assistance from both. It annoyed Hanoi that Beijing refused to cooperate with Moscow, rejecting Soviet calls for "united action" in support of the DRV and denying the Soviets access to Chinese air space for the delivery of war materials. As the war progressed after 1968, the DRV preferred the more sophisticated and modern weaponry of the Soviet Union and refused to side with China in the dispute.

Unhappy with what he perceived as Vietnamese ingratitude, Mao began cutting back on material aid to the DRV and by the summer of 1970 all Chinese support troops had left Vietnam. Hanoi not only resented Beijing's reduction in aid but also took great offense at its surprising rapprochement with the United States. Pham Van Dong formally requested that Mao cancel President Richard Nixon's 1972 visit to the PRC, but Mao refused. Mao and Zhou Enlai toasted Richard Nixon in Beijing as American bombers continued their destructive runs over the DRV. Although the PRC did not pressure the DRV to negotiate a peace settlement with the United States as Nixon had hoped, Vietnamese leaders could not help but remember the Geneva Conference and expected Chinese leaders to once again force Vietnam to make compromises that benefited China rather than Vietnam. By the time of the 1973 Paris Peace Accord which ended the fighting between the DRV and the United States, Hanoi had come to rely far more on the Soviets than the Chinese for weapons and supplies, including the tanks it used to launch the final campaign against South Vietnam in 1975. Having contributed massive support to the DRV and suffered over 1,000 Chinese soldiers killed and 4,000 wounded, China could only watch its former Vietnamese ally move closer to its greatest enemy, the Soviet Union.

China and the Khmer Rouge

The rapid withdrawal of U.S. military forces from Indochina in 1973 created a power vacuum in Southeast Asia. PRC leaders feared that Moscow intended to consolidate relations with the new pro-Soviet regimes in Vietnam, Cambodia, and Laos, and thereby encircle China. Moreover, the PRC now faced a unified Vietnam, renamed the SRV (Socialist Republic of Vietnam), with a strong and experienced military on its southern border. The deteriorating relations between China and Vietnam during the latter stages of the war against the United States, exacerbated by the Sino-American rapprochement, meant that the PRC now faced the possibility of hostile neighbors to both the north and the south.

In an attempt to counter Vietnam's increasingly dominant position in Indochina, China cultivated close relations with the Cambodian Communists, known as the Khmer Rouge. The Khmer Rouge shared with the Chinese a distrust of the Vietnamese and had little interest in joining any kind of Vietnam-dominated "Indochina Federation" sought by Hanoi. Khmer Rouge leader Pol Pot had long been suspicious of the Vietnamese and harbored ambitions to retake Cambodian territory that had centuries earlier come under Vietnamese rule. Relations between the DRV and the Khmer Rouge had deteriorated over the course of the war and military clashes between Khmer Rouge and PAVN (People's Army of Vietnam) troops took place as early as 1971. China hoped to build a relationship with the Khmer Rouge as a bulwark against Vietnamese, and therefore Soviet, influence in Indochina.

After the fall of the Cambodian capital Phnom Penh in April 1975, Khmer Rouge troops immediately began seizing territory from Vietnam which had formerly belonged to Cambodia and demanded that all Vietnamese troops leave Cambodian soil. In mid-1976, barely a year after establishing the new state of DK (Democratic Kampuchea), Pol Pot began to purge all Khmer Rouge he deemed to be pro-Vietnamese. He also ordered Khmer Rouge soldiers to cross into Vietnam to attack villages along the border. When Vietnam responded with attacks into Cambodia, Beijing warned Hanoi to halt its aggression against Cambodia and protested against alleged Vietnamese armed intrusions into Chinese territory. In early November 1978, Vietnam and the Soviet Union signed a Treaty of Friendship and Cooperation, clearly indicating that Hanoi had aligned itself with Moscow against China. Beijing continued to ship substantial military supplies and equipment to Cambodia, including Chinese fighter-bombers flown by Chinese-trained Cambodian pilots. Despite Chinese warnings, Vietnam launched an invasion of Cambodia in December 1978, sending 100,000 PAVN troops across the border. They routed the Khmer Rouge and captured Phnom Penh in early January. Vietnamese forces established a new Cambodian government, the PRK (People's Republic of Kampuchea), which maintained close relations with Vietnam. Chinese military leaders discussed sending PLA combat troops to Cambodia to defend the Khmer Rouge but ultimately rejected this option because of the logistical problems of supplying troops in Cambodia. Beijing instead planned a direct attack on Vietnam but waited until the completion of Deng Xiaoping's important visit to the United States in January 1979.[5]

The Sino-Vietnamese Border War

The PRC had multiple objectives in its attack on Vietnam. First, PLA troops intended to pacify the border region by pushing deeply into Vietnam in order to destroy military installations, artillery outposts, and defensive works. Second, the PLA would inflict casualties on the Vietnamese military in order to "punish" Vietnam for its attack on Cambodia. A third less tangible objective involved attempting to convince Hanoi to reconsider its relationship with Moscow by demonstrating China's regional military power and exposing Soviet unwillingness to support Vietnam. In this respect, the attack on Vietnam differed from previous military actions in Korea and on the Sino-Indian border, but resembled the 1969 Sino-Soviet border clashes, which Mao may have initiated for geopolitical rather than territorial reasons. Chinese public pronouncements featured the need to protect the border from Vietnamese aggression by launching a "counterattack in self-defense," but the unstated goal of the attack involved forcing a change in Vietnam's policies toward Cambodia and the Soviet Union.

From the outset, PRC leaders maintained that the attack would be limited and have a short duration, in part to avoid a larger war which would disrupt China's burgeoning modernization program under the new leader Deng Xiaoping and in part to complete the military action before the start of Vietnam's rainy season in April. Although the PRC did not anticipate a military reaction from the Soviet Union in response to the attack on Vietnam, Deng established two military fronts as a precaution. The Northern Front, commanded by Marshal Xu Xiangqian, included troops from several military regions in the north and prepared for a potential Soviet attack on the border. The Southern Front drew troops from most of the military regions, assembled under the command of General Xu Shiyou. This force totaled 300,000 PLA main force troops supported by regional forces and militia, which dealt

The China–Vietnam Border, 1979. From *Chinese Warfighting: The PLA Experience Since 1949,* ed. Mark A. Ryan, David M. Finkelstein, and Michael A. McDevitt (Armonk, NY: M.E. Sharpe, 2003). Copyright © 2003 by the CNA Corporation. Reprinted with permission of M.E. Sharpe, Inc.

primarily with logistical matters. The Southern Front assembled over 1,000 tanks and 1,500 pieces of artillery in preparation for the attack. On the other side of the border, the Vietnamese had 75,000–100,000 border troops and local militia along the border, backed up by perhaps as many as 200,000 PAVN main force troops in the Red River delta region. Although both sides had air and naval capabilities, neither committed them to the fighting.[6]

The battle plan called for a quick strike into northern Vietnam along five major routes and the capture of population centers along the way. Thousands of PLA soldiers infiltrated the border prior to the attack to conduct acts of sabotage and to destroy Vietnamese communications infrastructure. Early on the morning of February 17, 1979, Chinese artillery began shelling Vietnamese positions in preparation for an advance by tanks and infantry. PLA troops crossed the border at multiple locations and converged in columns on five provincial capitals: Lai Chau, Lao Cai, Ha Giang, Cao Bang, and Lang Son. Chinese troops encountered difficulties from the start of the attack, because of the rugged terrain of northern Vietnam which slowed their advance. In some areas, tanks and trucks could not pass, forcing the Chinese logistical chain to rely on human and animal transportation. The outdated PLA supply system forced some units to suffer serious shortages of food, water, and ammunition, even though only a few kilometers inside Vietnamese territory. Despite superior numbers, Chinese forces struggled against Vietnamese defenders, moving only several miles into Vietnam in the first days of the fighting. Chinese officials would later remark on the lack of field training that left many PLA troops unprepared for combat. In some cases Chinese artillery proved ineffective because of an inability to calculate accurately. As a result, infantry troops could not request indirect fire to support their attacks for fear of friendly fire.[7]

In contrast, the Vietnamese border troops and militia turned out to be better trained and equipped than the Chinese had anticipated. These troops fought tenaciously, utilizing a network of tunnels, caves, and trenches to slow the Chinese advance. The Vietnamese battle plan drew upon Maoist military strategy, calling for the border troops to inflict casualties on the Chinese attacking force while drawing them deeper into Vietnam where fresh PAVN units would then attack the weary Chinese forces. The PLA relied on its traditional tactics of applying overwhelming force against individual enemy positions and because they enjoyed a numerical advantage in battles with scattered Vietnamese border troops, PLA forces eventually succeeded in pushing fifty miles into Vietnam, capturing several cities and destroying military fortifications along the way.

On February 27, the PLA began the siege of Lang Son, an important stronghold that controlled the route to Hanoi and the Red River delta. The Chinese had no intention of marching on Hanoi, but they made a concerted effort to capture Lang Son nonetheless. The battle began with an artillery barrage followed by tank and infantry assaults by two divisions of PLA reinforcements. After several days of fighting, Chinese forces surrounded the city and took control of it on March 5. On that same day, the PRC government announced an immediate, unilateral ceasefire and gave the order for all PLA forces to withdraw from Vietnam. All Chinese soldiers who had participated in the attack had returned to Chinese territory by March 16, approximately one month after the initial assault.

This brief border war proved costly for both sides. The exact numbers are unclear, but King Chen's analysis of the available evidence yields an estimated of 125,000 combined casualties, 62,000 for the Vietnamese and 63,000 for the Chinese.[8] Considering that the Chinese had not even encountered PAVN main force units and fought against border troops and militia, these numbers indicated clear limits to the capabilities of the PLA. The brief war revealed problems with Chinese logistical systems and weaponry, neither of which had been updated for decades and proved inadequate for modern combat. The results of the war would spur a movement to upgrade and modernize the Chinese military in the next decade. Both sides claimed victory, but from Beijing's perspective the fighting brought mixed results at best. PLA troops succeeded in destroying defense installations on the Vietnamese side and inflicted significant casualties on the border forces. Yet the PLA performance did not amount to a strong display of regional power sufficient to force Hanoi to end its military action in Cambodia or to reconsider its relationship with the Soviet Union. The subsequent Soviet invasion of Afghanistan in December of 1979 and the dominant position of Vietnam in Indochina presented the Chinese leadership with possibility of Soviet encirclement.

Chinese Opposition to Vietnam's Occupation of Cambodia

In the wake of the Vietnamese invasion of Cambodia, Beijing found itself with no alternative to continued support of the Khmer Rouge in order to oppose Vietnamese domination of Indochina. Given the mixed results of the 1979 war, another Chinese attack on Vietnam offered little promise of forcing a withdrawal of Vietnamese troops from Cambodian soil. The remnants of the Khmer Rouge provided the only tool with which China could begin to work for the expulsion of the Vietnamese. Fortunately for Beijing, the Khmer Rouge depended heavily on Chinese material aid for its survival which meant that the Chinese leaders exercised significant influence over the Khmer Rouge. Prior to this point, China had only limited ability to influence the radical policies of Pol Pot and the Khmer Rouge, but after 1979 Beijing found itself with greater control over its now desperate Cambodian client.

In its attempt to drive Vietnamese troops out of Cambodia, China adopted an effective strategy of combining military and diplomatic pressure designed to drain Vietnamese military strength and exhaust its feeble economy. With regard to military pressure, China continued to supply the Khmer Rouge with weapons and advised Pol Pot's surviving forces to utilize guerrilla tactics to harass Vietnamese troops in Cambodia. The Khmer Rouge force of 30,000 troops could not hope to defeat PAVN forces and overthrow the new Vietnamese-supported PRK regime, but their presence and guerrilla operations necessitated a large deployment of up to 250,000 Vietnamese troops in Cambodia. Beijing capitalized on regional fears of Vietnamese expansion to prevail upon the government of Thailand for permission to transport supplies to the Khmer Rouge across Thai territory. Without a common border with Cambodia and with Vietnamese ships patrolling off the Cambodian coast, Thailand played a vital role in China's plans to sustain the Khmer Rouge as viable force against Vietnam. The Thai government continued to recognize the Khmer Rouge as the legitimate government of Cambodia and allowed its forces to move back and forth freely across the Thai–Cambodian border. The Khmer Rouge could avoid confrontation when prudent, using Thailand as a safe sanctuary much in the way Vietnamese troops had used Cambodia during the American war in Vietnam. Beijing therefore hoped the guerrillas could bog Hanoi down in protracted warfare, forcing the Vietnamese to expend more men and resources in a quagmire of its own making. In addition to providing military materials to the Khmer Rouge, the PRC maintained its own military forces on the Sino-Vietnamese border. By keeping alive the threat of a second attack on Vietnam, China forced Hanoi to prepare for a possible two front war and to keep as many as 200,000 troops on the Sino-Vietnamese border which otherwise would have been available for deployment in Cambodia.

On the diplomatic front, China attempted to prevent Hanoi from consolidating its position in Cambodia by organizing international opposition to the Vietnamese occupation. Beijing consistently defended DK as the legitimate government of Cambodia and portrayed Pol Pot's regime as a victim of foreign aggression in violation of international law. In the United Nations, of which the PRC became a member in 1971, Chinese representatives argued that Vietnam's invasion of Cambodia trampled underfoot the UN Charter and fundamental principles of international law and criticized the pro-Vietnamese PRK regime as a puppet supported by Vietnamese military force. China's efforts produced results as in November 1979 the United Nations adopted a resolution calling for the immediate withdrawal of all foreign forces from Cambodia.

China owed its diplomatic success in support of the Khmer Rouge to its ability to take advantage of the concerns of other Southeast Asian states, which feared an aggressive and expansion-minded Vietnam. Beijing described the Vietnamese invasion of Cambodia not as an isolated event but rather as a part of a master plan for Soviet–Vietnamese hegemony in Asia and a matter of international significance. Still, some Southeast Asian states perhaps feared China as much as Vietnam and proved reluctant to respond to China's call to defend DK. Furthermore, the near universal disgust for Pol Pot regime's domestic policies that brought about the death of more than one million Cambodians between 1975 and 1978 made it difficult for China to arrange international support for DK. For their part, Khmer Rouge leaders feebly admitted that they had committed excesses and serious mistakes. Beijing urged changes to the Khmer Rouge leadership and political program in order to improve its image. The Khmer Rouge responded by adopting a new political program which included a variety of social and political freedoms for the Cambodian people, such as freedom of speech, the right to form political parties, and the right to vote for a national assembly. A modest reshuffling of top offices followed, most notably with Khieu Samphan replacing the notorious Pol Pot as prime minister.

In order to strengthen the international opposition to the Vietnamese occupation, Beijing urged the Khmer Rouge to form a broad united front with other anti-Vietnamese Cambodian groups. Chinese leaders offered to supply arms and ammunition to the supporters of former ruler Prince Norodom Sihanouk and other Cambodian political groups in exchange for their participation in the united front with the Khmer Rouge. After prolonged negotiations, Norodom Sihanouk and Son Sann, leader of the Khmer People's National Liberation Front (KPNLF), met with Khieu Samphan in Kuala Lumpur in June 1982 to declare the formation of the CGDK (Coalition Government of Democratic Kampuchea). Sihanouk took the office of president with Khieu Samphan and Son Sann serving as vice-president in charge of foreign affairs and prime minister, respectively. These diverse groups exhibited little genuine cooperation and the alliance proved tenuous, but the coalition government provided Beijing with a larger military force with which to fight the Vietnamese and more acceptable representation for Cambodia in the international forum. As a result, a multitude of states recognized the new CGDK, including the United States, and joined China in a strict economic embargo of Vietnam. Vietnam's economy, already heavily dependent on massive Soviet aid, suffered greatly during its occupation of Cambodia.

Through these military, diplomatic, and economic pressures, China contributed to the gradual weakening of Vietnam to the point where its occupation of Cambodia became too costly to sustain. This campaign came at a relatively low cost to China while slowly draining the resources of Vietnam and its Soviet supporters. This practical strategy helped keep the Cambodian resistance alive until Mikhail Gorbachev began a program of significant change in the Soviet Union. His economic and political restructuring and his desire to normalize relations with China resulted in a drastic reduction in aid to Vietnam, forcing an end to the occupation of Cambodia. Unable to continue without Soviet support, Vietnam announced in April 1989 that it would unilaterally withdraw its troops by the end of September 1989. This announcement represented the realization of a military and foreign policy goal that China had pursued for ten years.

Although China's military and diplomatic pressure helped force Vietnam to end its occupation of Cambodia, the 1979 war served as a wake up call for PLA commanders. The lackluster performance of Chinese troops revealed that it had not maintained an effective training regimen and its weapons and equipment were outdated. In the next two decades, the PLA would focus on attempts to improve by reorganizing its forces, rethinking its traditional doctrine, and bringing its technology up to date.

The Chinese Military Since 1980

Mao's death in September 1976 marked the end of an era in which his views had decisively shaped the political and military policies of the PRC. Mao's influence would continue to guide PRC leaders in their fundamental goal of building a militarily strong and economically prosperous socialist state, but the end of the Maoist era opened the door for important changes to the way Chinese leaders pursued this goal. Under the leadership of Deng Xiaoping, the CCP would make dramatic changes to its political and economic policies, amounting to what some have called a "Second Revolution." The post-Mao emphasis on economic development and modernization had important implications for the PLA, which went through significant changes and faced new challenges, both internal and external, in the last two decades of the 20th century.

Deng Xiaoping and the "Four Modernizations"

Following Mao's death, his handpicked successor, Hua Guofeng, assumed the posts of Party Chairman and Chair of the MAC. In deciding political policy, Hua advocated following whatever policies Mao Zedong had supported. Unfortunately for Hua, many of the leading officials in the party, government, and military viewed this as a continuation of the Cultural Revolution which had wreaked havoc on the state and the Chinese people. Those who had suffered during the Cultural Revolution had no desire to see it continue. As a result, Hua did not enjoy strong support and his tenure as Mao's successor proved fleeting. In one of his few accomplishments after Mao's death, Hua conspired with Wang Dongxing, the head of Mao's personal bodyguard unit, to arrest the so-called "Gang of Four," which included Mao's widow Jiang Qing and three of her close supporters. Jiang had risen to great authority during the Cultural Revolution and for many Chinese represented the excesses and chaos of the last decade. Accused of counterrevolutionary activities and branded, ironically, as an anti-Mao rightist, Jiang Qing and the rest of the Gang of Four went on trial in 1980–1981, which resulted in long prison terms for all.

Removing Jiang from public power did little to secure Hua Guofeng's position as China's paramount leader. Deng Xiaoping, a veteran of the Long March and twice banished to the countryside during the Cultural Revolution, reemerged in 1977 at the head of a group of senior CCP and PLA officials who had no taste for Hua's continuation of Mao's policies. Deng and his supporters rehabilitated a number of capable officials who, like Deng, had been criticized by Red Guards and sent off to remote areas for "reeducation through labor." These men returned to the capital to begin implementing Deng's more practical policies designed to improve China's economic condition. Hua soon realized that his own inexperience in national politics and determination to cling to Mao's unpopular policies rendered him vulnerable to Deng and his vast network of political allies within the party, government, and military. Deng gradually squeezed Hua aside, taking for himself the chair of the MAC, reorganized in 1982 as the CMC (Central Military Commission), and then appointing his protégés Hu Yaobang and Zhao Ziyang as general secretary of the party and premier, respectively. By the end of 1980, Hua had quietly receded from the top levels of leadership, and Deng had emerged as China's paramount leader, a position he retained until his death in 1997.

In 1978, Deng began preparing for what some would call China's "Second Revolution," that is the incorporation of material incentives and capitalist-free market reforms in the Chinese economy. With the support of a group young protégés such as Hu and Zhao, Deng turned the PRC away from Mao's emphasis on political ideology and class struggle to a new focus on the "Four Modernizations." This program directed efforts to modernize China in four critical areas: agriculture, industry, science and technology, and national defense. Deng began with practical economic reforms in the agricultural sector, such as giving individual farmers greater control over their farms and responsibility for production. When these new policies proved successful and widely popular, Deng did the same in the industrial sector, giving managers greater responsibility in acquiring raw materials and resources, production, and compensation of workers. By introducing material incentives and free market reforms, opening up China to foreign investment and technology, and by allowing greater intellectual and cultural exchanges with foreign countries, Deng presided over a period of remarkable economic growth which featured dramatic increases in personal income in both rural and urban areas. This pragmatic approach, which Deng had advocated as far back as the early 1960s, found expression in an old Sichuan proverb, "It does not matter if it is a yellow cat or a black cat, as long as it catches mice."[1]

Deng Xiaoping recognized the need to improve Chinese military and national defense capabilities, but he deliberately placed the military as the last of the Four Modernizations. China's lack of resources made it impossible to upgrade PLA equipment and weapons, however great the need. Chinese soldiers still used weapons and equipment based on technology of the 1950s and 1960s and had not kept pace with developments of more modern armies of the world. The Sino-Soviet split and the departure of Soviet engineers and advisors in 1960 had serious consequences for China's military, which lost its only source of weapons and military technology. Deng gave priority to agricultural and industrial development, hoping that these areas would generate surplus funds that could then be used to purchase advanced military technology, which remained a long-term goal. As a result, the initial steps toward modernization of the Chinese military involved changes in organization and the way Chinese strategists conceived of future conflicts.

As a first step in military modernization, Deng began a force reduction program, designed to reduce the size of the PLA in order to transform it into a smaller, more effective force. Initial waves of demobilization and reorganization brought the PLA from 4 million total personnel down to approximately 3.5 million in the mid-1980s. Demobilization continued through the 1990s, bringing the PLA down to 2.5 million by the year 2000 and allowing for a reallocation of military funds into weapons purchases. While many demobilized soldiers simply returned to civilian life, militia and border patrol units underwent reorganization as a new force called the PAP (People's Armed Police). The 900,000 strong PAP took up the task of internal security, supporting the PSB (Public Security Bureau), allowing the PLA to concentrate on external threats and national defense. Regardless, the PLA would retain a secondary role in internal security, as had all military forces in China dating back to the Manchu conquest.[2]

People's War Under Modern Conditions

In addition to reducing its size, PLA strategists began to rethink their doctrinal principles which dated back to the 1930s and 1940s. The 1979 war with Vietnam had revealed the ineffectiveness of the PLA in dealing with an opponent of inferior numbers and relatively equal firepower, raising the question of how the PLA would fare in a war against a modern army that enjoyed a significant advantage in firepower and technology. Since 1949, PLA strategists had relied on Mao's strategy of People's War in planning for an attack on the PRC by either the United States or the Soviet Union. As of the 1969 border clashes, Chinese strategists believed the Soviet Union posed the greatest threat. The traditional strategy of People's War called for a retreat to the interior in the face of a superior enemy force. Once this force had been "lured deep" into Chinese territory, PLA main force units and militia would engage in mobile warfare and guerrilla attacks on enemy vulnerable points and lines of supply and communication. In the course of a protracted struggle, occupation of large parts of China, and perhaps even the use of tactical nuclear weapons, the enemy would gradually become bogged down in China's vast expanses. Eventually, Chinese forces would launch a general counteroffensive against the weakened and overextended enemy forces, driving them out of Chinese territory.

By the late 1970s, PLA strategists realized that developments in military technology made this strategy unappealing for mounting an effective defense against a potential Soviet attack. First, the mechanized forces of the Soviet Red Army could move so quickly that PLA planners doubted the ability of Chinese forces to succeed in a war of maneuver and mobile warfare. Second, advanced missile technology allowed the Soviets to attack virtually every remote corner of China from Soviet territory. This would deny the PLA a safe rear area, an essential part of People's War, without risk to Soviet forces. Therefore, PLA strategists made changes to the strategy of People's War in order to mount a successful defense against a technologically superior and more mobile enemy. They called this new strategy "People's War under Modern Conditions."

While retaining Mao's emphasis on "active defense," the new strategy rejected some of the core tenets of traditional Maoist military thinking, such as the initial strategic retreat and yielding of territory to the enemy force. In the event of a Soviet attack, the PLA planned to engage in positional warfare to defend important cities along the border, preventing the enemy force from penetrating deep into Chinese territory. The new strategy emphasized not protracted war but the importance of the first battle, as PLA forces would attempt to blunt the initial enemy assault. Once the enemy had been halted near the border, PLA main force units and militia would move behind enemy lines into Soviet territory to conduct mobile operations and guerrilla attacks on enemy supply lines. Once Soviet operations had been sufficiently disrupted, the PLA would launch a counteroffensive to push Soviet forces back across the border.[3]

In order to prepare to execute People's War under Modern Conditions, in the mid-1980s the PLA reorganized its thirty-five Army Corps into twenty-four Group Armies which featured integrated units. Each Group Army included 50,000–60,000 soldiers, combining infantry, armor, artillery, engineers, and other support units which had previously operated independently. The new Group Armies offered an integrated command for more effective centralized application. In addition to changes to the force structure, the CMC further reduced the number of military regions from eleven to seven (Beijing, Shenyang, Jinan, Nanjing, Guangzhou, Chengdu, and Lanzhou), increasing central control and efficiency. In 1988, the PLA restored all ranks and insignias which had been abolished in the 1960s, marking a renewed interest in professionalization of the military.

Local, Limited War

Even as the PLA made these doctrinal and organizational changes, strategists continued to rethink China's national defense strategy. The two superpowers had arrived at a Cold War stalemate in which neither side showed an inclination to take reckless action by attacking each other or the PRC. Instead of preparing for continental defense against a major attack by the USSR, the PLA began preparing for smaller engagements on China's periphery which might involve a variety of possible opponents. Chinese strategists now spoke in terms of "Local, Limited War" which required not massive mobilization of manpower but rather the rapid deployment of elite forces that relied on speed and mobility. Accordingly, each of the seven military regions assembled Rapid Response Units or "Fist" units, which can be deployed in less than twelve hours to meet any challenge to China's territorial sovereignty along its borders. In truth, the PLA had much more experience in this type of conflict, having fought border conflicts with India, the Soviet Union, and Vietnam. PLA strategists believed that the PRC's next military conflict would take place along the periphery, such as the Taiwan Straits or the South China Sea, where it claims sovereignty over disputed islands.

The 1991 Gulf War caught the attention of PLA commanders who saw this as exactly the kind of war of limited area and duration that they believed China would likely face in future conflicts. Moreover, it clearly demonstrated the high level of technology that characterized modern warfare, leading Chinese strategists to prepare for "Local, Limited War under High-Tech Conditions." The effectiveness of the American air campaign against Iraq in particular confirmed the belief of PLA strategists that they could no longer count on greater numbers to make up for technological deficiencies. As a result, in the 1990s the PLA emphasized acquisition and development of new technology and weapons.

Despite Deng's emphasis on economic development, China had fallen far behind the modern armies of the United States and Europe in terms of military technology. The collapse of the Soviet Union in 1991 opened up new opportunities for the PRC to purchase arms and military technology from the new Russian government which found itself in need of money. Increasing military budgets allowed the PLA to acquire helicopters, fighter planes, submarines and other naval vessels, missile and air defense systems, and other equipment from the Russians, who proved willing to sell advanced weapons and technology that the other Western powers would not. This equipment proved essential to the new national defense strategy which emphasized joint operations with increased roles for the People's Liberation Army Navy and the People's Liberation Army Air Force, which had traditionally played secondary roles in PLA infantry campaigns.

The consistent force reductions since the late 1970s, the reorganization of ground forces into combined arms Group Armies, and the drive for greater technology and more sophisticated weaponry are all parts of the attempt to transform the PLA from a manpower-based infantry force intended to defend the Chinese interior into a smaller, technology-based military force capable of projecting force along its periphery against a variety of opponents.

The Tian'anmen Square Demonstrations

While the PLA planned for future conflicts, internal pacification remained an important secondary role for the Chinese military. The economic reforms begun in the late 1970s produced dramatic changes in Chinese society, including rising personal incomes and rapid economic growth, but also social unrest. By the late 1980s, inflation, corruption, and nepotism among officials had led to widespread popular discontent which came to a head in 1989 when student demonstrators gathered in Tian'anmen Square in the center of Beijing and posed a direct challenge to the authority of the CCP. Deng Xiaoping and the Party leaders responded to this challenge by sending the PLA in to clear the Square in what many refer to as the Tian'anmen Square Massacre of June 4, 1989.

Large-scale student demonstrations first erupted in 1985 as young, educated Chinese called for greater political freedoms and civil liberties. Many proclaimed the need for a "Fifth Modernization," a term for democracy coined by dissident Wei Jingsheng, to accompany the economic reforms. Deng and most of the CCP leaders rejected these calls, maintaining that the economic reforms must take place in a stable political environment under the firm guidance of the CCP. Campus demonstrations across China in 1985 and 1986 revealed the depth of dissatisfaction among the students, who expressed frustration over favoritism shown the children of high-ranking officials and the lack of freedoms of speech, press, and association. As hundreds of thousands of students marched in protests in several cities, CCP leaders considered how to respond. General Secretary of the CCP Hu Yaobang expressed understanding of student frustrations and described them as well-meaning and patriotic. More conservative officials bristled at Hu's tolerance of the demonstrations which they believed only emboldened the students, whom they regarded as spoiled and ungrateful. Even though the demonstrations died down in early 1986, some officials urged Deng to remove Hu from his position. Deng agreed and forced Hu to resign as general secretary and to complete a self-criticism in January 1987. Zhao Ziyang took over as general secretary while Li Peng took Zhao's place as premier.

Hu's death of a heart attack in April 1989 sparked a new round of demonstrations that dwarfed those of previous years. Beijing college and university students went to the Monument to the People's Heroes in the center of Tian'anmen Square to lay wreaths and display banners eulogizing Hu. In addition to expressing their respect and admiration for Hu, some students put up posters on their campuses criticizing CCP leadership and calling for greater political freedoms. In late April, thousands of students from local universities descended on the Square to demonstrate for democracy and to present a petition to the government demanding a variety of changes. Others began hunger strikes, vowing not to eat until China had democracy. The government responded with editorials in the party newspaper *People's Daily,* criticizing the protestors for causing chaos and endangering economic development. Rather than dampen the students' spirits, the editorials angered and emboldened them.

The party leadership again split over how to deal with the students. The new premier Li Peng and other members of the politburo interpreted the demonstrations as premeditated attacks on the party and advocated action to suppress the movement. Zhao Ziyang, like Hu Yaobang before him, advocated tolerance and consideration for the issues the students raised. In some respects, each side sought to use the demonstrations to make political points. Li Peng hoped to slow the progress of economic liberalization in order to preserve order and stability. Zhao Ziyang advocated pushing ahead with economic reform despite the side effects and social unrest. The students became a pawn in the political struggle within the top levels of CCP leadership. Deng Xiaoping sided with the conservatives and ordered the PLA to prepare to support the PAP and PSB in restoring order around the Square. A few clashes took place between security forces and demonstrators, but the students tried hard to maintain order and avoid giving the government an excuse to use force against them. Regardless, in late April, Deng ordered the 38th Group Army from the Beijing Military Region to send troops into downtown Beijing. As PLA trucks carried troops toward the city center, Chinese citizens poured into the streets, blocked the roads, and stranded the troops in their trucks for hours. The bewildered young soldiers listened to the citizens plead with them not to use force against the demonstrators. The troops eventually withdrew back to their positions outside the city proper, giving the citizens the impression that they had succeeded and that the PLA would not use force against its own people. This incident proved an embarrassment for the PLA and the conservatives on the politburo.

On May 4, the 70th anniversary of the 1919 May Fourth student protests, tens of thousands of students marched to the Square in violation of city regulations against unapproved demonstrations. Joined by citizens of many walks of life, including journalists, workers, and even some police officers, the protests attracted the attention of the world. The growing movement humiliated the PRC leadership when Soviet leader Mikhail Gorbachev made a state visit to Beijing in mid-May. Not only did Gorbachev observe hundreds of thousands of demonstrators in the Square, but several official activities had to be canceled including plans to lay a wreath at the Monument to the People's Heroes. Such changes to the itinerary implied that the CCP leadership had lost control of the situation.

After Gorbachev's departure on May 18, Deng authorized a declaration of martial law in Beijing to take effect on the morning of May 20. The PLA had been moving away from internal security duties in the previous decade, but the PAP and PSB could not handle the crowds of demonstrators. Deng therefore assembled a large force on the outskirts of Beijing, many drawn from different military regions across China. When these troops attempted to enter the city to enforce the martial law decree, throngs of citizens again blocked the convoy trucks and prevented them from advancing toward the Square. At the time, the demonstrations had been losing steam, but the declaration of martial law and the attempt to bring PLA troops into the city, along with the citizens' success in blocking them, gave new life to the movement. Having twice faced down the PLA in the streets of Beijing, demonstrators again descended on the Square in massive numbers.

The humiliating experience of late May convinced Deng and the conservative leaders of the politburo that the situation required stronger measures. Some of the more than 150,000 PLA forces stationed outside of Beijing began quietly infiltrating the city and moving toward the Square. Young soldiers, unarmed and dressed in civilian clothes, emerged from the subway stations in small groups. They reassembled in specific locations near the Square, such as the compounds of the *People's Daily* newspaper, the Central Broadcast building, and Zhongshan Park. Other troops used a network of tunnels underneath the city constructed in the 1960s and 1970s to move into positions adjacent to the Square, such as the Great Hall of the People. Unmarked trucks brought weapons, equipment, and additional soldiers into the city.

The June 4 Crackdown

Deng designated June 3 as the date for the military action to remove demonstrators from the Square. The standing committee of the politburo met that afternoon for final preparations. The plan called for 50,000 PLA troops to converge on the Square from all directions. The initial assault would begin at 9:30 PM with infantry clearing the way for tanks and APCs. The actual clearing of the Square would take place between 1:00 and 6:00 AM on the morning of June 4. The politburo authorized the PLA, PAP, and PSB to take all measures necessary to deal with anyone who interfered with the movement of troops. Television announcements on the afternoon and evening of June 3 warned citizens to stay off the streets and away from Tian'anmen Square.

At approximately 9:30 PM on June 3, the operation began as PLA troops emerged from the Great Hall of the People and other locations around the Square. Others followed major roads from outside the city to converge on the Square. The violence began along the western approach on Chang'an Boulevard, where students had erected barricades in anticipation of another attempt to move soldiers into the Square. Demonstrators and citizens rushed into the streets to block the PLA as they had done before, but this time they faced fast moving APCs , which crashed through the barricades. The crowds responded by hurling rocks, bottles, and even Molotov cocktails at the military vehicles. PLA troops responded first with tear gas or by firing their weapons in the air, but then opened fire on the crowds. The vast majority of the deaths occurred not in the Square itself but in the streets as PLA forces descended on the city center from all sides.

By 1:00 AM, PLA soldiers from outside had arrived at the Square, coordinating with those who had been concealed in various locations nearby to seal off the Square. Still not believing that the PLA would use deadly force against them, many demonstrators thought the soldiers would fire only rubber bullets and held up quilts for protection. Loudspeakers ordered the remaining demonstrators to leave. Many did, but a few thousand remained at the base of the Monument to the People's Heroes. At 4:00 AM the lights in the Square went out in preparation for the final assault. At 4:30 AM, the lights came back on and the troops began entering the Square. Tanks and APCs trampled the ramshackle tents demonstrators had been using for shelter and ran over the "Goddess of Democracy" statue, built by Beijing art students. Representatives negotiated with PLA officers to arrange the evacuation of the last demonstrators, who filed out of the Square at gunpoint. By dawn, the Square fell quiet, under the complete control of the PLA.[4]

The exact number of deaths as a result of the June 4 military assault on the Tian'anmen Square demonstrators is unclear. Estimates range from a few hundred, the Chinese government reported 241 deaths of soldiers and civilians, to several thousand. Despite the fact that it faced an unarmed and largely unorganized opponent, the PLA saw significant losses of personnel and equipment. Hundreds of military vehicles, overturned and burned, littered the streets of Beijing. According to the government, PLA forces suffered 23 killed and 7,000 wounded. Rumors of a split among military units and a potential conflict between Group Armies proved exaggerated, but there is evidence that a number of senior officers disagreed with the decisions to declare martial law and use the PLA to suppress the demonstrations. The fact that more than 100 officers and 1,400 enlisted men faced charges of failing to do their duty may indicate that many soldiers had second thoughts about using force against unarmed citizens. Many of the soldiers involved had little training for such duties, and their inexperience and anxiety undoubtedly contributed to the violence.

The order to use force against the Tian'anmen Square demonstrators came directly from Deng Xiaoping, who justified the need to "be firm with these counterrevolutionary riots" in order to prevent "civil war." The operation ended the demonstrations and cowed the population, but the PLA suffered a loss of prestige both at home and at abroad. Many Chinese now view the PLA with suspicion and fear, and continue to identify the military as an instrument of internal suppression rather than external defense. Western governments reacted to the bloody events of June 4 by imposing an arms embargo on the PRC, hindering PLA efforts to acquire modern equipment, weapons, and technology.[5]

China, Taiwan, and the United States

Following the violent suppression of the 1989 demonstrations, the most important military issue China faced in the 1990s involved its relations with Taiwan and the United States. From the PRC perspective, reunification with Taiwan represents the final outstanding territorial issue of the Chinese revolution. It also has implications for the legitimacy of the CCP, which no longer justifies its rule as the vanguard of the workers and peasants but rather as the party that can protect the PRC's territorial integrity and restore China to a prominent status in Asia and the world. It remains the most important issue in the relationship between the PRC and the United States.

Prior to 1972, the PRC maintained a belligerent policy toward Taiwan, periodically shelling Nationalist-held islands off the coast and threatening to use force against Taiwan. The shelling of Jinmen and other offshore islands in the 1950s demonstrated Mao's policy of using limited military force to create tension in the Straits in order to threaten Taiwan and drive a wedge between the United States and Chiang Kai-shek's government. Rather than abandon the islands, Taiwan moved closer to the United States, signing a defense treaty in 1954 that committed the United States to Taiwan's defense. The PLA continued sporadic shelling of offshore islands for decades, but Mao decided to hold off on a military campaign to "liberate" Taiwan. In the meantime, the governments of both Mao Zedong and Chiang Kai-shek claimed to be the legitimate representative of all of China. Taiwan legislators continued to represent constituents across the Straits, and Chiang vowed to recapture the mainland from the communist "bandits." For his part, Mao used the threat of attack by Taiwan forces or infiltration of Chiang's spies to whip up support for his domestic campaigns and to keep the revolutionary fervor alive in the PRC.

The PRC position on Taiwan changed only with the Sino-American rapprochement in 1972. The long simmering Sino-Soviet rift, which broke into the open with the 1969 border clashes on the Wusuli River, helped Mao and other CCP leaders move toward better relations with the United States as a counterweight to the USSR, which now loomed as the greatest threat to China's security. At the same time, American President Richard Nixon and his National Security Advisor, and later Secretary of State, Henry Kissinger sought to improve relations with the PRC in order to ease international tension and to facilitate a negotiated settlement to the war in Vietnam. During Nixon's historic 1972 visit to Beijing both sides pledged to work toward normalizing relations, ending two decades of estrangement and hostility. This had significant implications for the American relationship with Chiang Kai-shek's government on Taiwan, which had already seen the PRC assume the China seat on the UN Security Council in 1971. In the Shanghai Communiqué, which summarized the position of each government, Nixon acknowledged that "there is but one China and that Taiwan is a part of China" and pledged to gradually withdraw American military personnel and installations from Taiwan. This "strategic ambiguity" fit the immediate needs of all three states, as both the PRC and the ROC agreed with the "one China" policy, but it left unanswered the question of which government served as the legitimate ruling authority over the "one China."

Both the United States and the PRC expressed a desire to establish official diplomatic relations, but the Chinese insisted that the United States break all official ties with Taiwan, remove all American military forces from the island, and abrogate the 1954 Treaty as preconditions. The Nixon and Ford administrations made no attempt to do so, but President Jimmy Carter and his National Security Advisor Zbigniew Brezinski made normalization of US–China relations a priority. In late 1978, the two governments agreed on another joint communiqué in which the United States recognized the PRC as the sole legal government of China, agreed to remove its military personnel from Taiwan, and abrogated the 1954 Treaty. The American Congress reserved the right to sell arms to the Taiwan government by passing the Taiwan Relations Act in 1979, which ensured that the United States would provide Taiwan with weapons sufficient to defend itself against a PRC attack. Deng Xiaoping fumed over the issue of arms sales to Taiwan but agreed to proceed with the establishment of diplomatic relations, which began on January 1, 1979. Deng overlooked the issue of arms sales to Taiwan in part to secure American support for China against the Soviet Union in preparation for the PRC's upcoming February 1979 attack on Vietnam. Yet Chinese negotiators continued to address this issue with their American counterparts, which resulted in a third Sino-American joint communiqué in 1982. The United States acceded to Chinese demands by reaffirming the "one China" policy and by promising to gradually reduce the quantity and quality of weapons sold to Taiwan. For its part, the PRC promised to take a peaceful approach to the issue of reunification of Taiwan with the mainland. The three joint communiqués of 1972, 1978, and 1982 formed the basis of Sino-American relations with regard to Taiwan.

The normalization of relations between the PRC and the United States and American promises to gradually end arms sales had a softening effect on PRC policy toward Taiwan. The earlier policy of maintaining tension in the Straits through periodic shelling of offshore islands gave way to a peaceful approach. In fitting with his overall policy of creating a secure environment in which to pursue economic development, Deng Xiaoping began encouraging greater contacts between the PRC and Taiwan, including trade and investment, postal contacts, and sports and cultural exchanges. In 1984, Deng unveiled the "one country, two systems" policy designed to facilitate the return of Chinese sovereignty to Hong Kong after over a century of British colonial rule. This policy designated Hong Kong as a special administrative region which would enjoy economic autonomy while submitting to PRC foreign and defense policy. Deng hoped that increasing economic and cultural ties would gradually bind Taiwan to the mainland and result in a peaceful reunification. Not surprisingly, Chiang Ching-kuo, who assumed power in Taiwan after the death of his father Chiang Kai-shek in 1975, rejected any such arrangement with a "three no" policy: no contact, no negotiation, and no compromise.

The PRC maintained the "peace offensive" until changes in Taiwan politics began to challenge the status quo of "strategic ambiguity." In 1988, Lee Teng-hui, a native Taiwanese, took over as president of the ROC at the death of Chiang Ching-kuo. His rise to power coincided with a democratization movement in the late 1980s and the emergence of the DPP (Democratic Progressive Party) which openly supported Taiwan independence. Lee continued to adhere to the one China policy, but PRC leaders feared that he harbored aspirations to split Taiwan from China, creating a "two China" or "one China, one Taiwan" policy. Lee sought to increase Taiwan's relations, both official and unofficial, with other states and to join international organizations such as the Asian Development Bank and the World Bank. Beijing did not oppose Taiwan's admission to international economic organizations but grew increasingly suspicious of Lee Teng-hui's intentions. For example, in January 1995, PRC President Jiang Zemin proposed negotiations on the issue of reunification, but Lee responded with a demand that the PRC first renounce the use of force against Taiwan as a prerequisite for talks.[6]

Beijing's apprehensions about Taiwan independence are rooted in larger strategic and geopolitical considerations. Chinese officials are keen to achieve reunification not only for the sake of completing the revolution but also because Taiwan poses a security risk to the PRC. Should Taiwan ally itself too closely with a foreign power hostile to the PRC, it could become a base for an attack. Moreover, as Andrew Nathan has pointed out, the PRC leadership is well aware that separatists in Tibet, Xinjiang, and Inner Mongolia might use Taiwanese steps toward independence as an encouragement to do the same. These territories make up nearly 35 percent of PRC territory.[7]

The Chinese government aspires to exert a certain degree of influence over Taiwan's foreign policy in order to protect its own interests and has tried different strategies to achieve this goal. Mao Zedong had hoped to create military tension in the Straits, ideally causing American officials to fear that Chiang's government on Taiwan would drag the United States into an unwanted war with the PRC, and thereby drive a wedge between the two allies. This policy did not achieve the desired result, so after 1979 Deng employed a peaceful approach which encouraged economic ties with Taiwan. The democratization of Taiwan and the rise of the independence movement led Deng and his colleagues to again reassess China's strategy. As a result, in 1995–1996 Beijing made a radical departure from the peaceful approach when it adopted a bellicose strategy of using military exercises and missile tests in the Taiwan Straits in an attempt to influence policy in both Taiwan and the United States.

Military Exercises in the Taiwan Straits

While the PRC had grown increasingly uncomfortable with political developments on Taiwan through the early 1990s, Lee Teng-hui's 1995 visit to the United States to attend his class reunion at Cornell University provided the catalyst for the abrupt change in Chinese policy. Chinese leaders saw this as a part of a pattern of recent American violations of the three joint communiqués. For example, in 1992, the George H. W. Bush administration sold F-16 fighter planes to Taiwan. This represented a significant increase in Taiwan's air defense capabilities and, from the Chinese perspective, violated the 1982 arms sales communiqué in which the United States promised to reduce the quality of weaponry it sold to Taiwan. In 1994, the Clinton administration expanded government to government contacts and upgraded its treatment of Taiwan officials. When in early 1995 the American Congress approved a visa for Lee Teng-hui's visit, describing it as a personal rather than an official visit, Beijing interpreted it as an indication that the United States encouraged Taiwan independence. China then adopted a new militant policy designed to convince the United States to revise its Taiwan policy and to intimidate Taiwanese leaders into abandoning their moves toward independence.

To make its desires clear, in July 1995 the PLA conducted military exercises in the Taiwan Straits, including combined air and naval operations and missile tests. Over the next several months, the PLA conducted three more such exercises, firing missiles into the waters off the coast of Taiwan, simulating a naval blockade of the island (and the American response), and even practicing for an amphibious assault. Chinese officials intended these military exercises as a warning to Taiwan leaders and voters, who headed to the polls in December for legislative elections. Taiwan voters continued to support the Guomindang and its "one China" policy, but the pro-independence DPP did better than expected by winning a significant number of seats in the legislature.

Beijing reacted by announcing another round of military exercises in the Straits scheduled for March 1996, just prior to Taiwan's presidential election. At the same time, the PRC press carried editorials warning against Taiwan independence and stating Beijing's willingness to use military force to prevent such a move. The PLA massed 100,000 troops in Fujian Province for these exercises and launched missiles that landed only twenty miles from major cities on Taiwan's coast. United States officials did not believe that the PRC actually intended to attack Taiwan but urged Chinese officials to cancel the exercises and to refrain from interfering in Taiwan politics. The Chinese privately informed American diplomats that the PLA would not attack but went ahead with the exercises in a show of determination to influence affairs in the Straits. In a similar show of resolve, the United States sent two carrier battle groups to the region. The PLA continued its missile tests, warning against foreign intervention in China's "domestic" affairs.[8]

The PLA completed its exercises as Taiwan voters returned Lee Teng-hui to the presidency. One could argue that Beijing succeeded in scaring voters away from the DPP candidates, but this is by no means clear. In fact, four years later in the

2000 presidential elections, Taiwan voters elected DPP presidential candidate Chen Shui-bian to office. Chen subsequently backed away from his party's pro-independence position in the interests of peaceful relations with the PRC, but unification seems unlikely anytime soon. On the other hand, the PLA exercises resulted in changes to American policy toward Taiwan. In the interests of reducing tensions in the Straits, the United States scaled back its arms sales, restricted Taiwanese officials to transit visas, and urged Lee Teng-hui to avoid action that might upset the status quo. In 1997, President Clinton visited Beijing for a summit meeting where he assured Chinese President Jiang Zemin that the United States did not support Taiwan independence. The PRC remains staunchly opposed to Taiwan independence and insists that it will use force to prevent Taiwan from pursing a separatist course. As a result, the Taiwan issue remains the most important point of focus for the PLA. At the present time, it is not clear that the PLA is capable of mounting a successful military campaign against Taiwan, even if the United States did not commit its forces to the island's defense.[9]

Notes

Chapter 1

1. Ralph Sawyer, trans., *Sun Tzu: The Art of War* (Boulder, CO: Westview Press, 1994), 33–37.

2. Edward L. Shaughnessy, "Historical Perspectives on the Introduction of the Chariot into China," *Harvard Journal of Asiatic Studies* 48, no. 1 (June 1988): 228.

3. Hsu Cho-yun, *Ancient China in Transition: An Analysis of Social Mobility, 722–222 B.C.* (Stanford: Stanford University Press, 1965), 55.

4. Joseph Needham and Robin Yates, eds., *Science and Civilization in China,* vol. 5, Part VI (Cambridge: Cambridge University Press, 1994), 120, 184.

5. John Minford, trans., *The Art of War* (New York: Penguin Books, 2002), 68.

6. Arthur Waldron, "The Problem of the Great Wall of China," *Harvard Journal of Asiatic Studies* 43, no. 2 (December 1983): 663; See also same author, *The Great Wall of China: From History to Myth* (Cambridge: Cambridge University Press, 1990).

7. David Graff, *Medieval Chinese Warfare, 300–900* (London: Routledge, 2002), 205–8.

8. On firearms in China see Kenneth Chase, *Firearms: A Global History to 1700* (Cambridge: Cambridge University Press, 2003).

9. Jack Weatherford, *Genghis Khan and the Making of the Modern World* (New York: Crown Publishers, 2004), 65.

10. Edward Dreyer, *Zheng He: China and the Oceans in the Early Ming Dynasty, 1405–1433* (New York: Pearson, Longman, 2006), 51.

11. Kenneth Swope, "Crouching Tiger, Secret Weapon: Military Technology Employed During the Sino-Japanese War, 1592–1598," *The Journal of Military History* 69 (January 2005): 41.

Chapter 2

1. Thomas Barfield, *The Perilous Frontier: Nomadic Empires and China* (Cambridge: Blackwell Publishers, 1989), 251.

2. Franz Michael, *The Origin of Manchu Rule in China: Frontier and Bureaucracy as Interacting Forces in the Chinese Empire* (New York: Octagon Books, 1965), 64–65.

3. Mark Elliott, *The Manchu Way: The Eight Banners and Ethnic Identity in Late Imperial China* (Stanford: Stanford University Press, 2001), 41.

4. Barfield, *The Perilous Frontier,* 256.

5. Joanna Waley-Cohen, *The Sextants of Beijing: Global Currents in Chinese History* (New York: W.W. Norton, 1999), 118–19.

6. Frederic Wakeman, *The Great Enterprise: The Manchu Reconstruction of Imperial Order in the Seventeenth Century,* vol. 1 (Berkeley: University of California Press, 1985), 163–202.

7. Frederick Mote, *Imperial China, 900–1800* (Cambridge: Harvard University Press, 1999), 808–15.

8. Wakeman, *The Great Enterprise,* 557–63.

9. Pamela Crossley, *Orphan Warriors: Three Manchu Generations at the End of the Qing World* (Princeton: Princeton University Press, 1990), 15, 50.

10. Elliott, *The Manchu Way,* 117, 177–78, 363.

11. Ralph Powell, *The Rise of Chinese Military Power, 1895–1912* (Princeton: Princeton University Press, 1995), 12.

12. Lawrence Kessler, *K'ang-hsi and the Consolidation of Ch'ing Rule, 1661–1684* (Chicago: University of Chicago Press, 1976), 78.

13. Jonathan Spence, "The K'ang-hsi Reign," in *The Cambridge History of China, Volume 9, Part One: The Ch'ing Empire to 1800,* ed. Willard J. Peterson (Cambridge: Cambridge University Press, 2002), 139.

Chapter 3

1. Crossley, *Orphan Warriors,* 19–26, 51.

2. James Hevia, *Cherishing Men from Afar: Qing Guest Ritual and the Macartney Embassy of 1793* (Durham: Duke University Press, 1995), 29–56.

3. Teng Ssu-yu and John K. Fairbank, *China's Response to the West: A Documentary Survey, 1839–1923* (New York: Atheneum, 1965), 19.

4. William T. de Bary, Wing-tsit Chan, and Chester Tan, eds., *Sources of Chinese Tradition,* vol. II (New York: Columbia University Press, 1960), 7.

5. Chang Pao-hsin, *Commissioner Lin and the Opium War* (Cambridge: Harvard University Press, 1964), 153–94.

6. Arthur Waley, *The Opium War Through Chinese Eyes* (London: Allen and Unwin, 1958), 84–85.

7. Crossley, *Orphan Warriors,* 108.

8. Peter Ward Fay, *The Opium War, 1840–1842: Barbarians in the Celestial Empire in the Early Part of the Nineteenth Century and the War by Which They Forced Her Gates Ajar* (Chapel Hill: University of North Carolina Press, 1975), 289–93.

9. Frederic Wakeman, *Strangers at the Gate: Social Disorder in South China, 1839–1861* (Berkeley: University of California Press, 1966), 17–19.

10. James Polachek, *The Inner Opium War* (Cambridge: Council on East Asian Studies, Harvard University Press, 1992), 164–67.

11. Frederic Wakeman, "The Canton Trade and the Opium War," in *The Cambridge History of China: Volume 10, Part One, Late Ch'ing 1800–1911,* ed. Denis Twitchett and John K. Fairbank (Cambridge: Cambridge University Press, 1978), 203–4.

12. John Wong has cast serious doubt on whether the British flag was indeed "hauled down" during the Arrow Incident. See John Wong, *Deadly Dreams: Opium, Imperialism, and the Arrow War (1856–1860) in China* (Cambridge: Cambridge University Press, 1998), 43–66.

Chapter 4

1. de Bary, Chan, and Tan, *Sources of Chinese Tradition vol. II,* 27.

2. Vincent Y.C. Shih, *Taiping Ideology: Its Sources, Interpretations, and Influences* (Seattle: University of Washington Press, 1967), 260–61.

3. Thomas Reilly, *The Taiping Heavenly Kingdom: Rebellion and the Blasphemy of Empire* (Seattle: University of Washington Press, 2004), 118–20.

4. Jonathan Spence, *God's Chinese Son: The Taiping Heavenly Kingdom of Hong Xiuquan* (New York: W.W. Norton, 1996), 127, 141.

5. Jen, *The Taiping Revolutionary Movement* (New Haven: Yale University Press, 1973), 89–91.

6. Spence, *God's Chinese Son,* 165–68.

7. Franz Michael, *The Taiping Rebellion: History and Documents,* vol. 1 (Seattle: University of Washington Press, 1966), 69.

8. Philip Kuhn, *Rebellion and Its Enemies in Late Imperial China: Militarization and Social Structure, 1796–1864* (Cambridge: Harvard University Press, 1970), 145–48.

9. On these rebellions see Elizabeth Perry, *Rebels and Revolutionaries in North China, 1845–1945* (Stanford: Stanford University Press, 1980), 96–151 and David G. Atwill, *The Chinese Sultanate: Islam, Ethnicity, and the Panthay Rebellion in Southwest China, 1856–1873* (Stanford: Stanford University Press, 2006).

10. Spence, *God's Chinese Son,* 249.

11. Jen, *The Taiping Revolutionary Movement,* 243.

12. On the Ever-Victorious Army see Caleb Carr, *The Devil Soldier: The American Soldier of Fortune Who Became a God in China* (New York: Random House, 1992).

Chapter 5

1. Benjamin Elman, "Naval Warfare and the Refraction of China's Self-Strengthening Reforms into Scientific and Technological Failure, 1865–1895," *Modern Asian Studies* 38, no. 2 (2003): 293–301.

2. Kwang-ching Liu and Richard Smith, "The Military Challenge: The North–West and the Coast," in *The Cambridge History of China, Volume 11: Late Ch'ing, 1800–1911, Part 2,* ed. John K. Fairbank and Kwang-ching Liu (Cambridge: Cambridge University Press, 1980), 202–7.

3. Stanley Karnow, *Vietnam: A History* (New York: Penguin, 1983), 74–85.

4. Lloyd Eastman, *Thrones and Mandarins: China's Search for a Policy During the Sino-French Crisis, 1880–1885* (Cambridge: Harvard University Press, 1967), 89–96.

5. Henry McAleavy, *Black Flags in Vietnam: The Story of a Chinese Intervention* (New York: McMillan, 1968), 225–58.

6. John Rawlinson, *China's Struggle for Naval Development, 1839–1895* (Cambridge: Harvard University Press, 1967), 118–25.

7. Liu and Smith, "The Military Challenge," 257–68.

8. Allen Fung, "Testing the Self-Strengthening Movement: The Chinese Army in the Sino-Japanese War of 1894–1895," *Modern Asian Studies* 30, no. 4 (October 1996): 1018–20.

9. S.C.M. Paine, *The Sino-Japanese War of 1894–1895: Perceptions, Power, and Primacy* (Cambridge: Cambridge University Press, 2003), 197–98.

10. Paine, *The Sino-Japanese War of 1894–1895,* 223–29.

Chapter 6

1. Powell, *The Rise of Chinese Military Power,* 51–80.

2. Joseph Esherick, *The Origins of the Boxer Uprising* (Berkeley: University of California Press, 1987), 216–22.

3. Paul Cohen, *History in Three Keys: The Boxers as Event, Experience, and Myth* (New York: Columbia University Press, 1997), 46–53.

4. Peter Fleming, *The Siege at Peking* (Oxford: Oxford University Press, 1983), 168–69.

5. Edward L. Dreyer, *China at War, 1901–1949* (New York: Longman, 1995), 19–20.

6. Edmund Fung, *The Military Dimension of the Chinese Revolution: The New Army and Its Role in the Revolution of 1911* (Vancouver: University of British Columbia Press, 1980), 20–34.

7. Stephen MacKinnon, "The Peiyang Army, Yuan Shih-k'ai, and the Origins of Modern Chinese Warlordism," *The Journal of Asian Studies* 32, no. 3 (May 1973): 413–23.

8. Edmund Fung, *The Military Dimension of the Chinese Revolution.*

9. Joseph Esherick, *Reform and Revolution in China: The 1911 Revolution in Hunan and Hubei* (Berkeley: University of California Press, 1976), 178–83.

10. Ernest Young, "Yuan Shih-k'ai's Rise to the Presidency," in *Revolution in China: The First Phase, 1900–1913,* ed. Mary Wright (New Haven: Yale University Press, 1968), 423.

11. Edward McCord, *The Power of the Gun: The Emergence of Modern Chinese Warlordism* (Berkeley: University of California Press, 1993), 165–66.

Chapter 7

1. Xu Guoqi, *China and the Great War: China's Pursuit of a New Identity and Internationalization* (Cambridge: Cambridge University Press, 2005), 203–33.

2. Arthur Waldron, "War and the Rise of Nationalism in Twentieth Century China," *The Journal of Military History* 57, no. 2 (October 1993): 98.

3. Mark Sheridan, *China in Disintegration: The Republican Era in Chinese History* (New York: The Free Press, 1975), 78–83.

4. Chow Tse-tsung, *The May Fourth Movement: Intellectual Revolution in Modern China* (Cambridge: Harvard University Press, 1960), 84–116.

5. Keiji Furuya, *Chiang Kai-shek, His Life and Times,* abridged English edition by Chang Chun-ming (New York: St. John's University Press, 1981), 56.

6. C. Martin Wilbur, *The Nationalist Revolution in China, 1923–1928* (Cambridge: Cambridge University Press, 1983), 33–37.

7. Tien Chen-ya, *Chinese Military Theory: Ancient and Modern* (Oakville, Ontario: Mosaic Press, 1992), 173. Specifically, the Law of Joint Responsibility stated that any commander who gives up his position without orders to do so faces execution. If troops abandon a commanding officer in the field, that officer's subordinates will be executed. Designed to ensure military discipline, it also served as a deterrent to bold action by officers in the field who might be held accountable if things went badly.

8. Peter Worthing, "The Road Through Whampoa: The Early Career of He Yingqin," *The Journal of Military History* 69, no. 4 (October 2005): 977–83.

9. C. Martin Wilbur and Julie Lien-ying How, *Missionaries of Revolution: Soviet Advisors and Nationalist China, 1920–1927* (Cambridge: Harvard University Press, 1989), 485.

10. Hans Van de Ven, *War and Nationalism in China, 1925–1945* (London: Routledge-Curzon, 2003), 105–20.

11. Dreyer, *China at War,* 143–46.

Chapter 8

1. F. F. Liu, *A Military History of Modern China, 1924–1949* (Princeton: Princeton University Press, 1956), 71–72.

2. Van de Ven, *War and Nationalism,* 142–44.

3. Chiang Kai-shek, "Essentials of the New Life Movement," in *Sources of Chinese Tradition, Volume II,* ed. William T. de Bary, Wing-tsit Chan, and Chester Tan (New York: Columbia University Press, 1960), 143–44.

4. Van de Ven, *War and Nationalism,* 153.

5. Donald Jordan, *China's Trial by Fire: The Shanghai War of 1932* (Ann Arbor: University of Michigan Press, 2001), 103–4.

6. Frederic Wakeman, "A Revisionist View of the Nanjing Decade: Confucian Fascism," *The China Quarterly* 150 (June 1997): 396.

7. Parks Coble, *The Shanghai Capitalists and the Nationalist Government, 1927–1937* (Cambridge: Council on East Asian Studies, Harvard University Press, 1980), 28–65.

8. Mao Zedong, *On Guerrilla Warfare,* trans. Samuel B. Griffith (Urbana: University of Illinois Press, 1961, 2000), 93.

9. Edgar Snow, *Red Star Over China,* 1st rev. ed. (New York, Bantam Books, 1978), 166–67.

10. Van de Ven, *War and Nationalism,* 344–46, 387.

11. Mao Zedong, "A Single Spark Can Start a Prairie Fire," *The Selected Works of Mao Zedong,* vol. I (Beijing: Foreign Languages Press, 1965), 124.

12. William Wei, *Counterrevolution in China: The Nationalists in Jiangxi During the Soviet Period* (Ann Arbor: University of Michigan Press, 1985), 101–25.

13. On the Long March see Harrison Salisbury, *The Long March: The Untold Story* (New York: Harper and Row, 1985).

Chapter 9

1. Jordan, *China's Trial By Fire,* 186–93.

2. Chiang Kai-shek, "Resistance to Aggression and Renaissance of the Nation July 1934", in *The Collected Wartime Messages of Generalissimo Chiang Kai-shek, 1937–1945,* vol. 1, ed. Chinese Ministry of Information (New York: John Day Company, 1946), 3.

3. Frederic Wakeman, *Spymaster: Dai Li and the Chinese Secret Service* (Berkeley: University of California Press, 2001), 173–82.

4. Lyman Van Slyke, *Enemies and Friends: The United Front in Chinese Communist History* (Stanford: Stanford University Press, 1967), 75–91.

5. James Crowley, *Japan's Quest for Autonomy: National Security and Foreign Policy, 1930–1938* (Princeton: Princeton University Press, 1966), 325–26.

6. Chiang Kai-shek, *Collected Wartime Messages of Generalissimo Chiang Kai-shek, 1937-1945,* vol. 1. Compiled by Chinese Ministry of Information (New York: The John Day Company, 1946).

7. Dreyer, *China at War,* 217.

8. See Masahiro Yamamoto, *Nanking: Anatomy of an Atrocity* (Westport, CT: Praeger, 2000) and Iris Chang, *The Rape of Nanking: The Forgotten Holocaust of World War II* (New York: Basic Books, 1997).

9. Marvin Williamson, "The Sino-Japanese War, 1937–1941," in *China's Bitter Victory: The War with Japan, 1937–1945,* ed. James C. Hsiung and Steven Levine (Armonk, NY: M.E. Sharpe, 1992), 139–40.

10. Lloyd Eastman, "Nationalist China During the Sino-Japanese War," in *The Cambridge History of China, Volume 13, Republican China, 1912–1949, Part 2,* ed. John K. Fairbank and Albert Feuerwerker (Cambridge: Cambridge University Press, 1986), 572–73.

11. Dreyer, *China at War,* 213.

12. On Stilwell and Chiang, see Van de Ven, *War and Nationalism in China,* 19–63.

13. William Whitson, *The Chinese High Command: A History of Communist Military Politics, 1927–1971* (New York: Praeger, 1973), 67.

14. Gregor Benton, *The New Fourth Army: Communist Resistance Along the Yangtze and the Huai, 1938–1941* (Berkeley: University of California Press, 1999), 565–91.

Chapter 10

1. Edward Dreyer, *China at War,* 316.

2. United States Department of State, *The China White Paper, August 1949,* Introduction by Lyman Van Slyke (Stanford: Stanford University Press, 1967), 214.

3. Steven Levine, *Anvil of Victory: The Communist Revolution in Manchuria, 1945–1948* (New York: Columbia University Press, 1987).

4. Lionel Chassin, *The Communist Conquest of China: A History of the Civil War, 1945–1949,* trans. Timothy Osato and Louis Gelas (Cambridge: Harvard University Press, 1965), 166.

5. Xu Guangqiu, *War Wings: The United States and Chinese Military Aviation, 1929–1949* Westport, CT: Greenwood Press, 2001), 208–9.

6. Lloyd Eastman, *Seeds of Destruction: Nationalist China in War and Revolution, 1937–1949* (Stanford: Stanford University Press, 1984), 225.

7. Suzanne Pepper, *Civil War in China: The Political Struggle, 1945–1949* (Berkeley: University of California Press, 1978), 16–34.

8. See Chen Yung-fa, *Making Revolution: The Communist Movement in Eastern and Central China, 1937–1945* (Berkeley: University of California Press, 1986) and Joseph Yick, *Making Urban Revolution: The CCP–GMD Struggle for Beijing–Tianjin, 1945–1949* (Armonk, NY: M.E. Sharpe, 1995).

9. Odd Arne Westad, *Decisive Encounters: The Chinese Civil War, 1946–1949* (Stanford: Stanford University Press, 2003), 6–13.

Chapter 11

1. See Nancy Bernhopf Tucker, *Patterns in the Dust: Chinese–American Relations and the Recognition Controversy, 1949–1950* (New York: Columbia University Press, 1983).

2. Chen Jian, *China's Road to the Korean War: The Making of the Sino-American Confrontation* (New York: Columbia University Press, 1994), 108–13.

3. Hao Yufan and Zhai Zhihai, "China's Decision to Enter the Korean War: History Revisited," *The China Quarterly* 121 (March 1990): 99.

4. Burton Kaufman, *The Korean War: Challenges in Crisis, Credibility, and Command* (New York: Knopf, 1986), 34.

5. Hao and Zhai, "China's Decision to Enter the Korean War," 105–6.

6. Chen, *China's Road to the Korean War,* 127, 159.

7. Sergei Goncharov, John Lewis, and Xue Litai, *Uncertain Partners: Mao, Stalin, and the Korean War* (Stanford: Stanford University Press, 1993), 175.

8. On Mao's theory of active defense see Paul Godwin, "Change and Continuity in Chinese Military Doctrine: 1949–1999," in *Chinese Warfighting: The PLA Experience Since 1949,* ed. Mark Ryan, David M. Finkelstein, and Michael A. McDevitt (Armonk, NY: M.E. Sharpe, 2003), 25–26.

9. Zhang Xiaoming, *Red Wings over the Yalu: China, the Soviet Union, and the Air War in Korea* (College Station: Texas A&M University Press, 2002), 96–97.

10. Zhang Shu Guang, *Mao's Military Romanticism: China and the Korean War, 1950–1953* (Lawrence, KS: University of Kansas Press, 1995), 167.

11. Richard Peters and Xiaobing Li, *Voices from the Korean War: Personal Stories of American, Korean, and Chinese Soldiers* (Lexington: University of Kentucky Press, 2004), 119.

12. Chen Jian, *Mao's China and the Cold War* (Chapel Hill: University of North Carolina Press, 2001).

13. Kathryn Weathersby, "Stalin, Mao, and the End of the Korean War," in *Brothers in Arms: The Rise and Fall of the Sino-Soviet Alliance, 1945–1963,* ed. Odd Arne Westad (Stanford: Stanford University Press, 1998), 108–9.

Chapter 12

1. "Talk with American Correspondent Anna Louise Strong," *Selected Works of Mao Tse-tung,* vol. IV (Beijing: Foreign Languages Press, 1965), 100.

2. Gordon Chang, *Friends and Enemies: The United States, China, and the Soviet Union, 1948–1972* (Stanford: Stanford University Press, 1990), 121.

3. Chen, *Mao's China and the Cold War,* 172–73.

4. Li Xiaobing, "PLA Attacks and Amphibious Operations During the Taiwan Straits Crisis of 1954–55 and 1958," in *Chinese Warfighting: the PLA Experience Since 1949,* ed. Mark Ryan, David Finkelstein, and Michael McDevitt, (Armonk, NY: M.E. Sharpe, 2003), 163.

5. Neville Maxwell, *India's China War* (New York: Pantheon Books, 1970), 260–62.

6. John Garver, *Protracted Contest: Sino-Indian Rivalry in the Twentieth Century* (Seattle: University of Washington Press, 2001), 79–83.

7. Melvyn Goldstein, *The Snow Lion and the Dragon: China, Tibet, and the Dalai Lama* (Berkeley and Los Angeles: University of California Press, 1997), 46–54.

8. Garver, *Protracted Contest,* 57.

9. Allen Whiting, "The Sino-Soviet Split," in *The Cambridge History of China Volume 14, The People's Republic, Part I: The Emergence of Revolutionary China, 1949–1965,* ed. Roderick MacFarquhar and John Fairbank (Cambridge: Cambridge University Press, 1987), 512.

10. Patrick Tyler, *A Great Wall: Six Presidents and China, An Investigative History* (New York: The Century Foundation, 1999), 48.

11. Thomas Robinson, "The Sino-Soviet Border Dispute: Background, Development, and the March 1969 Clashes," *The American Political Science Review* 66, no. 4 (December 1972): 1184–85.

12. Thomas Robinson, "The Sino-Soviet Border Conflicts of 1969: New Evidence Three Decades Later," in *Chinese Warfighting: The PLA Experience since 1949,* ed. Mark Ryan, David Finkelstein, and Michael McDevitt (Armonk, NY: M.E. Sharpe, 2003), 203.

Chapter 13

1. Zhai Qiang, *China and the Vietnam Wars, 1950–1975* (Chapel Hill: University of North Carolina Press, 2001), 26–33.

2. Kuo-kang Shao, "Zhou Enlai's Diplomacy and the Neutralization of Indo-China, 1954–1955," *The China Quarterly* 107 (September 1986): 494–99.

3. Zhang Xiaoming, " The Vietnam War, 1964–1969: A Chinese Perspective," *The Journal of Military History* 60, no. 4 (October 1996): 734.

4. Chen Jian, "China and the First Indo-China War, 1950–1954," *The China Quarterly* 133 (March 1993): 366–71, 378.

5. "Keng Piao's Report on the Situation of the Indochinese Peninsula," *Issues and Studies* XVII, no. 1 (January 1981): 78–96.

6. Harlan Jencks, "China's 'Punitive' War on Vietnam: A Military Assessment," *Asian Survey* XIX, no. 8 (August 1979): 807–9.

7. Edward C. O'Dowd and John F. Corbett, Jr., "The 1979 Chinese Campaign in Vietnam: Lessons Learned," in *The Lessons of History: The Chinese People's Liberation Army at 75,* ed. Laurie Burkitt, Andrew Scobell, and Larry M. Wortzel (Carlisle, PA: Strategic Studies Institute, 2003), 355–62.

8. King C. Chen, *China's War with Vietnam: Issues, Decisions and Implications* (Stanford: Hoover Institution Press, 1987), 114.

Chapter 14

1. Deng Xiaoping, "Restore Agricultural Production," *Selected Works of Deng Xiaoping (1938–1965)* (Beijing: Foreign Languages Press, 1992), 293.

2. David Shambaugh, "The People's Liberation Army and the People's Republic at 50: Reform at Last," *The China Quarterly* 159 (September 1999): 663–64.

3. Ellis Joffe, "'People's War Under Modern Conditions': A Doctrine for Modern War," *The China Quarterly* 112 (December 1987): 556–66.

4. Timothy Brook, *Quelling the People: The Military Suppression of the Beijing Democracy Movement* (Stanford: Stanford University Press, 1999), 134.

5. Andrew Nathan and Perry Link, eds., *The Tian'anmen Papers* (New York: Public Affairs, 2001), 219, 420, 436.

6. Zhao Suisheng, "Military Coercion and Peaceful Offence: Beijing's Strategy of National Reunification with Taiwan," *Pacific Affairs* 72, no. 4 (Winter 1999–2000): 503.

7. Andrew Nathan, "China's Goals in the Taiwan Straits," *The China Journal* 36 (July 1996): 87–88.

8. Robert Ross, "The 1995–1996 Taiwan Strait Confrontation: Coercion, Credibility, and the Use of Force," *International Security* 25, no. 2 (Autumn 2000): 109–12.

9. Michael O'Hanlon, "Why China Cannot Conquer Taiwan," *International Security* 25, no. 2 (Autumn 2000): 51–86.

Selected Bibliography

Atwill, David G. *The Chinese Sultanate: Islam, Ethnicity, and the Panthay Rebellion in Southwest China, 1856–1873.* Stanford: Stanford University Press, 2006.

Bachman, David. "Military Modernization and Civil–Military Relations in China Toward the Year 2020." *American Asian Review* 19, 3 (Fall 2001): 1–34.

Barfield, Thomas. *The Perilous Frontier: Nomadic Empires and China.* Cambridge: Cambridge University Press, 1989.

Beeching, Jack. *The Chinese Opium Wars.* New York, London: Harcourt Brace Jovanovich, 1975.

Benton, Gregor. *New Fourth Army: Communist Resistance Along the Yangtze and the Huai, 1938–1941.* Berkeley: University of California Press, 1999.

Bland, Larry I., ed.*George C. Marshall's Mediation Mission to China, December 1945–January 1947.* Lexington, VA: George C. Marshall Foundation, 1998.

Brook, Timothy. *Documents on the Rape of Nanking.* Ann Arbor: University of Michigan Press, 1999.

———. *Quelling the People: The Military Suppression of the Beijing Democracy Movement.* Stanford: Stanford University Press, 1999.

Carr, Caleb. *The Devil Soldier: The American Soldier of Fortune Who Became a God in China.* New York: Random House, 1992.

Chang, Gordon. *Friends and Enemies: The United States, China, and the Soviet Union, 1948–1972.* Stanford: Stanford University Press, 1990.

Chang, Hsin-pao. *Commissioner Lin and the Opium War.* Cambridge: Harvard University Press, 1964.

Chang, Iris. *The Rape of Nanking: The Forgotten Holocaust of World War II.* New York: Basic Books, 1997.

Chang, Jui-te. "Nationalist Army Officers During the Sino-Japanese War, 1937–1945." *Modern Asian Studies* 30, 4 (October 1996): 1033–56.

Chang, Pao-min. *The Sino-Vietnamese Territorial Dispute.* New York: Center for Strategic and International Studies, Georgetown University, Praeger, 1986.

Chase, Kenneth. *Firearms: A Global History to 1700.* Cambridge: Cambridge University Press, 2003.

Chassin, Lionel. *The Communist Conquest of China: A History of the Civil War, 1945–1949.* Translated by Timothy Osato and Louis Gelas. Cambridge: Harvard University Press, 1965.

Ch'en, Jerome. "Defining Chinese Warlords and Their Factions." *Bulletin of the School of Oriental and African Studies* 31, 3 (1968): 563–600.

Chen, Jian. "China and the First Indo-China War, 1950–1954." *The China Quarterly* 133 (March 1993): 85–110.

———. *China's Road to the Korean War: The Making of the Sino-American Confrontation.* New York: Columbia University Press, 1994.

———. *Mao's China and the Cold War.* Chapel Hill: University of North Carolina Press, 2001.

Chen, King C. *China's War with Vietnam, 1979: Issues, Decisions, and Implications.* Stanford: Hoover Institution Press, Stanford University, 1987.

Chen, Yung-fa. *Making Revolution: The Communist Movement in Eastern and Central China, 1937–1945.* Berkeley: University of California Press, 1986.

Chere, Lewis M. *Great Britain and the Sino-French War: The Problems of an Involved Neutral, 1883–1885.* Ann Arbor: Western Conference of the Association of Asian Studies, 1980.

Cherepanov, Aleksander Ivanovich. *The Northern Expedition of the National Revolutionary Army of China: Notes of a Military Advisor.* Translated by Caroline Rodgers and Lydia Holubnycky. New York: Columbia University, n.d.

Ch'i, Hsi-sheng. *China at War: Military Defeats and Political Collapse, 1937–1945.* Ann Arbor: University of Michigan Press, 1982.

Chinese Ministry of Information, ed . *The Collected Wartime Messages of Generalissimo Chiang K'ai-shek, 1937–1945.* 2 Vols. New York: The John Day Company, 1946.

Chow Tse-Tsung. *The May Fourth Movement: Intellectual Revolution in Modern China.* Cambridge: Harvard University Press, 1960.

Chu, Samuel C., and Kwang-ching Liu, eds. *Li Hung-chang and China's Early Modernization.* Armonk, NY, London: M.E. Sharpe, 1994.

Coble, Parks. *The Shanghai Capitalists and the Nationalist Government, 1927–1937.* Cambridge: Council on East Asian Studies, Harvard University Press, 1980.

Cohen, Paul. *History in Three Keys: The Boxers as Event, Myth, and Experience.* New York: Columbia University Press, 1997.

Cohen, Warren I. *America's Response to China: A History of Sino-American Relations.* New York: Columbia University Press, 1990.

———. "Who Fought the Japanese in Hunan? Some Views on China's War Effort." *Journal of Asian Studies* 27, 1 (November 1967): 111–15.

Crossley, Pamela Kyle. *Orphan Warriors: Three Manchu Generations at the End of the Qing World.* Princeton: Princeton University Press, 1990.

Crowley, James B. *Japan's Quest for Autonomy: National Security and Foreign Policy, 1930–1938.* Princeton: Princeton University Press, 1966.

Dai, Yingcong. "A Disguised Defeat: The Myanmar Campaign of the Qing Dynasty." *Modern Asian Studies* 38, 1 (February 2004): 145–89.

De Bary, William T., Wing-tsit Chan, and Chester Tan, eds. *The Sources of Chinese Tradition.* 2 Vols. New York: Columbia University Press, 1960.

Deng, Xiaoping, *Selected Works of Deng Xiaoping (1938–1965).* Beijing: Foreign Languages Press, 1992.

Di Cosmo, Nicola. *The Diary of a Manchu Soldier in Seventeenth-Century China.* Richmond: Curzon, 2001.

Dreyer, Edward. *China at War, 1901–1949.* New York: Longman, 1995.

———. *Zheng He: China and the Oceans in the Early Ming Dynasty, 1405–1433.* New York: Pearson Longman, 2006.

Dreyer, June Teufel. *Chinese Defense and Foreign Policy.* New York: Professors World Peace Academy, Paragon House, 1988.

Dryburgh, Marjorie. *North China and Japanese Expansion, 1933–1937.* Richmond: Curzon, 2000.

Eastman, Lloyd. "Nationalist China During the Sino-Japanese War, 1937–1945." In *The Cambridge History of China, Volume 13, Republican China, 1912–1949, Part 2*, edited by John K. Fairbank and Albert Feuerwerker, 547–608. Cambridge: Cambridge University Press, 1986.

———. *Seeds of Destruction: Nationalist China in War and Revolution, 1937–1945*. Stanford: Stanford University Press, 1984.

———. *Throne and Mandarins: China's Search for a Policy During the Sino-French Controversy, 1880–1885*. Cambridge: Harvard University Press, 1967.

Elliott, Mark C. *The Manchu Way: The Eight Banners and Ethnic Identity in Late Imperial China*. Stanford: Stanford University Press, 2001.

Elman, Benjamin A. "Naval Warfare and the Refraction of China's Self-Strengthening Reforms into Scientific and Technological Failure, 1865–1895." *Modern Asian Studies* 38, 2 (May 2004): 283–326.

Esherick, Joseph. *The Origins of the Boxer Uprising*. Berkeley: University of California Press, 1987.

———. *Reform and Revolution in China: The 1911 Revolution in Hunan and Hubei*. Berkeley: University of California Press, 1976.

Eto, Shinkichi and Harold Z. Schiffrin. *China's Republican Revolution*. Tokyo: University of Tokyo Press, 1994.

Fay, Peter Ward. *The Opium War, 1840–1842: Barbarians in the Celestial Empire in the Early Part of the Nineteenth Century and the War by Which They Forced Her Gates Ajar*. Chapel Hill: University of North Carolina Press, 1975.

Feuerweker, Albert. *Rebellion in Nineteenth-Century China*. Ann Arbor: University of Michigan Center for Chinese Studies, 1975.

Fleming, Peter. *The Siege at Peking*. Oxford: Oxford University Press, 1983.

Fogel, Joshua A. *The Nanjing Massacre in History and Historiography*. Berkeley: University of California Press, 2000.

Fung, Allen. "Testing the Self-Strengthening: The Chinese Army in the Sino-Japanese War of 1894–1895." *Modern Asian Studies* 30, 4 (October 1996): 1007–31.

Fung, Edmund S.K. *The Military Dimension of the Chinese Revolution: The New Army and Its Role in Revolution of 1911*. Vancouver: University of British Columbia Press, 1980.

Furuya, Keiji. *Chiang K'ai-shek, His Life and Times*. Abridged English edition by Chang Chun-ming. New York: St. John's University Press, 1981.

Garver, John W. "Chiang Kai-shek's Quest for Soviet Entry into the Sino-Japanese War." *Political Science Quarterly* 102, 2 (Summer 1987): 295–316.

———. *Protracted Contest: Sino-Indian Rivalry in the Twentieth Century*. Seattle: University of Washington Press, 2001.

———. "Sino-Vietnamese Conflict and the Sino-American Rapprochement." *Political Science Quarterly* 96, 3 (Autumn 1981): 445–64.

George, Alexander L. *The Chinese Communist Army in Action: The Korean War and Its Aftermath*. New York: Columbia University Press, 1967.

Gibson, Michael Richard. "Chiang Kai-shek's Central Army, 1924–1938." PhD diss., George Washington University, 1985.

Gilks, Anne. *The Breakdown of the Sino-Vietnamese Alliance, 1970–1979*. Berkeley: Institute of East Asian Studies, University of California, Center for Chinese Studies, 1992.

Godwin, Paul H.B. "Changing Concepts of Doctrine, Strategy and Operations in the Chinese People's Liberation Army, 1978–1987." *The China Quarterly*, 112 (December 1987): 572–90.

Goldstein, Melvyn. *The Snow Lion and the Dragon: China, Tibet, and the Dalai Lama.* Berkeley and Los Angeles: University of California Press, 1997.

Goncharov, Sergei N., John W. Lewis, and Xue Litai. *Uncertain Partners: Stalin, Mao, and the Korean War.* Stanford: Stanford University Press, 1993.

Graff, David A., and Robin Higham, eds. *A Military History of China.* Boulder, CO: Westview, 2002.

———. *Medieval Chinese Warfare, 300–900.* London: Routledge, 2002.

Hao, Yufan, and Zhai Zhihai. "China's Decision to Enter the Korean War: History Revisited." *The China Quarterly,* 121 (March 1990): 94–115.

Hevia, James. *Cherishing Men from Afar: Qing Guest Ritual and the Macartney Mission of 1793.* Durham: Duke University Press, 1995.

Hood, Steven J. *Dragons Entangled: Indochina and the China–Vietnam War.* Armonk, NY: M.E. Sharpe, 1992.

Hsi, Angela N.S. "Wu San-Kuei in 1644: A Reappraisal." *The Journal of Asian Studies* 34, 2 (February 1975): 443–53.

Hsiung, James, and Steven Levine, eds. *China's Bitter Victory: The War with Japan, 1937–1945.* Armonk, NY: M.E. Sharpe, 1992.

Hsu, Cho-yun. *Ancient China in Transition: An Analysis of Social Mobility, 722–222 B.C.* Stanford: Stanford University Press, 1965.

Jen, Yu-wen. *The Taiping Revolutionary Movement.* New Haven: Yale University Press, 1973.

Jencks, Harlan. "China's 'Punitive' War on Vietnam: A Military Assessment." *Asian Survey* XIX, 8 (August 1979): 801–15.

Joffe, Ellis. "'People's War Under Modern Conditions': A Doctrine for Modern War." *The China Quarterly* 55 (December 1987): 555–71.

Jordan, Donald. *The Northern Expedition: China's National Revolution of 1926–1928.* Honolulu: University of Hawaii Press, 1976.

———. *China's Trial by Fire: The Shanghai War of 1932.* Ann Arbor: University of Michigan Press, 2001.

Karnow, Stanley. *Vietnam: A History.* New York: Penguin, 1983.

Kataoka, Tetsuya. *Resistance and Revolution: The Communists and the Second United Front.* Berkeley: University of California Press, 1974.

Kaufman, Burton. *The Korean War: Challenges in Crisis, Credibility, and Command.* New York: Knopf, 1986.

"Keng Piao's Report on the Situation of the Indochinese Peninsula." *Issues and Studies* 17, 1 (January 1981): 78–96.

Kessler, Lawrence D. *K'ang-hsi and the Consolidation of Ch'ing Rule, 1661–1684.* Chicago: University of Chicago Press, 1976.

Kuhn, Philip. *Rebellion and Its Enemies in Late Imperial China: Militarization and Social Structure, 1796–1864.* Cambridge: Harvard University Press, 1970.

Lary, Diana, and Stephen R. MaKinnon. *The Scars of War: The Impact of Warfare on Modern China.* Vancouver: University of British Columbia Press, 2001.

Lattimore, Owen. *China Memories: Chiang Kai-shek and the War Against Japan.* Tokyo: Tokyo University Press, 1991.

Lawson, Eugene K. *The Sino-Vietnamese Conflict.* New York: Praeger, 1984.

Levine, Steven I. *Anvil of Victory: The Communist Revolution in Manchuria, 1945–1948.* New York: Columbia University Press, 1987.

———. "A New Look at American Mediation in the Chinese Civil War: The Marshall Mission and Manchuria." *Diplomatic History* 3, 4 (1979): 349–75.

Li, Nan. "Organizational Changes of the PLA, 1985–1997." *The China Quarterly,* 158 (June 1999): 314–49.

―――. "The PLA's Evolving Warfighting Doctrine, Strategy and Tactics, 1985–1995: A Chinese Perspective." *The China Quarterly* 146 (June 1996): 443–63.

Li, Xiaobing, Allan R. Millett, and Yu Bin, eds. *Mao's Generals Remember Korea.* Lawrence: University Press of Kansas, 2001.

Lilley, James, and David L. Shambaugh. *China's Military Faces the Future.* Armonk, NY: M.E. Sharpe, 1999.

Liu, F.F. *A Military History of Modern China, 1924–1949.* Princeton: Princeton University Press, 1956.

Liu, Kwang-ching, and Richard Smith. "The Military Challenge: the North–West and the Coast." In *The Cambridge History of China, Volume 11, Part 2: The Late Ch'ing, 1800–1911,* edited by John K. Fairbank and Kwang-ching Liu, 202–73. Cambridge: Cambridge University Press, 1980.

Liu, Xuechang. *The Sino-Indian Border Dispute and Sino-Indian Relations.* Lanham, MD: University Press of America, 1994.

McAleavy, Henry. *Black Flags in Vietnam: The Story of a Chinese Intervention.* New York: McMillan, 1968.

McClaran, John P. "U.S. Arms Sales to Taiwan: Implications for the Future of Sino-U.S. Relationship." *Asian Survey* 40, 4 (July–August 2000): 622–40.

McCord, Edward. *The Power of the Gun: The Emergence of Modern Chinese Wardlordism.* Berkeley: University of California Press, 1993.

MacKinnon, Stephen R. "The Peiyang Army, Yüan Shih-k'ai and the Origins of Modern Chinese Warlordism." *Journal of Asian Studies* 32, 3 (May 1973): 405–23.

Mao Zedong. *On Guerrilla Warfare.* Translated by Samuel Griffith. Urbana: University of Illinois Press, 1961, 2000.

―――. *The Selected Works of Mao Zedong.* 5 Vols. Beijing: Foreign Languages Press, 1965.

Maxwell, Neville. *India's China War.* New York: Pantheon Books, 1970.

Michael, Franz H. *The Origin of Manchu Rule in China: Frontier and Bureaucracy as Interlocking Forces in the Chinese Empire.* New York: Octagon Books, 1965.

―――. *The Taiping Rebellion: History and Documents.* 3 Vols. Seattle: University of Washington Press, 1966.

Mote, Frederick. *Imperial China, 900–1800.* Cambridge: Cambridge University Press, 1999.

Mulvenon, James C., and Richard H. Yang, eds. *The People's Liberation Army in the Information Age.* Santa Monica, CA: Rand, 1999.

Mulvenon, James. "The Limits of Coercive Diplomacy: The 1979 Sino-Vietnamese Border War." *Journal of Northeast Asian Studies* 14, 3 (1995): 68–88.

Nathan, Andrew. "China's Goals in the Taiwan Strait." *The China Journal* 36 (July 1996): 87–93.

Nathan, Andrew, and Perry Link, eds. *The Tian'anmen Papers.* New York: Public Affairs, 2001.

Needham, Joseph, and Robin Yates, eds. *Science and Civilization in China,* Volume 5 Part VI. Cambridge: Cambridge University Press, 1994.

Nelson, Harvey. *The Chinese Military System: An Organizational Study of the Chinese People's Liberation Army.* Boulder, CO: Westview Press, 1977.

O'Dowd, Edward C., and John F. Corbett, Jr. "The 1979 Chinese Campaign in Vietnam: Lessons Learned." In *The Lessons of History: The Chinese People's Liberation Army at 75,* edited by Laurie Burkitt, Andrew Scobell, and Larry M. Wortzel, 353–78. Carlisle, PA: Strategic Studies Institute, 2003.

O'Hanlon, Michael. "Why China Cannot Conquer Taiwan." *International Security* 25, 2 (Autumn 2000): 51–86.

Paine, S.C.M. *The Sino-Japanese War of 1894–1895: Perception, Power, and Primacy.* New York: Cambridge University Press, 2003.

Pepper, Suzanne. *Civil War in China: The Political Struggle, 1945–1949.* Berkeley: University of California Press, 1978.

Perry, Elizabeth J., ed. *Chinese Perspectives on the Nien Rebellion.* White Plains, NY: Sharpe, 1982.

———. *Rebels and Revolutionaries in North China, 1845–1945.* Stanford: Stanford University Press, 1980.

Peters, Richard, and Xiaobing Li. *Voices from the Korean War: Personal Stories of American, Korean, and Chinese Soldiers.* Lexington: University Press of Kentucky, 2004.

Polachek, James M. *The Inner Opium War.* Cambridge, MA: Harvard University, Council on East Asian studies, 1992.

Porter, Gareth. "Hanoi's Strategic Perspective and the Sino-Vietnamese Conflict." *Pacific Affairs* 57, 1 (Spring 1984): 7–25.

Powell, Ralph L. *The Rise of Chinese Military, 1895–1912.* Princeton: Princeton University Press, 1955.

Rawlinson, John L. *China's Struggle for Naval Development, 1839–1895.* Cambridge: Harvard University Press, 1967.

Reilly, Thomas. *The Taiping Heavenly Kingdom: Rebellion and the Blasphemy of Empire.* Seattle: University of Washington Press, 2004.

Robinson, Thomas W. "Chinese Military Modernization in the 1980s." *The China Quarterly* 90 (June 1982): 231–52.

———. "The Sino-Soviet Border Dispute: Background, Development and the March 1969 Clashes." *American Political Science Review* 66, 4 (December 1972): 1175–1202.

Ross, Robert S. "The 1995–1996 Taiwan Strait Confrontation: Coercion, Credibility, and the Use of Force." *International Security* 25, 2 (Autumn 2000): 87–123.

———. *The Indochina Tangle: China's Vietnam Policy, 1975–1979.* New York: Columbia University Press, 1988.

Ryan, Mark A., David M. Finkelstein, and Michael A. McDevitt, eds. *Chinese Warfighting: The PLA Experience Since 1949.* Armonk, NY: M.E. Sharpe, 2003.

Salisbury, Harrison. *The Long March: the Untold Story.* New York: Harper and Row, 1985.

Sandler, Stanley. *The Korean War: No Victors, No Vanquished.* Lexington: University Press of Kentucky, 1999.

Scobell, Andrew. *China's Use of Military Force: Beyond the Great Wall and the Long March.* New York: Cambridge University Press, 2003.

Shambaugh, David L. *Modernizing China's Military: Progress, Problems, and Prospects.* Berkeley: University of California Press, 2002.

———. "The People's Liberation Army and the People's Republic at 50: Reform at Last." *The China Quarterly* 159 (September 1999): 660–72.

Shambaugh, David L., and Richard Yang. *China's Military in Transition.* New York: Oxford University Press, 1997.

Shao, Kuo-kang. "Zhou Enlai's Diplomacy and the Neutralization of Indo-China, 1954–1955." *The China Quarterly* 107 (September 1986): 483–504.

Shaughnessy, Edward L. "Historical Perspectives on the Introduction of the Chariot into China." *Harvard Journal of Asiatic Studies* 48, 1 (June 1988): 189–237.

Sheridan, Mark. *China in Disintegration: The Republican Era in Modern China.* New York: The Free Press, 1975.

Shih, Vincent Y.C. *Taiping Ideology: Its Sources, Interpretations, and Influences.* Seattle: University of Washington Press, 1967.

Snow, Edgar. *Red Star Over China.* 1st rev. ed. New York: Bantam Books, 1978.

Spector, Stanley. *Li Hung-chang and the Huai Army: A Study in Nineteenth-Century Chinese Regionalism.* Seattle: University of Washington Press, 1964.

Spence, Jonathan D. *God's Chinese Son: The Taiping Heavenly Kingdom of Hong Xiuquan.* New York: W.W. Norton, 1996.

———. "The K'ang-hsi Reign." In *The Cambridge History of China, Volume 9 Part 1: The Ch'ing Empire to 1800,* edited by Willard J. Peterson, 120–82. Cambridge: Cambridge University Press, 2002.

Spence, Jonathan D., and John E. Wills. *From Ming to Ch'ing: Conquest, Region, and Continuity in Seventeenth-Century China.* New Haven: Yale University Press, 1979.

Stueck, William. *Rethinking the Korean War: A New Diplomatic and Strategic History.* Princeton: Princeton University Press, 2002.

Sun Tzu. *The Art of War.* Translated by Ralph Sawyer. Boulder, CO: Westview Press, 1994.

Sun Zi. *The Art of War.* Translated by Jack Minford. New York: Penguin, 2002.

Sutton, Donald S. "German Advice and Residual Warlordism in the Nanking Decade: Influence on Nationalist Military Training and Strategy." *The China Quarterly* 91 (September 1982): 386–410.

Swope, Kenneth M. "Crouching Tiger, Secret Weapon: Military Technology Employed in the Sino-Japanese War, 1592–1598." *The Journal of Military History* 69 (January 2005), 11–42.

Tanner, Harold M. "Guerillas, Mobile and Base Warfare in Communist Military Operations in China, 1945–1947." *The Journal of Military History* 67, 4 (October 2003): 1177–1222.

Teng, Ssu-yu, and John K. Fairbank, eds. *China's Response to the West: A Documentary Survey, 1839–1923.* New York: Atheneum, 1965.

Tien, Chen-Ya. *Chinese Military Theory: Ancient and Modern.* New York, Lanham: Mosaic Press, 1992.

Tuchman, Barbara W. *Stilwell and the American Experience in China, 1911–1945.* New York: Grove Press, 1971.

Tucker, Nancy Bernhopf. *Patterns in the Dust: Chinese–American Relations and the Recognition Controversy, 1949–1950.* New York: Columbia University Press, 1983.

Tyler, Patrick. *A Great Wall: Six Presidents and China, an Investigative History.* New York: The Century Foundation, 1999.

United States Department of State, *The China White Paper, August 1949.* Introduction by Lyman Van Slyke. Stanford: Stanford University Press, 1967.

Van de Ven, Hans. "The Military in the Republic." *The China Quarterly* 150 (June 1997): 352–74.

———. *War and Nationalism in China, 1925–1945.* London: RoutledgeCurzon, 2003.

———, ed. *Warfare in Chinese History.* Leiden; Boston: Brill, 2000.

Van Slyke, Lyman P. "The Battle of the Hundred Regiments: Problems of Coordination and Control During the Sino-Japanese War." *Modern Asian Studies* 30, 4 (October 1996): 979–1005.

———. *Enemies and Friends: United Front in Chinese Communist History.* Stanford: Stanford University Press, 1967.

Vertzberger, Yaacov. *Misperception on Foreign Policymaking: The Sino-Indian Conflict, 1959–1962.* Boulder, CO: Westview Press, 1984.

Wakeman, Frederic E., Jr. "The Canton Trade and the Opium War." In *The Cambridge History of China, Volume 10, Part 1: The Ch'ing Empire to 1800,* edited by Dennis Twitchett and John K. Fairbank, 163–212. Cambridge: Cambridge University Press, 1978.

———. *The Great Enterprise: The Manchu Reconstruction of Imperial Order in Seventeenth-Century China.* 2 Vols. Berkeley: University of California Press, 1985.

———. *Spymaster: Dai Li and the Chinese Secret Service.* Berkeley: University of California Press, 2001.

———. *Strangers at the Gate: Social Disorder in South China, 1839–1861.* Berkeley: University of California Press, 1966.

Waldron, Arthur. *From War to Nationalism: China's Turning Point, 1924–1925.* Cambridge: Cambridge University Press, 1995.

———. *The Great Wall of China: From History to Myth.* Cambridge: Cambridge University Press, 1990.

———. "The Problem of the Great Wall of China." *Harvard Journal of Asiatic Studies* 43, 2 (December 1983): 643–63.

———. "War and the Rise of Nationalism in Twentieth-Century China." *The Journal of Military History* 57, 5 (October 1993): 87–104.

Waley, Arthur. *Opium War Through Chinese Eyes.* London: Allen and Unwin, 1959.

Waley-Cohen, Joanna. *The Sextants of Beijing: Global Currents in Chinese History.* New York: W.W. Norton, 1999.

Weatherford, Jack. *Genghis Khan and the Making of the Modern World.* New York: Crown Publishers, 2004.

Wei, William. *Counterrevolution in China: The Nationalists in Jiangxi During the Soviet Period.* Ann Arbor: University of Michigan Press, 1985.

Westad, Odd Arne, ed. *Brothers in Arms: The Rise and Fall of the Sino-Soviet Alliance, 1945–1963.* Stanford: Stanford University Press, 1998.

———. *Cold War and Revolution: Soviet–American Rivalry and the Origins of the Chinese Civil War.* New York: Columbia University Press, 1993.

———. *Decisive Encounters: The Chinese Civil War, 1946–1950.* Stanford: Stanford University Press, 2003.

Whiting, Allen S. *China Crosses the Yalu.* Stanford: Stanford University Press, 1960.

———. *The Chinese Calculus of Deterrence: India and Indochina.* Ann Arbor: University of Michigan Press, 1975.

———. "The Sino-Soviet Split." In *The Cambridge History of China, Volume 14, The People's Republic of China, Part I: The Emergence of Revolutionary China, 1949–1965,* edited by Roderick MacFarquhar and John K. Fairbank, 478–538. Cambridge: Cambridge University Press, 1987.

Whitson, William W. with Chen-hsia Huang. *The Chinese High Command: A History of Communist Military Politics, 1927–1971.* New York: Praeger Publishers, 1973.

Wilbur, C. Martin. *The Nationalist Revolution in China, 1923–1928.* Cambridge: Cambridge University Press, 1983.

Wilbur, C. Martin, and Julie Lien-ying How. *Missionaries of Revolution: Soviet Advisors and Nationalist China, 1920–1927.* Cambridge: Harvard University Press, 1989.

Wong, J. Y. *Deadly Dreams: Opium, Imperialism, and the Arrow War (1856–1860).* New York: Cambridge University Press, 1998.

Wright, Mary. *China in Revolution: The First Phase, 1900–1913.* New Haven: Yale University press, 1968.

Wu, Tien-wei. *The Sian Incident: A Pivotal Point in Modern Chinese History.* Ann Arbor: Center for Chinese Studies, University of Michigan, 1976.

Xiang, Lanxin. *Mao's Generals: Chen Yi and the New Fourth Army.* Lanham, MD: University Press of America, 1998.

Xu, Guangqiu. *War Wings: The United States and Chinese Military Aviation, 1929–1949.* Westport, CT: Greenwood Press, 2001.

Xu, Guoqi. *China and the Great War: China's Pursuit of a New Identity and Internationalization.* Cambridge: Cambridge University Press, 2005.

Yamamoto, Masahiro. *Nanking: Anatomy of an Atrocity.* Westport, CT: Praeger, 2000.

Yick, Joseph K.S. *Making Urban Revolution in China: The CCP–GMD Struggle for Beiping–Tianjin, 1945–1949.* Armonk, NY: M.E. Sharpe, 1995.

Young, Ernest. "Yuan Shih-k'ai's Rise to the Presidency." In *Revolution in China: The First Phase,* edited by Mary Wright, 419–42. New Haven: Yale University Press, 1968.

Zarrow, Peter. *China in War and Revolution, 1895–1949.* New York: RoutledgeCurzon, 2005.

Zhai, Qiang. *China and the Vietnam Wars, 1950–1975.* Chapel Hill: University of North Carolina Press, 2001.

Zhang, Shu Guang. *Mao's Military Romanticism: China and the Korean War, 1950–1953.* Lawrence: University Press of Kansas, 1995.

Zhang, Xiaoming. *Red Wings over the Yalu: China, the Soviet Union and the Air War in Korea.* College Station: Texas A&M University Press, 2002.

———. "The Vietnam War, 1964–1969: A Chinese Perspective." *The Journal of Military History* 60, 4 (October 1996): 731–62.

Zhao, Suisheng. "Military Coercion and Peaceful Offence: Beijing's Strategy of National Reunification with Taiwan." *Pacific Affairs* 72, 4 (Winter 1999–2000): 495–512.

Index

About the Author

PETER WORTHING is Associate Professor of History at Texas Christian University. He has a PhD in modern Chinese History from the University of Hawaii. He is the author of *Occupation and Revolution: China and the Vietnamese August Revolution of 1945* (2001) and several articles on Chinese military history in journals such as *The Journal of Military History, Modern China,* and *The Journal of American–East Asian Relations.*